CLASSROOM RESOURCES FOR INSTRUCTORS USING

Focus on Writing

PARAGRAPHS AND ESSAYS

CLASSROOM RESOURCES FOR INSTRUCTORS USING

Focus on Writing

PARAGRAPHS AND ESSAYS

SECOND EDITION

Linda J. Stine

Lincoln University

Linda J. Stengle

Lincoln University

Bedford/St. Martin's

Boston ■ New York

Manufactured in the United States of America.

5 4 3 2 1 0
f e d c b a

For information, write: Bedford/St. Martin's, 75 Arlington Street, Boston, MA 02116   (617-399-4000)

ISBN: 978-0-312-60343-4

Acknowledgments

Cyril O. Houle, "Seven Keys to Effective Learning." From *Responsibilities: A College Reader* by Edward Quinn, ed. Published by Harper & Row. Copyright © 1987. Reprinted by permission of David Houle.

Erika Lindemann, excerpt from *A Rhetoric for Writing Teachers, 4th Edition.* Copyright © 2001. Reprinted with permission of Oxford University Press and Erika Lindemann.

Barbara Walvoord and Hoke Smith, excerpts from "Coaching the Process of Writing." From *New Directions for Teaching and Learning: Teaching Writing in All Disciplines.* Copyright © 1982 by Jossey-Bass. Reprinted with permission of John Wiley & Sons, Inc.

Contents

PART THREE   *Teaching FOCUS ON WRITING: A Chapter-by-Chapter Guide*   87

PART FOUR   *Additional Resources*   139

PART FIVE   *Answers to Exercise Items*   175

Focus on Writing

PARAGRAPHS AND ESSAYS

PART ONE

Designing and Teaching the Course

1

Teaching FOCUS ON WRITING: An Introduction

Choosing the right textbook is an important first step toward teaching a successful class. This chapter contains additional resources that will guide you through your *next* steps: using the components of the text effectively, putting together a comprehensive syllabus and set of first-week handouts, and getting your class off to a successful beginning. (For chapter-by-chapter advice on teaching with *Focus on Writing*, see Part Three of this manual.)

Overview of *Focus on Writing:* Goals and Features

Focus on Writing is made up of three self-contained but interrelated sections. The first section, Writing Paragraphs and Essays (Units 1–3), introduces students to the writing process and the characteristics of good paragraphs and essays. The second section, Revising and Editing Your Writing (Units 4–7), covers basic principles of revising and editing. This part functions as both a workbook and a handbook, with clearly presented rules for grammatical and stylistic correctness along with a variety of practice exercises. It includes a chapter that specifically addresses ESL issues (Chapter 30). The third section, Becoming a Critical Reader (Unit 8), focuses on reading skills. Its practical advice is followed by nineteen professional and student essays exemplifying each of the developmental patterns introduced in the first section. Most instructors will prepare a syllabus that combines writing instruction (Units 1–3) with grammar instruction (Units 4–7) and refers to readings in Unit Eight as models and as subjects for discussion as appropriate.

Answers to odd-numbered exercises are included at the end of the student text so that students can monitor their own progress. (Instructors who prefer to make all answers available to their students will find them starting on page 175 of this manual in a form convenient for photocopying.) Appendix A, Strategies for College Success, contains practical advice to help students succeed in their college careers. Appendix B, Using Research in Your Writing, offers tips on writing research papers and features a student paper written according to MLA guidelines. A list of standard editing symbols appears on the page facing the back cover.

The premise of *Focus on Writing* is that students develop writing skills most effectively by practicing them within the context of their own writing. For that reason, most chapters start with a writing prompt—to which the student is directed later in the chapter as a means for applying and testing that chapter's main concepts— and then end with a final review. Even if you choose to use your own writing prompts rather than those in *Focus on Writing*, you will do well to maintain this basic structure, which keeps bringing the students back to their own words. In this way, they will learn the chapter content better because they are learning it for a purpose. Even more important, they will become better, more aware, and more confident writers.

Supplemental Materials for Teaching *Focus on Writing*

In addition to this manual, ancillary material available to adopters of *Focus on Writing* includes the following:

- *Teaching Developmental Writing: Background Readings*, **Third Edition.** This anthology contains more than two dozen articles by professional writers providing background information on topics of interest to developmental writing instructors. The articles, by experts such as Mina Shaughnessy, Mike Rose, Peter Elbow, and Constance Weaver, are accompanied by analytical introductions, informative headnotes, and practical suggestions on how you might use the readings in your classroom.

- *Supplemental Exercises for FOCUS ON WRITING*, **Second Edition.** These exercises provide additional practice for students working on Units 4–7. Answers to all exercises appear at the end of the book so that students can work independently.

- *Diagnostic and Mastery Tests for FOCUS ON WRITING*, **Second Edition.** These tests correspond to the coverage in *Focus on Writing.* The Sentence Skills Diagnostic Test is keyed to Exercise Central so that students who need extra help in any area can get it online. *Diagnostic and Mastery Tests* is available in print and can also be downloaded from the *Focus on Writing* Web site.

- *Transparency Masters.* These reproducible forms include model student essays, student examples of the stages of paragraph and essay writing, and uncorrected student essays from the Chapter Reviews to be used for in-class editing activities. The transparency masters are available as files that can be downloaded from the *Focus on Writing* Web site.

- *Bedford/St. Martin's ESL Workbook*, **Second Edition,** offers additional exercises to nonnative speakers.

- *Testing Tool Kit* CD-ROM allows instructors to create customized tests and quizzes from a pool of nearly 2,000 questions.

- *Make-a-Paragraph Kit* CD-ROM offers "Extreme Paragraph Makeover" animation to teach students about paragraph development, as well as additional writing and grammar practice exercises.

- *Exercise Central 3.0.* This collection of grammar exercises is comprehensive, easy to use, and convenient for you and your students. Multiple exercise sets on every grammar topic, at a variety of levels, allow students to get as much practice as they need. Customized lesson plans and instant feedback enables both students and instructors to assess student progress. *Exercise Central* can be accessed at **bedfordstmartins.com/ exercisecentral**. For more information see Chapter 3, page 37, of this manual.

- *Re:Writing Basics.* This easy-to-navigate Web site contains help with the writing process, tips on college success, and other resources for the developmental writing class. It is accessible through **bedfordst martins.com/rewritingbasics**.

- *Writing Class.* At one easy-to-use site, students can see if there is a new assignment, complete the activity, and check back to find out how they did. There are options for building online discussions, adding multimedia tutorials, and more.

- *The FOCUS ON WRITING Web Site.* This Web site, **bedfordstmartins.com/focusonwriting**, features downloadable versions of this ancillary as well as *Diagnostic and Mastery Tests* and the transparency masters and other helpful resources. This site also provides access to *Exercise Central, Re:Writing Basics,* and many more student and instructor resources.

- *The Bedford Research Room.* At **bedford stmartins.com/researchroom**, you'll find links to research tools, guided tutorials, teaching help, and more.

Day One/Week One: Setting the Tone

Your goal in the first few classes is to help students become acquainted with you, with each other, with your expectations, and with the course. These initial meetings establish the tone for the semester—even when, as is often the case, they involve abbreviated classes devoted to red-tape issues (taking attendance, distributing class materials, etc.). You may not be able to accomplish all the following goals in the first week of teaching, but you should keep them in mind as you begin the semester.

- *Get students used to participating actively.* Make sure that each student gives at least one oral contribution during the first class, even if it occurs within a small-group activity when class size prevents large-group participation. A typical opening-day exercise pairs students who haven't met and asks each one to interview and then introduce the other. It is helpful to assign specific interview directions: name, why the partner has chosen to enroll at this particular school at this particular time, what he or she can contribute to the class, any special hopes and/or fears, and one interesting thing others should know. (For large classes meeting in a fifty-minute time frame, students will have to introduce one another within smaller groups to meet time constraints.)

- *Introduce yourself.* Let the student know the person as well as the professor. Tell them how you prefer to be addressed and how they can reach you outside class. One way to do the latter, and to encourage collaborative activities, is to have students fill out a class directory. Put your own contact information on the list as well, and then photocopy it and distribute it to each student during the next class period.

- *Require students to write something on the first day.* Even if they just write a few sentences, this will break the ice and emphasize that your class will indeed follow the textbook's advice and focus on writing. Some instructors start with a diagnostic essay. Others require freewriting that will eventually be used in an assignment or a brief paragraph expressing the student's primary goal for the semester. (See Writing History Questionnaire, p. 141, and Essay Directions for Writing History Assignment, p. 142, in Part Four of this manual.)

- *Get an overview of your students' grammar background.* Many instructors administer a general grammar diagnostic, such as those found in *Diagnostic and Mastery Tests to Accompany FOCUS ON WRITING* or at Exercise Central. Depending on your class focus, you may prefer to test grammar skills through a standardized, multiple-choice test or by having students proofread and correct a brief essay into which representative grammar errors have been introduced. Using the same diagnostic as a posttest at the end of the semester will give both you and your students a valuable picture of the skills that have been learned in the course.

- *Review the main points of the class syllabus.* As class members follow along on their syllabus, give them a general overview of the course—what kinds of activities a typical class period will include, what students will be expected to do in and out of class, what they will have learned by the end of the semester. Define any terms that students might not understand, such as the difference between *skim* and *read* in assignment directions.

- *Be encouraging.* Acknowledge that the class may be feeling overwhelmed as they consider all this work at once. Assure them that you are there to help break tasks down into manageable chunks and that following the syllabus is their key to success.

- *Clarify class policies.* Go over the main policy points in class, and assign as homework reading the section in the syllabus or course pack in which policies on absences, late work, and so on are spelled out in their entirety.

- *Introduce the text.* Explain how it's structured and how it will be used in and outside class. You may want to assign "A Student's Guide to Using *Focus on Writing*" and Appendix A, Strategies for College Success, as homework reading and then use it as the basis of a small-group discussion in the next class period. Remember, too, that developmental writers will probably not be familiar with college textbooks, so it is helpful to explain the purpose and use of features such as glossaries, checklists, and appendixes.

- *Be well organized.* One of your main responsibilities as a teacher of developmental students is to model the kinds of behavior that ensure academic success. Have all first-day handouts and assignments ready, with enough to go around. Plan and monitor class time carefully; don't ask students to start a task they won't have time to finish. Many instructors find it useful to write out a brief lesson plan for each class period that specifies goals, materials, activities, time frames, and assignments. The advantage of writing down plans on paper is that you then have a place to note any changes you want to make the next time you teach that lesson. For a guide to constructing lesson plans, see the section below.

- *Involve the students in establishing writing goals and standards.* See the sequence of activities described in Getting Started in Chapter 5 of this manual, for one suggested approach.

- *Use humor where appropriate.* Jokes, cartoons, and funny observations are good tension relievers. Be careful, though—students tend to take instructors' statements literally (as we learned the hard way with a student who worked the night shift, after we joked about which one of us to call with problems that arose at 4 a.m.).

Structuring the Semester: Planning Your Syllabus and Sequence of Class Assignments

As you plan the semester, you will be considering the sequence of tasks that you want students to perform and then the kinds of class activities that will help them accomplish these tasks. Your institution may require a standard syllabus form for all writing classes. If not, the following checklist outlines the typical sections.

CHECKLIST FOR CREATING A SYLLABUS

☑ **Course Name and Number, Number of Credits Granted.** Write out the official name, the abbreviated name, and the course number as it will appear on the students' transcripts. Include the number of credits students will earn or, if applicable, the class's noncredit status.

☑ **Date, Time, and Place of Class.** Include the semester, time of day, building, and classroom location.

☑ **Prerequisites, If Any.** This enables you and your students to double-check students' eligibility for the class.

☑ **Your Name and How to Reach You.** You may want to include your office phone number, office hours, fax number, email address, and course Web site address. Some instructors also include their home phone; this, of course, is up to you.

☑ **Course Description.** Some institutions require the use of an approved course description as found in the course catalog. Otherwise, in a brief paragraph, describe the overall purpose of the class. For example: *This course provides computer-assisted and teacher-directed writing practice. In a laboratory setting, students will review and refine their grammar and editing skills while learning word-processing applications as tools for producing effective professional writing.*

☑ **Course Goals.** State course goals in terms of what the course will do for the students. For example: *The course will review and provide opportunities for students to practice the conventions of Standard Written English.*

☑ **Student Objectives.** If your institution does not require the use of an approved list, state your objectives as clear descriptions of the outcomes you expect students to achieve. For example: *Students will learn to identify and correct basic grammar problems in class exercises and in their own writing.*

☑ **Topics to Be Studied.** List the general topics the course will cover, such as the kinds of writing to be produced, stages of the writing process, and peer- and self-editing techniques.

☑ **Requirements of the Course.** Provide clear, measurable requirements. For example: *Students will demonstrate an understanding of basic word processing by producing and revising all essays on computer.*

☑ **Class Policies.** Be clear and specific about each of these; doing this provides structure for the students and protection for you in any grading disputes that may arise.

Grading. Mention all components that are graded and what percentage of the final grade each component represents.

Absences

Classroom behavior

Accommodating disabilities

Assignment formatting requirements

Penalty for late assignments

Plagiarism (See p. 143 of this manual for a Sample Policy on Plagiarism.)

Requirements for advancing to the next level

☑ **Textbooks (Required and Supplementary).** Specify the edition, if more than one exists; whether complete or shortened versions are required; and whether any ancillary materials such as computer software are needed. Students often purchase books online or at locations other than the college bookstore, so be precise in your descriptions.

☑ **Additional Materials Needed.** These might include three-ring binders, blank computer disks, and so on.

Once you have created a general syllabus, specifying overall goals and policies, your next step is to plan the schedule for the semester. Developmental writing students function best with clear, concise, written guidelines. Presentation of your class assignment schedule is vital to their success.

Starting on p. 9 are seven abridged weekly assignment schedules illustrating possible approaches for classes that emphasize sentence- and paragraph-level skills as well as for classes that focus on essay writing. The modular construction of *Focus on Writing* makes it easy for you to adapt the text to your needs. A typical sequence would move students from simple writing tasks (description and narration) to more complicated challenges (classification and argumentation), from serious grammar errors (subject-verb agreement, sentence boundary problems, and verb formation) to less serious issues of mechanics, and from basic stylistic considerations (sentence variety) to more sophisticated concepts (shifts in person, parallel construction, and active vs. passive voice). How much you cover, of course, depends on the level of your students and the length of class time.

The final planning activity narrows your focus to the individual class period. Lesson plans do not have to be elaborate, but before going into class you should have carefully thought through, and preferably written down, at least five aspects of each lesson. First, state your objectives in terms of student outcomes: *By the end of this period, students will be able to _____ .* We recommend that you make a practice of mentioning these objectives to the students at the beginning of each class, perhaps even writing them on the chalkboard, so students will have a framework into which to fit the day's activities. Such previewing is especially helpful for students who learn best when they see the big picture first. Second, give the rationale: explain why you are doing these particular things at this particular point in the term. Third, write down the materials you will need (handouts, audiovisual equipment, special paper, etc.). Fourth, list the steps to be followed in class and the estimated time frame for each. Fifth, note any plans you have for determining whether students achieved the objectives. After the class is over, but while it's still fresh in your mind, jot down any changes you want to remember for the next time you go through this process.

Sample Class Schedules

Following are a variety of sample assignment schedules that show how you might use *Focus on Writing* for either ten- or sixteen-week semesters, depending on whether your class goal is (a) to move students from sentence to paragraph fluency, (b) to move students from paragraph to essay-level competency, or (c) to help students write essays in a variety of rhetorical modes. One additional model assumes a class with a research paper/portfolio emphasis.

CLASS SCHEDULE (16 Weeks)
Emphasis on Sentence Structure and the Paragraph

(Students practice composing a variety of paragraphs; emphasis is on developing fluency and on editing for correctness and clarity.)

WEEK ONE

In-class activities: Course overview; introduction to text; overview of the writing process; writing and grammar diagnostics
Homework:
Reading: "A Note to Students"; Chapter 1 (Understanding the Writing Process)
Writing: Journal entries

WEEK TWO

In-class activities: Drafting a paragraph; topic sentences and paragraph unity; exercises on identifying subjects and verbs
Homework:
Reading: Chapter 3 (Using Exemplification); Chapter 15 (Writing Simple Sentences)
Writing: Exemplification paragraph, draft 1; continue journal

WEEK THREE

In-class activities: Peer review for paragraph development; exercises on basic sentence patterns
Homework:
Reading: Chapter 2 (TESTing Your Paragraphs); Chapter 22 (Sentence Fragments)
Writing: Exemplification paragraph, revised; continue journal

WEEK FOUR

In-class activities: Peer review for paragraph coherence; exercises on identifying and correcting sentence fragments; in-class writing practice
Homework:
Reading: Chapter 4 (Using Narration); Chapter 16 (Writing Compound Sentences)
Writing: Narrative paragraph, draft 1; continue journal

WEEK FIVE

In-class activities: Telling a story: paragraph organization; outlining; exercises on combining sentences
Homework:
Reading: Chapter 5 (Using Description); Chapter 17 (Writing Complex Sentences)

Writing: Narrative paragraph, revised; continue journal

WEEK SIX

In-class activities: Peer review: narrative paragraph; recognizing and creating complex sentences
Homework:
Reading: Chapter 7 (Using Cause and Effect); Chapter 21 (Run-Ons)
Writing: Cause-and-effect paragraph, draft 1; continue journal

WEEK SEVEN

In-class activities: Exercises on identifying and eliminating run-ons; structuring a cause-and-effect paragraph
Homework:
Reading: Appendix A, section 7 (Exam-Taking Strategies); Chapter 18 (Writing Varied Sentences)
Writing: Cause-and-effect paragraph, revised; continue journal

WEEK EIGHT

In-class activities: In-class midterm; exercises on sentence combining
Homework:
Reading: Chapter 26 (Verbs: Past Tense); Chapter 27 (Verbs: Past Participles)
Writing: Continue journal

WEEK NINE

In-class activities: Sentence combining, continued; exercises on verb tense and verb formation; midterm assessment and goal setting
Homework:
Reading: Chapter 8 (Using Comparison and Contrast); Chapter 28 (Nouns and Pronouns)
Writing: Comparison-and-contrast paragraph, draft 1; continue journal

WEEK TEN

In-class activities: Structuring comparison-and-contrast paragraphs; exercises on pronoun use

Homework:
Reading: Chapter 31 (Using Commas)
Writing: Comparison-and-contrast paragraph, revised; continue journal

WEEK ELEVEN
In-class activities: Comma use and misuse; peer review: comparison-and-contrast paragraph
Homework:
Reading: Chapter 9 (Using Classification); Chapter 10 (Using Definition); Chapter 34 (Understanding Mechanics)
Writing: Classification/definition paragraph, draft 1; continue journal

WEEK TWELVE
In-class activities: Proofreading exercises; structuring classification paragraphs; in-class writing practice
Homework:
Reading: Chapter 35, section E (Commonly Confused Words); Chapter 24 (Illogical Shifts)
Writing: Classification/definition paragraph, revised; continue journal

WEEK THIRTEEN
In-class activities: Peer review: classification paragraphs; exercises on avoiding illogical shifts of tense, voice, and number

Homework:
Reading: Chapter 25 (Dangling and Misplaced Modifiers); Chapter 11 (Using Argument)
Writing: Argument paragraph, draft 1; complete journal

WEEK FOURTEEN
In-class activities: Writing to a specific audience; structuring effective arguments; identifying and correcting misplaced modifiers; begin grammar review (sentence structure)
Homework:
Reading: Chapter 19 (Using Parallelism)
Writing: Argument paragraph, revised

WEEK FIFTEEN
In-class activities: Peer review: argument paragraphs; exercises on parallelism; continue grammar review (verb formation and agreement)
Homework:
Reading: Chapter 20 (Using Words Effectively)
Writing: Argument paragraph, final draft

WEEK SIXTEEN
In-class activities: In-class writing final; final grammar exam

CLASS SCHEDULE (10 Weeks)
Emphasis on Sentence Structure and the Paragraph

(Students practice composing a variety of paragraphs; emphasis is on developing fluency and editing for correctness and clarity.)

WEEK ONE
In-class activities: Course overview; introduction to text; overview of the writing process; writing and grammar diagnostics
Homework:
Reading: "A Note to Students"; Chapter 1 (Understanding the Writing Process); Chapter 15 (Writing Simple Sentences)
Writing: Begin journal

WEEK TWO
In-class activities: Drafting a paragraph; topic sentences and paragraph unity; exercises on identifying subjects and verbs
Homework:
Reading: Chapter 22 (Sentence Fragments); Chapter 4 (Using Narration)
Writing: Narrative paragraph; journal entries

WEEK THREE
In-class activities: Peer review for paragraph coherence; exercises on identifying and correcting sentence fragments; in-class writing practice
Homework:
Reading: Chapter 16 (Writing Compound Sentences); Chapter 17 (Writing Complex Sentences); Chapter 5 (Using Description)
Writing: Descriptive paragraph, draft 1; journal entries

WEEK FOUR
In-class activities: Peer review: descriptive paragraph; recognizing and creating compound and complex sentences; adding concrete detail
Homework:
Reading: Chapter 21 (Run-Ons)
Writing: Descriptive paragraph, revised; journal entries

WEEK FIVE
In-class activities: Exercises on identifying and eliminating run-ons; in-class midterm; organization and outlining
Homework:
Reading: Chapter 23 (Subject-Verb Agreement); Chapter 7 (Using Cause and Effect)

Writing: Cause-and-effect paragraph, draft 1; journal entries

WEEK SIX
In-class activities: Identifying causes and effects; peer review: cause-and-effect paragraph; exercises on subject-verb agreement
Homework:
Reading: Chapter 26 (Verbs: Past Tense); Chapter 27 (Verbs: Past Participles)
Writing: Cause-and-effect paragraph, revised; journal entries

WEEK SEVEN
In-class activities: Structuring comparison-and-contrast paragraphs; exercises on past tense and perfect tenses
Homework:
Reading: Chapter 31 (Using Commas); Chapter 34 (Understanding Mechanics); Chapter 8 (Using Comparison and Contrast)
Writing: Comparison-and-contrast paragraph; journal entries

WEEK EIGHT
In-class activities: Proofreading for mechanics; structuring classification paragraph
Homework:
Reading: Chapter 18 (Writing Varied Sentences); Chapter 9 (Using Classification); Chapter 10 (Using Definition)
Writing: Classification paragraph, draft 1; journal entries

WEEK NINE
In-class activities: Peer review: classification paragraph; editing for sentence variety and style; grammar review
Homework:
Reading: Chapter 19 (Using Parallelism); Appendix A, section 7 (Exam-Taking Strategies)
Writing: Classification paragraph, revised; complete journal assignment

WEEK TEN
In-class activities: In-class writing final; final grammar quiz

CLASS SCHEDULE (16 Weeks)
Emphasis on the Paragraph and the Essay

(Students spend the first half of the semester practicing paragraph-level writing, moving to complete essays in the second half. Emphasis is on editing for correctness and style.)

WEEK ONE
In-class activities: Course overview; introduction to text; overview of the writing process; writing and grammar diagnostics
Homework:
Reading: "A Student's Guide to Using *Focus on Writing*"; Chapter 15 (Writing Simple Sentences)
Writing: Narrative paragraph; writing experiences

WEEK TWO
In-class activities: Choosing topics; structuring effective paragraphs; identifying sentence parts
Homework:
Reading: Chapter 1 (Understanding the Writing Process); Chapter 22 (Sentence Fragments)
Writing: Descriptive paragraph, draft

WEEK THREE
In-class activities: Supporting topic; adding concrete details; identifying and correcting sentence fragments
Homework:
Reading: Chapter 5 (Using Description); Chapter 16 (Writing Compound Sentences); Chapter 17 (Writing Complex Sentences)
Writing: Descriptive paragraph, revised

WEEK FOUR
In-class activities: Peer review; editing for paragraph coherence; sentence-combining exercises
Homework:
Reading: Chapter 21 (Run-Ons); Chapter 2 (TESTing Your Paragraphs)
Writing: Introduction and conclusion for descriptive paragraph

WEEK FIVE
In-class activities: Identifying and correcting run-ons; editing for paragraph unity; structuring process paragraph
Homework:
Reading: Chapter 6 (Using Process); Chapter 23 (Subject-Verb Agreement)
Writing: Process paragraph, draft

WEEK SIX
In-class activities: Editing for logical transitions; exercises on subject-verb agreement; in-class writing practice
Homework:
Reading: Chapter 8 (Using Comparison and Contrast); Chapter 26 (Verbs: Past Tense); Chapter 27 (Verbs: Past Participles)
Writing: Process paragraph, revised

WEEK SEVEN
In-class activities: Structuring comparison-and-contrast paragraphs; exercises on verb formation and tense
Homework:
Reading: Appendix A, section 7 (Exam-Taking Strategies); Chapter 35, section E (Commonly Confused Words)
Writing: Comparison-and-contrast paragraph

WEEK EIGHT
In-class activities: In-class midterm
Homework:
Reading: Chapter 12 (Writing an Essay); Chapter 31 (Using Commas); Chapter 32 (Using Apostrophes)
Writing: None

WEEK NINE
In-class activities: Choosing and supporting a thesis; exercises on punctuation; structuring classification essays
Homework:
Reading: Chapter 34 (Understanding Mechanics); Chapter 9 (Using Classification); Chapter 14, section G (Classification)
Writing: Classification essay, draft 1

WEEK TEN
In-class activities: Peer review: classification essay draft; exercises on mechanics; writing for different audiences
Homework:
Reading: Chapter 13 (Writing Introductions and Conclusions); Chapter 18 (Writing Varied Sentences)
Writing: Classification essay, revised

WEEK ELEVEN
In-class activities: Creating effective introductions and conclusions; exercises on varying sentence style
Homework:
Reading: Chapter 19 (Using Parallelism); Chapter 14, section I (Argument)
Writing: Proposal for argument essay

WEEK TWELVE
In-class activities: Deciding on argument topic; organizing arguments; exercises on parallel construction
Homework:
Reading: Chapter 20 (Using Words Effectively); Chapter 11 (Using Argument)
Writing: Argument essay, draft 1

WEEK THIRTEEN
In-class activities: Exercises on effective wording; peer review: argument essay
Homework:
Reading: Chapter 24 (Illogical Shifts); Chapter 28 (Nouns and Pronouns)
Writing: Argument essay, revised

WEEK FOURTEEN
In-class activities: Editing for style and correctness; exercises on pronoun use, avoiding shifts in person, number, and voice; begin grammar review
Homework:
Reading: Chapter 25 (Dangling and Misplaced Modifiers)
Writing: Argument essay, final draft

WEEK FIFTEEN
In-class activities: Exercises on modifiers; continue grammar review; practice in-class essays
Homework:
Reading: Review grammar as needed
Writing: Preparation for in-class final

WEEK SIXTEEN
In-class activities: In-class final; final grammar exam

CLASS SCHEDULE (10 Weeks)
Emphasis on the Paragraph and the Essay

(Students spend the first half of the semester practicing paragraph-level writing, moving to complete essays in the second half. Focus is on editing for correctness and style.)

WEEK ONE
In-class activities: Course overview; introduction to text; overview of the writing process; writing and grammar diagnostics
Homework:
Reading: "A Note to Students"*;* Chapter 15 (Writing Simple Sentences)
Writing: Narrative paragraph: writing experiences

WEEK TWO
In-class activities: Choosing topics; structuring effective paragraphs; identifying sentence parts
Homework:
Reading: Chapter 1 (Understanding the Writing Process); Chapter 22 (Sentence Fragments)
Writing: Descriptive paragraph, draft

WEEK THREE
In-class activities: Supporting a topic; adding concrete details; identifying and correcting sentence fragments
Homework:
Reading: Chapter 5 (Using Description); Chapter 16 (Writing Compound Sentences); Chapter 17 (Writing Complex Sentences)
Writing: Descriptive paragraph, revised

WEEK FOUR
In-class activities: Sentence-combining exercises; editing for paragraph unity; structuring process paragraphs
Homework:
Reading: Chapter 6 (Using Process); Chapter 2 (TESTing Your Paragraphs); Chapter 21 (Run-Ons)
Writing: Process paragraph, draft

WEEK FIVE
In-class activities: Identifying and correcting run-ons; peer review; in-class midterm
Homework:
Reading: Chapter 23 (Subject-Verb Agreement); Chapter 26 (Verbs: Past Tense); Chapter 12 (Writing an Essay)
Writing: Process paragraph, revised

WEEK SIX
In-class activities: Exercises on subject-verb agreement; choosing and supporting a thesis
Homework:
Reading: Chapter 9 (Using Classification); Chapter 14, section G (Classification); Chapter 27 (Verbs: Past Participles)
Writing: Classification essay, draft

WEEK SEVEN
In-class activities: Exercises on verb formation, tense; peer review; structuring effective introductions and conclusions
Homework:
Reading: Chapter 13 (Writing Introductions and Conclusions); Chapter 18 (Writing Varied Sentences); Chapter 31 (Using Commas)
Writing: Classification essay, revised

WEEK EIGHT
In-class activities: Stating and supporting a point of view; organizing an argument essay; exercises on sentence variety
Homework:
Reading: Chapter 11 (Using Argument); Chapter 14, section I (Argument); Chapter 32 (Using Apostrophes); Chapter 34 (Understanding Mechanics); Chapter 35, section E (Commonly Confused Words)
Writing: Argument essay, draft

WEEK NINE
In-class activities: Grammar and mechanics review; peer editing
Homework:
Reading: Appendix A, section 7 (Exam-Taking Strategies); Chapter 19 (Using Parallelism); Chapter 20 (Using Words Effectively)
Writing: Argument essay, revised

WEEK TEN
In-class activities: In-class final; final grammar exam

CLASS SCHEDULE (16 Weeks)
Emphasis on the Essay

(Students write and revise six essays with the aid of peer review groups. Class focus is on issues of correctness during the first half of the semester and on issues of style during the second half.)

WEEK ONE
In-class activities: Course overview; introduction to text; establish goals and standards; write diagnostic essay
Homework:
Reading: "A Note to Students;
Chapter 12 (Writing an Essay);
Chapter 23 (Subject-Verb Agreement)
Writing: Freewriting: writing experiences

WEEK TWO
In-class activities: Review subject-verb agreement; writing process; introduction to peer review
Homework:
Reading: Chapter 4 (Using Narration);
Chapter 14, section B (Narration);
Chapter 22 (Sentence Fragments)
Writing: Essay 1 (narration)

WEEK THREE
In-class activities: Identifying and correcting sentence fragments; practicing idea generation techniques; developing concrete detail; peer review
Homework:
Reading: Chapter 5 (Using Description);
Chapter 16 (Writing Compound Sentences);
Chapter 17 (Writing Complex Sentences)
Writing: Essay 1, revised

WEEK FOUR
In-class activities: Sentence combining; practice organizational schemes; peer review; practice in-class writing
Homework:
Reading: Chapter 14, section C (Description);
Chapter 21 (Run-Ons);
Chapter 2 (TESTing Your Paragraphs)
Writing: Essay 2 (description)

WEEK FIVE
In-class activities: Identifying and correcting run-ons and comma splices; composing effective paragraphs; peer review

Homework:
Reading: Chapter 7 (Using Cause and Effect); Chapter 31 (Using Commas)
Writing: Essay 2, revised

WEEK SIX
In-class activities: Editing for comma correctness; creating effective introductions and conclusions; peer review
Homework:
Reading: Chapter 14, section E (Cause and Effect); Chapter 26 (Verbs: Past Tense); Chapter 27 (Verbs: Past Participles); Chapter 13 (Writing Introductions and Conclusions)
Writing: Essay 3 (cause and effect)

WEEK SEVEN
In-class activities: Exercises on correct verb use; practicing effective revising, editing, and proofreading
Homework:
Reading: Chapter 34 (Understanding Mechanics); Chapter 32 (Using Apostrophes); Appendix A, section 7 (Exam-Taking Strategies)
Writing: Essay 3, revised

WEEK EIGHT
In-class activities: Review of mechanics and punctuation; midterm
Homework:
Reading: Chapter 8 (Using Comparison and Contrast); Chapter 35 (Understanding Spelling)
Writing: None

WEEK NINE
In-class activities: Midterm assessment; practice with commonly confused words; structuring comparison-and-contrast essays
Homework:
Reading: Chapter 14, section F (Comparison and Contrast); Chapter 18 (Writing Varied Sentences); Chapter 36 (Reading Critically)
Writing: Essay 4 (comparison and contrast)

WEEK TEN
In-class activities: Editing for style: sentence variety; peer review
Homework:
Reading: Chapter 9 (Using Classification); Chapter 19 (Using Parallelism)
Writing: Essay 4, revised

WEEK ELEVEN
In-class activities: Editing for style: parallel construction; structuring classification essays; peer review
Homework:
Reading: Chapter 14, section G (Classification);
Chapter 20 (Using Words Effectively)
Writing: Essay 5 (classification)

WEEK TWELVE
In-class activities: Editing for style: wording; peer review; in-class writing practice
Homework:
Reading: Chapter 11 (Using Argument); Chapter 25 (Dangling and Misplaced Modifiers)
Writing: Essay 5, revised

WEEK THIRTEEN
In-class activities: Editing for style: modifiers; peer review; structuring effective arguments

Homework:
Reading: Chapter 14, section I (Argument); Chapter 24 (Illogical Shifts); review grammar trouble spots
Writing: Plan Essay 6 (argument)

WEEK FOURTEEN
In-class activities: Editing for style: consistency; peer review; begin grammar review
Homework:
Reading: Chapter 28 (Nouns and Pronouns)
Writing: Essay 6 (argument)

WEEK FIFTEEN
In-class activities: Editing for style: pronoun use; continue grammar review; final peer review
Homework:
Reading: Review as needed
Writing: Essay 6, revised

WEEK SIXTEEN
In-class activities: In-class final; final grammar exam

CLASS SCHEDULE (10 Weeks)
Emphasis on the Essay

(Students write and revise five essays; focus is on editing for correctness and clarity.)

WEEK ONE
In-class activities: Course overview; introduction to text; establish goals and standards; write diagnostic essay
Homework:
Reading: "A Note to Students"; Chapter 12 (Writing an Essay); Chapter 4 (Using Narration); Chapter 14, section B (Narration); Chapter 23 (Subject-Verb Agreement)
Writing: Essay 1 (narration)

WEEK TWO
In-class activities: Review subject-verb agreement; discuss writing process; structuring narrative essays
Homework:
Reading: Chapter 5 (Using Description); Chapter 22 (Sentence Fragments)
Writing: Essay 1, revised

WEEK THREE
In-class activities: Identifying and correcting sentence fragments; practicing idea generation techniques; developing concrete detail
Homework:
Reading: Chapter 14, section C (Description); Chapter 2 (TESTing Your Paragraphs); Chapter 16 (Writing Compound Sentences); Chapter 17 (Writing Complex Sentences)
Writing: Essay 2 (description)

WEEK FOUR
In-class activities: Sentence combining; practicing organizational schemes; composing effective paragraphs
Homework:
Reading: Chapter 21 (Run-Ons); Chapter 36 (Reading Critically); Appendix A, section 7 (Exam-Taking Strategies)
Writing: Essay 2, revised

WEEK FIVE
In-class activities: Identifying and correcting run-ons and comma splices; reading effectively: finding the main point; in-class midterm
Homework:
Reading: Chapter 8 (Using Comparison and Contrast); Chapter 14, section F (Comparison and Contrast); Chapter 31 (Using Commas); Chapter 13 (Writing Introductions and Conclusions)
Writing: Essay 3 (comparison and contrast)

WEEK SIX
In-class activities: Editing for comma correctness; creating effective introductions and conclusions; structuring comparison-and-contrast essays
Homework:
Reading: Chapter 9 (Using Classification); Chapter 26 (Verbs: Past Tense); Chapter 27 (Verbs: Past Participles); Chapter 35, section E (Commonly Confused Words)
Writing: Essay 3, revised

WEEK SEVEN
In-class activities: Exercises on correct verb use; practicing effective revising, editing, and proofreading; structuring classification essays
Homework:
Reading: Chapter 14, section G (Classification); Chapter 18 (Writing Varied Sentences); Chapter 19 (Using Parallelism)
Writing: Essay 4 (classification)

WEEK EIGHT
In-class activities: Editing for style: sentence variety, parallel structure; in-class writing practice
Homework:
Reading: Chapter 11 (Using Argument); Chapter 24 (Illogical Shifts)
Writing: Essay 4, revised

WEEK NINE
In-class activities: Editing for style: illogical shifts; structuring effective arguments; grammar review
Homework:
Reading: Chapter 14, section I (Argument); Chapter 25 (Dangling and Misplaced Modifiers); Chapter 20 (Using Words Effectively)
Writing: Essay 5 (argument)

WEEK TEN
In-class activities: Editing for clarity and conciseness; in-class final

CLASS SCHEDULE (15 Weeks)
Emphasis on the Research Paper and/or the Portfolio

WEEK ONE
Grammar: Identifying subjects and verbs
Writing: Writing and grammar diagnostics; writing process; description

WEEK TWO
Grammar: Sentence fragments
Writing: Description essay draft

WEEK THREE
Grammar: Subject-verb agreement
Writing: Revised description essay due; narration freewrite

WEEK FOUR
Grammar: Verb tense and formation
Writing: Peer review

WEEK FIVE
Grammar: Compound sentences
Writing: Narrative and critique due; library instruction; introduction to research paper

WEEK SIX
Grammar: Complex sentences
Writing: Comparison-and-contrast freewrite

WEEK SEVEN
Grammar: Avoiding run-ons and comma splices
Writing: Library research

WEEK EIGHT
Grammar: Sentence combining for variety

Writing: Comparison-and-contrast essay due; practice for midterm

WEEK NINE
Grammar: Commas; mechanics; commonly confused words
Writing: Midterm; classification freewrite

WEEK TEN
Grammar: Illogical shifts
Writing: Work on classification essay

WEEK ELEVEN
Grammar: Parallel construction
Writing: Library research; classification essay due

WEEK TWELVE
Grammar: Quoting and citing sources
Writing: Conferences; portfolio workshop

WEEK THIRTEEN
Grammar: Review
Writing: In-class writing practice

WEEK FOURTEEN
Grammar: Review
Writing: Portfolios due

WEEK FIFTEEN
Grammar: Final exam
Writing: In-class final

2

Thirty-Two Teaching Tips

It's not unusual for developmental writing instructors to be given little or no time for preparation before they plunge into a new term of teaching. The following tips are designed to help you get started with a minimum of difficulty and to help you teach effectively throughout the semester.

1. Familiarize yourself with the classroom ahead of time. If possible, visit the classroom and see what kind of chalkboard or other equipment is available and whether there is ample space for students and instructor. Find out who does the duplicating and where requests should be dropped off and picked up. Put in your copy request early.

2. Gather everything you need for the first day of class. Make sure you have the following items: the syllabus, class policies, assignments, some sort of writing diagnostic tool, the textbook, and a lesson plan that includes an ice-breaking activity. (See Chapter 1 of this manual for more information on the first day of class.)

3. Consider making a class directory. Pass around a sheet of paper on the first day of class, and ask students to list their email addresses. Put your own contact information at the top, and make copies for everyone. Encourage students to use the list to consult one another about assignments and to contact you about problems or emergencies.

4. Plan an ice-breaker. Start with an activity that will allow you and the students to get to know one another. This can be as simple as having students introduce themselves or as elaborate as planning scavenger hunts in which

students ask questions about one another's backgrounds. Whether simple or complex, an ice-breaker will give you an idea of the types of students in the class and will encourage the students to network among themselves. (See Chapter 1 of this manual for more information on the first day of class.)

Consider using the following set of ice-breaking activities to prepare students for a homework reading assignment in Appendix A, "Strategies for College Success." Be sure to save time for a general class discussion in which students compare notes.

a. Interview a partner about what he or she did to prepare for the semester.

b. In a group of three or four students, compare biorhythms. Are you a morning or an evening person? Where and when do you study best?

c. In a small group, generate a list of the five most important places to know on campus, and then report back to the class.

d. With a partner, discuss your time management strategies. What has worked for you and what hasn't?

e. In small groups, discuss your favorite extracurricular activities. How will you ensure that your study schedule leaves time for these activities?

5. Combat nervousness with preparation. It's good to be prepared, nervous or not, but if you are particularly worried, you may want to work away those jitters with a detailed lesson plan for the day. Remember that some activities will go more quickly or more slowly than you anticipate, so it is a good idea to have backup plans ready. After a couple of classes, you'll develop a feel for how long it might take your students to complete a particular activity, but there will always be surprises. (See Chapter 1 of this manual for more information on what to address in lesson plans.)

6. Don't overcomplicate activities. New instructors sometimes design complicated activities for developmental writing students. However, it's better to focus on a single three- or four-step in-class activity. For example, have students work in groups of three to compare their answers to grammar exercises. Then have the students reconcile disagreed-upon answers and report their findings to the rest of the class.

7. Mix activities. Use a variety of teaching strategies to get the message across. Consider mixing lectures with small-group activities, games, or one-on-one instruction. Students vary widely in their learning styles and needs, so you shouldn't rely on one approach. The class will be more enjoyable for you and your students if the activities are varied.

8. Remember that developmental writers have a wide range of skills. Not everyone who participates in a developmental writing class will have trouble with sentence fragments. Some will have minor problems with style and organization, and others will have trouble constructing basic sentences. A writing diagnostic tool, even if it is just a brief essay, will help you identify the different skill levels in your class. Depending on your assessment of the students, you may want to adjust the lesson plans to focus more or less on particular topics. You may also want to consider breaking the class into groups according to skill level and dividing your time accordingly. Determining skill levels also gives you a chance to see if any students have been placed inappropriately and should be moved to a higher- or lower-level writing class.

9. Respect and believe in your students. An inability to write well is not an indication of poor character. Many students are highly motivated and passionately invested in the course. They recognize the value of a diploma and know they must write better to get one. Try not to see your students solely in terms of their writing limitations. They all have gifts and talents in other areas. Appreciate their gifts, and try to find ways of using these to enrich the class.

10. Work to reduce fear. Many developmental writing students have spent twelve or more years being frustrated by writing tasks. They may have been told they're stupid, may have received failing grades, and may be scared to death of a college-level writing course. It can be helpful to have students talk about their best and worst writing experiences. (For a sample discussion and assignment on the theme of students' writing experiences, see pp. 64–65 in Chapter 7 of this manual.) This act alone may help the students feel more comfortable with their participation in the course because they will realize that others have had similar experiences. Communicate your encouragement and understanding of their situation. Let your students know that they can ask questions and get help at any time.

11. Expect varying degrees of progress. Just as developmental writers arrive at your class with different skill levels, they will progress at different rates. It may take one student one lecture to identify and correct a sentence fragment, but another will need the entire semester just to figure out what an incomplete sentence is. Don't expect all students to begin correcting their writing errors after they've received a week of instruction. It took years for their writing problems to develop, and it will take time and practice to correct them.

12. Remember that education is collaboration. Some students will fail despite your best efforts. Emphasize from the beginning that the course is a partnership: the instructor has responsibilities, and the students have responsibilities. Sometimes issues in students' lives interfere with class work, and they simply can't be successful at that particular time. Sometimes fear and anxiety keep students from progressing. Expect that some students will not make progress no matter how well you do your job.

13. Know the text. Many students will work faithfully and diligently in their workbooks. They will have questions about their homework and will ask for explanations. Be prepared. Make sure that your presentation of concepts is in sync with the textbook's. Try to use the same language whenever possible. Read the preface to the text — especially "A Note to Students," which offers valuable insights for instructors as well.

14. Get your students to focus. Do whatever is necessary to get your students' attention: tell jokes, have students teach each other, change seating arrangements. Focusing may be difficult for many of your students, and they may tune out to avoid being overly frustrated by writing. However, you must hold their interest if they are to progress.

15. Have students write, write, write. The developmental writing student has missed out on an entire childhood of writing properly. Many developmental writing students have not had the advantage of hearing grammatically correct English spoken at home, either. The only way to supplant poor writing habits is through practice. If a student is having serious problems with certain aspects of grammar or syntax, consider advising him or her to do all the exercises in a related chapter in the workbook. Students who request or need more practice can be directed to *Supplemental Exercises for FOCUS ON WRITING* or to the *Exercise Central* online grammar exercise bank.

16. Repeat key concepts. Some people respond well to a lecture; others don't. Expect to repeat key concepts many times during the semester, and try to use some of the same language over and over. During your initial explanation, describe the writing concept clearly, in several ways, visually and verbally. Sum up the concept with a catchphrase such as "Never start a sentence with 'such as.'" Afterward, use the catchphrase frequently to help students associate the concept in practice. The hope is that these catchphrases will come to mind when students are using problematic words or punctuation in their writing.

17. Small-group activities are important. Research has shown that students who don't feel comfortable participating in front of the whole class will participate in small groups. Incorporate small-group activities into your lesson plan, particularly if you teach long sessions. Have students in small groups edit each other's work, identify key points of reading material, and review textbook exercises. (See Chapter 5 of this manual for more ideas on collaboration.)

18. Plan some in-class editing time. At the end of each session, allow time for students to make last-minute changes to their papers and to ask questions one on one. Students who don't acquire good writing habits from workbook exercises are more likely to improve when mistakes in their work are pointed out to them and explained. Give students time to edit each other's work. You can be called in to resolve disputes. Try to see that students are not mismatched during this activity. Less skilled but persuasive students can sometimes talk more highly skilled students into making errors.

19. Be patient. Patience is a virtue in every situation, but particularly in the teaching of developmental writing. Students may ask the same question over and over; you may still be reminding students of the difference between topic and thesis at the end of fifteen weeks of instruction. This, however, is the nature of the course. Identify progress where you see it, and don't expect students' skill levels to exceed yours at the end of the semester (though they may!). It may be helpful to compare the diagnostic essays written on the first day of class to current assignments as a measure of your students' progress. They may be doing better than you think. At the end of the course, return these essays to the students so that they too can see the progress they've made.

20. Avoid red ink. Your students have a long history of getting back papers covered with criticisms and poor grades written in red. Consider using a different color ink. Students may develop a similar aversion to green ink by the end of the semester, but the green sends a message that this course is different and that the instructor doesn't wish to cause students any more pain over writing. Green can be taken by students as a signal to move forward with their writing, whereas red signifies "stop." Another option is to write your comments in pencil. This allows you to change your mind and doesn't "shout" your comments quite so loudly. Whatever the color, try to avoid telling students they are wrong. Use euphemisms such as "What would be your second choice?" or "If you had to pick another answer, what would it be?" In a tolerant environment, students feel more comfortable and are more daring with class participation.

21. Attend to physical comfort. Do what you can to make sure your students are physically comfortable within the classroom. Make sure there is ample space to sit and work and that everyone can see and hear you. You may not have much control over the room temperature and lighting, but you should do what you can to optimize the environment. Some instructors start class with a snack; others schedule a coffee break halfway through long sessions. Try to anticipate your students' physical needs so that they won't distract from your instruction.

22. Make assignments orally and in writing. Be very clear about due dates and policies regarding promptness in assignments. Distribute an assignment schedule on the first day of class so that there will be no excuse for students not knowing when something is due. Tell students that they are responsible for turning assignments in on time, whether or not they attend class. Encourage students to use their class directories to make arrangements with other students if necessary. Remind them of your expectations each time you make an assignment. Provide a detailed written description of essay assignments that includes planning and organizing strategies and perhaps a sample. The preparation involved will pay off when students clearly understand what is due.

23. Make assignments stimulating. Keep in mind that developmental writers are adults who have complex opinions on a wide variety of topics. They will not appreciate overly simplistic assignments. They often want to express their views in writing and are anxious to practice their new skills in a meaningful way. Give them meaty subjects to write about. Draw ideas from current events and the editorial pages of national newspapers. Let students make controversial arguments. Not only will they exercise their critical thinking skills, but they will be much more motivated to produce good writing.

24. Do all the assignments yourself. Follow the instructions you've given for writing assignments. Were you bored with the assignment? If so, chances are your students will be, too. Was the assignment too time-consuming? If so, break it down to be accomplished over several classes, or modify it so that it is shorter. Following this tip requires you to proofread assignment sheets carefully—an added benefit because grammatical mistakes by the teacher can be embarrassing!

25. Set expectations for appropriate behavior. Announce your course requirements. Be clear about when homework is due and what happens when papers are late. Take attendance at the beginning of class to send a message about tardiness. Don't allow students to make fun of each other or to be openly hostile. If you are courteous with the students, they will usually reflect that demeanor. Let students know clearly that you are in charge and intend to enforce class rules fairly but firmly.

26. Keep a teaching journal. After each class, jot down notes about what worked and what didn't. You may have designed an activity that was too complicated, or you may have miscalculated time in your lesson plan. You'll appreciate having this information when you plan the next semester. You might also jot down your expectations of students and whether or not they were borne out. If you have a student who seems unlikely to pass the course, keep track of your efforts to assist his or her progress.

27. Enlist the support of colleagues. The advice and aid of another instructor can save you a lot of frustration and aggravation. If you are fortunate enough to work with other developmental writing teachers, ask for copies of their lesson plans and assignment schedules. They may also be able to point you in the direction of other resources, answer your questions about course material, and walk you through the intricacies of campus administration.

28. Consider online resources. Check out writing sources on the Internet. Purdue University and the University of Maine have excellent online writing labs, as do many other universities. There are also many networks for writing teachers that offer everything from ESL resources to jokes to classroom activity ideas. If you can't find a colleague close by with whom to share your classroom experiences, you can certainly find someone online. (See Chapter 3 of this manual for more information on teaching with technology. In addition, the Bedford/ St. Martin's Web site (**bedfordstmartins.com**) includes various resources for instructors, including online versions of *The Bedford Bibliography for Teachers of Writing* and *The Bedford Bibliography for Teachers of Basic Writing*.)

29. Find time for your own professional growth. Go to conferences, subscribe to journals, and take time to reflect on your growing teaching skills. These activities can be a refreshing break from teaching and can give you a new perspective on developmental writing. Consider joining the Conference on College Composition and Communication (CCCC), which includes in its membership a subscription to *College Composition and Communication*, as well as information on its annual spring conference. Subscription information is available at **ncte.org/ cccc** or by writing to the National Council of Teachers of English (1111 W. Kenyon Road, Urbana, IL 61801-1096). Another important journal for developmental writing teachers is *JBW: Journal of Basic Writing*, P.O. Box 465,

Hanover, PA 17331. Additionally, the Conference on Basic Writing, a CCCC special-interest group, publishes *BWe: Basic Writing e-Journal,* an electronic journal devoted to developmental writing: **orgs.tamu-commerce.edu/CBW/ASU/journal-1 .html**.

30. Develop your own style. Trust yourself. Make your own decisions about what suits your personality and your particular students. It's good to emulate other instructors, but ultimately you'll find what works best for you. Give thought to what makes you comfortable in the classroom. As you relax, so will your students.

31. Keep your sense of humor. It's okay to laugh about some of the problems you experience in your class. Your students will be demanding, and you'll run into sticky situations. Several times a semester you may fret about whether your students are actually learning anything. Of course they are, but that's not always easy to see. We comfort ourselves by reflecting on the importance of self-esteem. If nothing else, we've made our students feel better about their writing ability. This helps us keep things in perspective, and soon we're back in the classroom smiling again. Learn to laugh, and you'll be fine.

32. Treat your students like writers. Give your students assignments for real audiences with real purposes and high expectations. As much as possible, ensure that they have the support writers need to succeed: appropriate tools, clear goals, frequent feedback, and an atmosphere of encouragement.

3

Using Technology in the Classroom

A central goal of any writing course is to equip students with the communication skills they will need to be successful both in and out of school. It's difficult to envision a career today that does not require some level of technology skills, be it for data keeping, research, marketing, internal correspondence, product development, manufacturing, or repair. In addition to the important goal of teaching marketable skills, there are many reasons to add a computer component to a developmental writing class.

The Top Ten Reasons for Using Computers in Your Writing Classes

Reason 10: Computer use may reinforce habits of precision. Students are forced to attend to detail when they work on computers. Typing a semicolon instead of a colon, or improperly capitalizing a word, will prevent them from getting to the Internet resource they're looking for. Spell checkers underline typos, and grammar checkers point out irregular spacing. At least in theory, sloppiness becomes harder to ignore, and the virtue of precision becomes more obvious.

Reason 9: New kinds of style and format issues become important. Visual learners may find that they are good at a writing skill they hadn't even known *was* a writing skill because more than verbal skills are called into play. Writing on a computer involves making judgments about design elements such as font, page layout, and the kind of bullets to use in lists.

Reason 8: Students take increased pride in the professional appearance of their work. Although the professional appearance of word-processed text can lead to a false sense of security, it can also be a source of pride and an incentive to make a paper's content as impressive as its appearance.

Reason 7: New ways of "publishing" student writing emerge. Developmental writers rarely have the chance to see their words published in any form; thus they miss one of the major rewards of writing and one of the main incentives to keep working to get it right. Desktop publishing offers this opportunity, and the Internet expands it by enabling students to enter a worldwide conversation with scholars, authors, and other people of all types. Students can publish their essays on a class home page, and ESL students can practice real-life conversation in chat rooms.

Reason 6: Students find themselves writing for more and different audiences. Writing in a lab setting is a social activity. Words displayed on a computer screen seem more public than do the same words written on a sheet of paper tucked in a notebook. Students always seem to be commenting on something they see on someone else's monitor or asking a neighbor to look at something on their own. When classes are connected to the Internet, this social aspect is magnified. Students have new opportunities to take on the role of both author and critic. Those who have grammar questions can visit tutors in online writing labs, unhampered by barriers of time and location.

Reason 5: The classroom shifts from teacher-centered to student-centered. Anyone glancing into a computer classroom notices immediately that the instructor is no longer the focal point of all activity. Developmental writing students tend to come to the classroom without much sense of autonomy, believing that only the instructor knows the "right" way to write and fearing that whatever that right way might be, it's probably beyond their grasp. Mastering a tool like word processing empowers them, helping them gain control as writers and as students.

Reason 4: Student writing becomes central to class instruction and activity. Instructors don't have to rely on convenient, but not very useful, "canned" examples. Student texts, once digitized, can be shared in a lab, projected onto a screen, printed as needed, tried out and analyzed in multiple formats, and commented on unobtrusively with a word processor's Comment feature.

Reason 3: Students write and revise more because they can do so with less effort. At the computer, students seem to get more involved with their own words. Sentences or paragraphs can be moved around quickly. Words on-screen are clearer than scratched-out handwriting, they can be manipulated to provide the writer with a more objective perspective, and only the unwanted words have to be retyped. This last factor motivates everyone and helps students with learning disabilities, who often introduce errors when recopying correct prose. However, we don't want to suggest that computer use in itself turns every student into an effective editor. Students frightened by technology may initially revise less, while the ease of making mechanical changes may interfere with more substantive editing for others. Guidance by the instructor is essential to show students why, how, and when to revise, but at least with computers the revision is less arduous.

Reason 2: Learning becomes more active. Talking takes a backseat to doing. Although adult students, especially, prefer learning situations in which they are actively involved and can see the real-world usefulness of a task, all students regardless of age benefit from the opportunity to make their own knowledge. With technology, many barriers fall—between student and teacher, between student and student, between students and their learning institutions, between students and the outside world, between knowledge and action.

Reason 1: That's how people write today. Instructors used to ask whether research has shown that people write better with computers. This question has become moot, as a glance around any high school, college campus, or library proves. For better or worse, the computer is the writing tool of choice—especially among younger students. The question we should be asking now is, Given that my students will be writing with computers, both in school and on the job, how can I help them use this tool effectively?

Teaching a Computer-Intensive Writing Course: Common Concerns

Even if you believe that computers can have a positive effect on students in general, you may be worried that the effect on your particular class and students might not be wholly positive. Following are typical concerns voiced by new instructors. Luckily, the experiences of writing teachers over the past decade or two have produced some useful answers.

Effects on Teaching

I'll have less time to teach writing because I'll be spending too much time teaching technology. This is a serious issue because class time is always at a premium in a writing course. If you do have to teach technical skills, you can do so in a way that models and reinforces good writing practice. A creative instructor will find many ways to fit instructions on cutting and pasting, for instance, into a sentence-combining activity, or grammar and spell checker use into a lesson on editing versus revising. You'll find that teaching computer skills in the context of the writing process enhances, rather than detracts from, your writing instruction.

You can also save time by being proactive: distribute handouts with step-by-step explanations for all the basic computer tasks in language students can understand, avoiding technical jargon wherever possible. (If you're lucky, you might get your institution's computer center staff to write out these instructions, but you will probably still have to customize them for your students.) Refer frequently to these computer directions in your assignment instructions. For example, a reminder in bold type at the end of a homework assignment to save the draft on a floppy disk and on the hard drive can prevent class time from being wasted while a student searches for an essay on a mysteriously blank disk. Come to class early, if possible, so individual students' computer problems can be addressed before the class begins. Remind students of the technical support available at your institution's computer labs, writing center, or library.

I'm not a computer expert myself. I'm worried that I won't know enough to answer questions that come up. Relax. You're not there to teach computing, just writing. If you use word processing for your own writing, you know more than enough to help students do the same. Share your experience, keep the class focused on writing issues, and direct technical questions to the technical staff. One of the most important behaviors you can model for your students is learning how to find answers to questions you don't understand.

How can I make sure I take advantage of the opportunities offered by a computer-intensive classroom? Technology is a means, not an end. Focus on whether students are learning what they need to learn about writing, not on whether you have used every technological bell and whistle available to help them learn it. This doesn't mean you should teach the same way in a lab setting as you would in a traditional classroom, but you don't have to use computers just because they're there. Many instructors continue to write their comments on printed copies of student papers, for instance, even when papers are submitted electronically. The instructors find it faster and easier, and they feel students can access the comments more conveniently.

You may find it helpful to keep a teaching journal in which you jot down your thoughts, successful techniques, lessons you want to present differently next time, things you should have told the students before a certain activity, equipment you need to get, skills you need to learn, or changes you need to make to class activities. As you teach, you'll learn what works and what doesn't, and you'll begin to build your own repertoire of tips and tricks. Another excellent way to pick up teaching ideas is to join one

of the electronic discussion groups focusing on computers and composition. (See the list of Internet resources near the end of this chapter.)

I'll have to spend a lot more time preparing for class, not to mention trying to keep up with all the hardware and software changes. True, technology is not labor saving. But it can help you to teach more creatively and effectively, and after all, that's why you're in this profession. All sorts of new options will open up. You can demonstrate how a grammar point works with motion and color and other visual cues, or you can let students hear what they've written as they make decisions about sentence style. Talk to instructors who are presently teaching in computer classes because they are often among the most enthusiastic and motivated of composition faculty.

Effects on Students

Using computers will simply add another layer of complexity to the writing task, overtaxing my students' already-strained working memory and causing their writing to suffer. Yes and no. A student with no previous keyboarding or computing experience, or someone with computer anxiety, will probably be distracted initially. This usually subsides relatively quickly, and the student's sense of accomplishment and control over the technical process may even translate into a sense of control over the writing process. The "fun" of word processing—with its ease of revision, uniformity of appearance, and new tools for editing—can go far toward eliminating the fear and dislike of writing prevalent among developmental writers. Be sure to demonstrate a little computer "magic" early on: how to use the Replace command in the Edit menu to change the misspelling of a frequently used word, for example, or how to use the Properties function to count words. Make your students aware of the Undo command (CTRL + Z), which "undoes" the most recent typing and editing. Show students that this intimidating machine can help with tasks they consider important. Reassure them that it will soon become a trusted friend.

I've heard that it's harder to read from the screen than from paper. If my students have problems with proofreading anyway, why would I want to put an additional barrier in front of them? A number of problems are associated with reading from monitors: readers have trouble gauging the length of paragraphs; they don't see errors easily; and they have difficulty keeping the structure of the entire document in mind when they can see only one screen at a time. What to do? Encourage students to print out drafts frequently. Show them how to make the text bigger by using the Zoom function or by increasing the type size as they proofread. Give them simple tips for judging paragraph length—for example, a paragraph that fills the entire screen may be too long, whereas three or four paragraphs visible on one screen are probably short and choppy.

Problems with Technical Support

All my students seem to use different software, not to mention the Mac/PC problem. If you're teaching in a computer classroom, incompatibility can be an extra headache. Establish good relationships with your school's computer support staff, and advocate for the purchase of the latest versions of word-processing software and conversion drivers so that your computers can convert older software as well as accommodate the wide range of word-processing programs that students use at home and work. Teach students to change formats with the Save As rather than Save command so that they know, for example, how to save a WordPerfect document in Word format or how to use a Mac to change a Windows file to Mac format.

Our computer labs are notorious for breakdowns. What if I've planned a collaborative activity and find that our network is down and students can't exchange papers? Technological breakdowns are inevitable. There's not much you can do to prevent them, but the best you can do is anticipate the possibility and have an alternate plan ready. Even though technology may provide a better way to reach class objectives, it is rarely the only way.

I've got enough problems already without adding technology issues to the list of things to worry about in my classroom. It's true that equipment will malfunction, computers will "eat" homework, and in-class activities you planned with care won't work because of some software problem that never occurred when you were practicing at home. On the positive side, you will get to review all aspects of your course (content, structure, activities, as-

signments, and desired outcomes) through the lens of technology—a chance for reflective growth that is valuable to experienced and new instructors alike.

Tips for In-Class Activities

In-class activities like the ones below can encourage students to exploit the power of computers throughout the writing process. Students profit from thinking about what they've done and why, so you should allow adequate time for discussion after activities.

An important reminder: It is just as unproductive to take over students' keyboards as it is to take over their papers. No matter how impatient you are, let a student fix his or her problem rather than fixing it yourself. That way, students will gain the confidence to repeat these fixes outside of class.

Inventing

- Have students practice freewriting at the computer, once with the monitor on and once with the monitor off. The two options appeal to different kinds of writers. Students who find their creativity stimulated by seeing words like to watch their thoughts unfolding on the monitor. Perfectionists who tend to write slowly and painstakingly often find the "invisible freewriting" liberating: they can't see their mistakes, so they don't have to stop and correct them. Be sure to link the freewriting practice with an upcoming assignment, so students are producing a useful product while they're developing a new skill.

- If your class is online, have students brainstorm a topic together in a chat room or by instant messaging.

- Let students converse about assignment ideas face-to-face and via email, and then discuss the advantages and disadvantages of each approach.

Selecting and Arranging Ideas

- Have students list all their ideas and then cut and paste them into logical order. Boldface the general headings, and leave the supporting ideas in regular type, indented one tab space, so that the shape of the essay shows clearly.

- If you're a fan of formal outlines, demonstrate your word processor's Outline function, and then have students try it on their own topics. Remind them that they can keep their outline on-screen (or in a separate window) and just type the draft in between outline items, deleting the "skeleton" of the outline at the end. This is an easy way to maintain an essay's focus.

Drafting

- Encourage students to copy and paste unused ideas into a separate "idea" file for later use.

- Suggest that students type ideas or questions that occur to them during the drafting process in capital letters, boldface, or a different color. Later, these comments can easily be deleted or pasted elsewhere.

Revising/Editing/Proofreading

It's at the later stages of the writing process that computers can be most helpful. Here is just a brief sampling of classroom applications.

- Ask your lab technicians to set up a separate network drive for your class with two kinds of folders: one that is read-only, in which you save grammar exercises and other files that you want students to use in class but not change permanently, and one with read/write privileges so that the students can share and modify files in class and you can access all student files from your computer.

- Encourage frequent printouts during revision. Moving back and forth between screen and paper copy is a good way for students to gain the necessary distance for revising.

- If you have a projector or LCD panel, project a student's draft on a screen and model effective peer review behavior by leading the class in a group editing session.

- After students save a separate copy of a draft with a new name (important!), have them delete everything but the first and last paragraph of the draft. Then ask them to

check for consistency of focus by making sure the opening and closing ideas relate to, but don't simply repeat, one another.

- Have students delete everything but the first and last sentences of all paragraphs to check for logical transitions.

- Have students switch disks or seats and highlight in red what they think is the topic sentence of each paragraph of their partner's essay. Then see if the author agrees. Or have the author scramble sentences within a paragraph and see if a partner can put them back in the original sequence.

- Have students delete the first paragraph of their essay. A partner reads the rest of the essay and then writes an introductory paragraph; students compare the two versions. They then do the same with the conclusion.

- Put on the network or student disks a simple macro (an automated sequence of commands) that replaces each period with two carriage returns, thus breaking text into a list of separate sentences. Students can then scroll to the bottom of the list, read from end to beginning, check lengths of sentences, check for sentence completeness, and so on. Suddenly the essay looks more like a workbook exercise, and errors are easier to see.

- Have students enlarge the type a few sizes or use the Zoom function so that problems become more visible.

- Have students switch the font style before editing, in order to gain some distance from the original text.

- Show your class how to use the Find command to edit for individual trouble areas. With a little ingenuity, you can teach students to be their own grammar checkers and give them much more control over their writing. (See suggestions in Part Three of this manual for examples of how to use this command with the various grammar and style issues covered in different chapters.)

The more you engage in these kinds of activities in class, the more you are emphasizing that writing is never "finished" and that computers enable writers to manipulate their texts easily and fearlessly.

Frequently Asked Questions about Teaching Writing with Computers

Do students write better with computers? Valid research on this question is sparse, and the results are mixed. Measurable improvements in writing take time to develop. It's difficult to find research showing that *anything* significantly improves writing over the course of one semester. It is also difficult to isolate the effect of one factor from the effects of all the other variables in an instructional setting. However, it is probably fair to say that technology has not been found to have any significantly negative results and that (anecdotally at least) students report a more positive attitude toward writing and their own academic abilities when they're learning in a lab setting.

Students like to write with computers. This in itself is a powerful argument for making the tool available to developmental writing students, who tend to be reluctant, fearful writers with negative views of their own ability.

Will slow typists be at a disadvantage? Your class will probably exhibit quite a range of typing ability, from students with clerical backgrounds who are technologically adept to others who have never set finger to keyboard. In a computer classroom, this range can cause a bit of chaos in the beginning, but it also provides a good opportunity for students to get to know one another. Acknowledge the initial confusion, and ask the class to bear with it, promising that it won't last. Pair experts with novices when you assign activities at first: this is an esteem builder for the helpers, and the students being helped often learn more easily from peers than from a teacher. Plan group exercises in which newcomers can choose to watch and learn until they get over their fears. Generally, after the first three or four weeks of class, everyone will have developed enough fluency that in-class work won't be a problem. Let slow typists know that initially they may have to spend more time than others in producing their assignments. Assure them that their hard work will pay off: the keyboarding skills they develop will help them not only in your class but also across the curriculum and on the job.

What kinds of software programs are most useful? Many kinds of writing software are available: invention programs, organization tools, style analyzers, voice-powered word processors, speech synthesizers. More is not always better, though. The best tool you can give a developing writer is a clear understanding of a standard word-processing program such as Word or WordPerfect.

Once students have learned to use a word processor, help them use it efficiently. Show them how to organize their work in different folders. Insist that they keep backup copies on a mass storage device like a USB flash drive. Explain the importance of naming files logically so that they can still be found later in the semester. Show how to turn the Spell Check and Grammar Check features on and off. Require students to print draft versions in large type with triple spacing for easy proofreading. Above all, show them how to use spell checkers and grammar checkers effectively; don't assume they will do so automatically.

You may want to try out voice recognition software (such as the *Dragon NaturallySpeaking* or IBM's ViaVoice) to see if your students benefit from it. Many developmental writers can talk about their ideas fluently but freeze when they have to write them down. Being able to speak their ideas into a computer can help them overcome their writer's block. Be aware, though, that voice recognition software requires a period of "training" — it's far from plug-and-play. It also will not miraculously cure grammar problems, as fervently as students might wish it could. Students who have trouble seeing basic errors in their typed drafts may be helped by freeware such as ReadPlease (**readplease.com**) that allows them to use simple cut-and-paste functions to hear their essay read aloud in a variety of voices and at a variety of speeds.

Should I encourage students to compose on-screen? Everyone has different ideas about what works best. Some people need the feel of a favorite pen or the reassuring scratch of a pencil to get words flowing, so you should never insist on a one-size-fits-all approach to computer use. However, it is useful to require that all students, at some point, compose directly on the computer and then spend time in class discussing their reactions to the process. Unless you insist, many students will never try on-screen writing. Force the issue. If they like the process, it can be a good time-saver for them. They'll never know until they try.

What class size works best in a laboratory setting? Computer lab classes of fifteen to twenty students are usually considered optimal. Even with fifteen, you'll often feel you've run a marathon by the end of the class, racing from computer to computer giving advice, helping with technical problems, moving the faster students ahead, and helping the slower ones keep up. Although you probably won't be making the final decisions on this matter, you, as an experienced instructor with knowledge of computer classrooms, can be a persuasive advocate for reasonable class size. Insist on capping class size at a level that allows you to have one or more unused computers available to accommodate the inevitable breakdowns in equipment.

How big a problem are computer viruses? Viruses are certainly an issue you'll want to discuss at the beginning of the term, reminding students of the need to have good virus protection on their home computers. If you are planning to have students email work to you, be sure you have the latest protection on your home and office computers, preferably the type that includes weekly or monthly Internet updates. You'll need that kind of protection to stay worry free.

What are the pros and cons of spell checkers? The Spell Check function is invaluable to developmental writers. At one time or another, you've probably asked students what the hardest part of writing is for them and heard, "I'm a terrible speller." It's easy to ignore such an answer because you know that spelling is a small and essentially unimportant part of writing, but for students, worries about spelling can crowd out more productive concerns. An early introduction to spellchecking can eliminate a major source of writing anxiety. See the box below for the most common problems with spell checkers. You may also want to point students to Chapter 35 of *Focus on Writing*, Understanding Spelling.

■ Four Common Types of Spellcheck Abuse

- *An indiscriminate user replaces any highlighted word with the first option, assuming that the computer must be right even if the answer doesn't seem to make sense.* Spend some time early on talking about when and why to use the various options (Ignore, Ignore All, Add, Change, Change All) the spell checker offers.

- *A student spellchecks incessantly, correcting every typo even in a first draft.* If you notice that kind of writing behavior, discuss when to spellcheck and why. You may want to turn off the Check As You Go feature in the software used in your classroom lab if you find it is drawing students' attention to surface errors when they should be thinking about global concerns. Show them how to de-select that function on their home computer, too.

- *A student doesn't use the spell checker at all. He or she turns in final drafts riddled with typos.* Adopt a zero-tolerance policy, explaining that misspellings in a final draft indicate that the writer didn't care enough to take advantage of available tools. One paper returned ungraded because it wasn't spellchecked is usually enough to ensure a quick change in habits.

- *A student assumes that a spellchecked document will be error-free.* Remind students that spell checkers will not find *there/their* kinds of errors. Encourage students to keep a list of their own frequently misused words close to their computer and use the Find or Search command to check their final drafts for these words to make sure they are used appropriately. To reinforce that this exercise is important, have students practice it in class.

What about grammar checkers? Most instructors think these do more harm than good because they confuse students with complicated terminology and false error warnings. Unfortunately, anxious students will probably use them anyway, so it is important to discuss what a grammar checker can and cannot do. Let students know that it will often miss more errors than it finds. Worse, it will find errors where there are none. Run a sample paragraph through the grammar checker, and have your class analyze the results. Stress that students should trust their own instincts, not the machine, and should not automatically change or delete a passage just because the grammar checker questions it.

Despite its limitations as an editing tool, a grammar checker can be used creatively as a teaching tool. During a lesson on subject-verb agreement, for instance, you could have students de-select every option in the grammar check but that one and then have them grammar-check their essay. As a class or in small groups, they could discuss the results, seeing if they agree with errors pointed out and if they can beat the machine by finding errors it missed.

What about distance learning? Would an online developmental writing class be successful? Although we cannot address this important question in depth here, we offer a few questions to consider before moving a class online.

1. How well do you know the software your institution uses to put courses on the Web? Where can you turn for training and assistance?

2. What makes your present writing course successful, and which, if any, of those features cannot easily be reproduced online? Can chat rooms or bulletin boards house effective peer review groups? What will replace the tension-releasing laughter? How will you know when a student is struggling if you can't look at his or her face and body language? What will motivate a student to meet deadlines?

3. If you take your class online, should you build in face-to-face meetings during the course of the semester so that students have a chance to learn the faces behind the names — yours included — that will be appearing on their computer screens? Should you start with an on-campus orientation before moving into your virtual classroom? Is there a place on your course page where students' pictures are posted along with their email addresses? Is your own picture there?

4. Developmental writing students often need extra encouragement and personal attention from their instructors. How can you meet that need online? What kind of phone, fax, and email access will you make available? Will the twenty-four-hour access that email offers make up for the loss of face-to-face meetings? Can audio clips on a Web site help? Does your school have a toll-free number students can use if they want to talk with you?

5. Do all students have the equipment necessary to take the kind of course you're designing: reliable and available phone lines, adequate modem speed, sound capabilities, sufficient memory? Prepare your classes with the lowest common denominator in mind. If you are planning to put lengthy materials online, for example, consider whether this will create a financial burden for students who want to print them out.

6. Will your students know their way around computers well enough to be able to upload and download files, send email attachments, enter chat rooms, and perform all the other functions you have built into the course? Although teachers of developmental writers find many technologically adept students in their classes, they also frequently report that classes seem to have more than their share of students with little or no knowledge of computers. What would happen to these students if your course went online? What assistance is available to help them access online material (in the form of initial orientation, training, and ongoing technical support)? Is there a twenty-four-hour help desk available? Are there traditional classroom sections available to students who lack the skills, resources, or confidence to prosper online? Are clearly written, basic instructions available for everything the student is going to need to do — instructions that take into

account the different kinds of hardware and software that might be used?

7. Basic writers often struggle with reading comprehension, and on-screen reading adds another layer of difficulty. How will you compensate for the lack of oral interaction when oral feedback plays such an essential role in a developmental writing class?

8. The basic components of any online course include (a) a course overview and syllabus; (b) "lecture" material; (c) a calendar indicating when assignments will be due, information will be shared, and tasks will be started; (d) a convenient system for student-student and student-teacher email contact; (e) links to relevant Internet resources; (f) a chance to discuss topics asynchronously via bulletin boards or class journals; (g) chat rooms or MOOs where students can meet together in real time; (h) a system for submitting assignments and receiving feedback; and (i) technical support and directions for how to access it. How will you supply each of these? Can you anticipate which component might cause special problems for developmental writing students?

9. How will you know students are doing their own work?

One way to find answers to these questions is to take an online course yourself and experience the advantages and disadvantages firsthand. Keep in mind, however (as we stress in Chapter 10 of this manual, Accommodating Learning Styles), that you are likely to learn differently than your students do, be more at ease in a text-based world, and have better computer facilities and skills.

If you are not fortunate enough to have course-management software like Blackboard or WebCT available, you can add—or at least try out—online components by using free resources such as Yahoo Groups (**groups.yahoo .com**). These resources allow you to add basic e-components to your course, such as a class email group, a document depository for uploading and downloading files, a calendar, and a class chat room. While you and the students will have to put up with advertising and some junk mail, you'll find these e-groups a quick and easy way to try out online activities.

Once you add an online component—even a minimal one—to your writing class, you will discover all sorts of new teaching opportunities. In a typical writing assignment, groups of students might "meet" in their chat room at a specified time to brainstorm ideas. (Such groups should be kept small; ideas scroll by quickly, and chat rooms work best when students are involved in activities like brainstorming that don't require much two-way conversation or structure.) Students then print out a transcript of the chat session for reference as they develop a working thesis, which they email to you for approval. Once approved, the working thesis is posted on the class bulletin board where other students can suggest ideas for what to address in the resulting essay, questions to answer, and sources to consult for contradicting or supporting examples. Preliminary drafts are posted on the same bulletin board for comment. (Comments can be formulated according to standard guidelines you prepare or in answer to specific questions the author poses, or both.)

Before students begin to revise their drafts, ask them to email you a summary of the comments they received and their resulting revision plan so that you can add your own recommendations. After revising, pairs of students work together in real time to polish the final draft using the conferencing feature of their Internet browser. If such meetings are not feasible, final peer review can take place via the class bulletin board.

Despite the additional headaches—technology problems, access issues, and increased demands on their time—instructors tend to find that pedagogical advantages of online learning outweigh the disadvantages. Timid voices can be heard when class discussion is moved online and students are free to participate at their own rate of speed and skill. Working students can participate in research and group projects that they would not otherwise be able to join. The energy created by Web-based communication via chat rooms, email, and discussion lists helps unite and empower socially and geographically isolated students. Students often write more, and enjoy it more, when working online. They also tend to learn more, because online assignments force students to play a more active role in the learning process. Finally, and perhaps most important, when you move your basic writing class online, your students become a part of the persistent conversation that the Internet has created; you will be helping these students find a voice and begin to view themselves as writers.

Internet Resources for Writing Instructors

Regardless of your question or interest concerning computers and writing, you will find a wealth of online information and resources. Following are a few recommended sites to get you started.

- Use the searchable list of lists at **lists.topica .com** to join discussion groups, such as

  Conference on Basic Writing (CBW-L) **orgs.tamu-commerce.edu/CBW/ASU/listserv .html**

  Alliance for Computers and Writing (ACW-L) **www2.nau.edu/~acw-p/**

  Writing Program Administration (WPA-L) **wpacouncil.org/wpa-1**

- Read electronic journals, such as those listed below. Some have print versions, which you may prefer.

  Campus Technology **campustechnology.com**

  Computer-Mediated Communication Magazine **december.com/cmc/mag/**

  Computers and Composition **bgsu.edu/cconline/**

  Currents in Electronic Literacy **currents.dwrl.utexas.edu**

  Kairos **kairos.technorhetoric.net**

  T.H.E. Journal **thejournal.com**

- Become familiar with useful Web sites, such as

  The *Focus on Writing* Web site **bedfordstmartins.com/focusonwriting**, with downloadable ancillaries, useful links, and access to *Exercise Central* and to the *Bedford Bibliography for Teachers of Basic Writing*. You will also want to visit Bedford/St. Martin's main

site at **bedfordstmartins.com**, which offers a variety of disciplinary resources.

Purdue University's Online Writing Lab owl.english.purdue.edu/owl, offering a large collection of resources for writers, instructors, and students.

CUNY WriteSite writesite.cuny.edu/grammar/index.html, offering grammar references, interactive exercises, and a program for evaluating error patterns.

English Grammar on the Web www2.gsu.edu/~wwwesl/egw/index1.htm, offering resources for ESL/EFL instructors, including reference materials, links, and class activities.

Guide to Grammar and Writing grammar.ccc.commnet.edu/grammar, with rules for writers, listed both by revision type (paragraph-level, word-level, etc.) and in a comprehensive index.

On Using the Computer as a Writing Tool papyr.com/hypertextbooks/comp1/computer .htm, offering tips to instructors or students on how to get the most out of a word processor.

Grammar Hotline Directory tcc.edu/students/resources/writcent/gh/ hotlinol.htm, providing up-to-date contact information for grammar hotlines throughout the United States and Canada.

University of Victoria's Hypertext Writer's Guide web.uvic.ca/wguide/, offering general information on essays, paragraphs, sentences, words, and many other writing-related topics.

Merriam-Webster Online merriam-webster.com, offering links to online dictionaries and thesauruses.

Writing@CSU writing.colostate.edu/, containing, among many useful writing aids, good resources for students with learning disabilities and for non-native English speakers.

The Internet TESL Journal's Activities for ESL Students a4esl.org, offering interactive quizzes of use as class or individual activities.

- Read up on the literature. The Computer and Literacy Studies section of the *CCCC*

Bibliography and the Basic Writing Reading List at the Conference on Basic Writing Web site listed on page 37 are good places to start.

• Attend conferences. The most useful information in this rapidly changing field is exchanged at scholarly meetings that bring together theorists, practitioners, and vendors:

National Association for Developmental Education (**nade.net**) in late winter

Conference on College Composition and Communication (**ncte.org/cccc**) in the spring

International Society for Technology in Education (**center.uoregon.edu/ISTE/2010/**) in early summer

EDUCAUSE (**educause.edu**) in the fall

Additional Online Resources from Bedford/St. Martin's

The Bedford/St. Martin's Web site (**bedford stmartins.com**) contains a wealth of writing resources, two of which—the English Research Room and *Exercise Central*—will be of special interest to developmental writing students and teachers. The English Research Room houses interactive tutorials that will help your students use the Internet more effectively, along with research links to hundreds of useful sites, including online writing centers, dictionaries, thesauruses, LitLinks (a collection of more than 500 literature sites), and TopLinks (a searchable database of sites with information on commonly chosen writing topics, like affirmative action, ethics, gender, and environmental issues). It also contains links to pedagogical resources on such issues as teaching with technology, ESL, plagiarism, learning disabilities, and teacher training.

Exercise Central, the online collection of grammar exercises available to students and instructors using *Focus on Writing*, helps students improve their grammar knowledge and skills. This resource is particularly useful when you don't have time to go over basic grammar in detail. A link to *Exercise Central* is available at the Web site for *Focus on Writing* (**bedford stmartins.com/focusonwriting**). *Exercise Cen-*

tral includes many exercise sets that your students can use for further practice. At the end of each exercise, students receive immediate feedback for each response, correct or incorrect.

When students enter *Exercise Central* through the Web site for *Focus on Writing* at **bedfordstmartins.com/focusonwriting**, they will gain access to a customized lesson plan based on the book's table of contents. The customized lesson plan keeps track of the exercises students have completed. After students have completed one exercise, they can check the Your Status section to see how they have done. If they have not mastered a skill, they may be directed to practice further with another exercise set at the same level. (Links to other developmental exercises are included in the customized lesson plan.) If students have done well on the first exercise set, they may want to practice further with another exercise set at a higher level. (Links to more difficult exercise sets are also included in the customized lesson plan.) Whenever students sign in, they can check their customized lesson plan to see which topics they have mastered and which exercises they have completed.

As an instructor, you can view reports on individual students or all students at once. If you have several classes or sections, you can even set up customized reports that will show you results for each class or section separately. The first time you sign in as an instructor, you will be asked to supply some information about yourself, your class, and your institution. This enables Bedford/St. Martin's to verify that you are an instructor. Once the registration process is complete, you will be sent a password by email. When you sign in using this password, you will gain access to the instructor area of *Exercise Central*.

As part of the sign-in procedure, you will be asked to give your email address. If you want to see reports on students' exercises, you should tell them to type in your email address when they sign in. This identifies you as their instructor. Then, when you sign in as an instructor with the same email address, you will be able to view reports on all students who have supplied your email address.

The standard reporting option allows you to view exercise results either one student at a time or for all students at once. If you choose the latter, you can see the results for a single exercise set or for all exercise sets at once. The standard reporting option groups all your students together. For instructors who teach multiple courses or multiple sections, it is also possible to create custom reports. You can use the custom reports to set up smaller groups of students (e.g., all the students in one section of English 101). Complete directions for using the standard reports and creating customized reports are included on the Web site for *Exercise Central* (**bedfordstmartins.com/exercisecentral**).

Incorporating Critical Thinking

Many colleges and universities now require that instructors adopt curriculum-wide approaches to teaching and learning. A common practice is to require instructors in all disciplines to integrate critical thinking into their course work. Academicians are recognizing that the rapid growth of available information will make it necessary for students not only to learn what they are taught but also to analyze and create solutions to problems. There is also a widely held perception that students retain skills better than facts and that the teaching of thinking skills will thus prepare students to adapt successfully to a constantly changing environment. The developmental writing course offers many opportunities for students to develop their thinking skills.

What Is Critical Thinking?

Critical thinking has been defined as "the careful and deliberate determination of whether to accept, reject, or suspend judgment about a claim" (Moore and Parker 3). Basically, critical thinking is the use of informal argument or logic. It involves an ability to ask a comprehensive set of questions designed to evaluate a claim. Students who exercise critical thinking can react critically to their textbook or to the information in a reading assignment, form their own arguments, and evaluate the quality of others' arguments. They can separate fact from opinion and determine whether the proponent of a position has offered sufficient and appropriate supporting evidence. Students will use these skills to make sure the positions expressed in their own written work are supported by an acceptable amount of evidence and not by mere opinion.

There are some misconceptions about what constitutes critical thinking. Many people feel that critical thinking leads to the belief that all opinions are equally worthy. On the contrary, critical thinking leads students to evaluate the facts that form the basis of opinions and to ascertain whether these facts have been applied properly. The result should be the student's formulation of a unique viewpoint on the subject instead of a benign acceptance of the arguments that have been presented. True critical thinking is not simply discussion, and it does not cause students to become preoccupied with trivial details. Most important, critical thinking is a set of skills that can be developed, not a talent with which someone is born. Like any other skill, critical thinking improves with practice.

Course Components That Encourage Critical Thinking

When you emphasize critical thinking in your classroom, you are recognizing that the uncritical absorption of information is not useful and that students must learn to evaluate and apply information. In a course emphasizing critical thinking, classroom activities and writing assignments should be structured so that students mature in the way they react to information. As they do so, new and reasoned approaches will begin to take the place of poor learning habits.

The developmental writing course is an excellent setting for teaching critical thinking skills, which have the advantage of being interesting and appealing to nontraditional students in particular. A common failing of developmental writing courses is their almost exclusive focus on grammar exercises and very simple writing assignments. Writing assignments that exercise critical thinking skills and develop sound grammar and style often have the dual advantage of (1) making students feel that their work is important and (2) giving them the opportunity to comment on an important issue in a thoughtful, logical manner.

If your course promotes critical thinking and basic writing, it will have several easily identifiable characteristics. Students will talk more than you will. Classroom instruction will cover a broad range of ideas, concepts, and problems. Students will relate their own experiences to classroom material. They will be free to share ideas and opinions openly. Students will discuss the effects of egocentricity, ethnocentricity, bias, prejudice, and one-sidedness on thinking. Students will be encouraged to join small- and large-group discussions in order to share information and learn from each other. You will summarize key points and lines of reasoning developed by the class. Essay assignments will give students the opportunity to react to and evaluate the material presented. Completed essays will be clearly reasoned and exhibit improved writing skills.

Such attention to careful reasoning brings an extra bonus to the writing teacher. Problems that students have with grammar and style often clear up on their own when you help students clarify their thinking on the topic they are struggling with. Be sure, of course, that the reasoning with which students support their ideas, not the ideas themselves, is the focus of criticism.

Aspects of Critical Thinking

To help you design lessons that develop critical thinking skills, we present a list of thirty-five aspects of critical thinking that Richard Paul, director of research at the Center for Critical Thinking at Sonoma State University, developed with editor A. J. A. Binker (Paul 305–49). Some items overlap, but the list offers a sound conceptual framework for critical thinking.

1. *Thinking Independently.* Students discover information and use their knowledge, skills,

and insights to draw their own conclusions. Instead of simply discussing ideas from texts, students brainstorm or argue positions with each other. Collaborative activities at the end of each chapter in *Focus on Writing* are a good place to start.

2. *Developing Insight into Egocentricity or Sociocentricity.* Everyone has some egocentric or sociocentric tendencies. Your goal is to help students identify such tendencies and discuss how they impair critical thinking practices. Choose reading or journal activities that help promote these insights.

3. *Exercising Fair-Mindedness.* Students learn to reconstruct another's opinion and reasoning accurately, rather than exaggerating or distorting an opponent's ideas so as to make them easier to refute. Show students how to summarize texts objectively, waiting until later to insert their own ideas.

4. *Exploring Thoughts Underlying Feelings and Feelings Underlying Thoughts.* Students learn to assess how their emotions and feelings relate to their thought processes. They ask why someone thinks or feels a certain way, how that person interprets the situation, and what conclusions the person has formed. Peer review groups provide excellent opportunities to practice this skill.

5. *Developing Intellectual Humility and Suspending Judgment.* Students learn to suspend judgment until they have adequate information and admit that there are some limits to their knowledge. Pair students who took opposing sides on argumentation topics (see *Focus on Writing,* Chapter 11, for ideas), and ask them to read each other's paragraphs and then discuss what they learned.

6. *Developing Intellectual Courage.* You foster the development of intellectual courage by ensuring an open atmosphere and urging students to question or disagree without penalty. Set the tone for class discussions both by your actions and in your directions for peer review activities.

7. *Developing Intellectual Good Faith or Integrity.* Students assess the consistency in their own opinions and are aware of inconsistencies when they occur. Construct peer review activities carefully with this goal in mind.

8. *Developing Intellectual Perseverance.* Confusion is a necessary stage in the development of thinking skills. Students recognize that confusion and frustration will occur, and they realize that they are able to continue applying their new skills nonetheless. Long-term assignments give students the opportunity to grapple with difficult and complex issues. You suggest techniques to assess their progress such as asking good questions and ruling out irrelevant information. Asking students to analyze changes between early and final drafts can make this process more visible to them.

9. *Developing Confidence in Reason.* You give students opportunities to demonstrate their reasoning and persuade each other. Students learn, for example, to identify the difference between persuasion and intimidation. The section on argumentation in *Focus on Writing* (Chapter 11) presents a variety of opportunities for students to practice this critical thinking skill.

10. *Refining Generalizations and Avoiding Oversimplifications.* When students oversimplify, you ask them questions to deepen their understanding of an issue. When faced with generalizations, you ask students to give examples of instances when a generalization does not apply. Charge peer response groups with pointing out any questionable generalizations, explaining what the problem is and how to express the idea more effectively.

11. *Comparing Analogous Situations: Transferring Insights to New Contexts.* Students apply an insight to situations parallel to those mentioned in the text. Chapter 37 (Readings for Writers) in *Focus on Writing* provides a rich source of examples.

12. *Developing One's Perspective: Creating or Exploring Beliefs, Arguments, or Theories.* Students develop their perspective through extended thought, discussion, and writing. They are able to explain how something they've learned in class has changed their personal beliefs or outlook. If you use journals in class, ask for such reflection in one of the entries toward the end of the semester.

13. *Clarifying Issues, Conclusions, or Beliefs.* You encourage students to reflect before developing conclusions. Students practice identifying all relevant issues and information in a text or oral argument before constructing their response. Requiring students to work through all the major stages of the writing process can help to ensure this kind of careful thought.

14. *Clarifying and Analyzing the Meanings of Words and Phrases.* You help students understand the meaning of unfamiliar words and phrases by paraphrasing them, having students give examples that demonstrate their understanding, and discussing the use to which the word or phrase might be put. See also Chapter 20 (Using Words Effectively) in *Focus on Writing*.

15. *Developing Criteria for Evaluation: Clarifying Values and Standards.* Students discuss the criteria they use in evaluating written material. (See p. 50 in Chapter 5 of this manual, Facilitating Collaboration, for an example of this type of exercise.)

16. *Evaluating the Credibility of Sources of Information.* You select a controversial issue for discussion and have students check multiple sources for information. Students then discuss why they think each source is credible or not. Students can also consider their personal experience relative to a topic under discussion and examine the effect of experience on their opinions. The Internet is a good source of material for this sort of information. Consider asking students to research material on the same issue from a .gov, .edu, and .com site.

17. *Questioning Deeply: Raising and Pursuing Root or Significant Questions.* You discuss rules, institutions, or ideals and ask why they exist and what purpose they serve. Following this discussion, students identify a significant question and gather related information. Show students how they can follow this kind of process to narrow general essay topics and develop well-focused thesis statements.

18. *Analyzing or Evaluating Arguments, Interpretations, Beliefs, or Theories.* You encourage students to argue and modify their positions when presented with ones that are more logical and better formulated. You help students identify and evaluate assumptions, clarify

issues, and recognize contradictions. For instance, you might (a) select a controversial point of view and have students brainstorm all the reasons to support that viewpoint, (b) then think of all the reasons against it, and (c) finally decide which reasons on both sides make the strongest argument.

19. *Generating or Assessing Solutions.* You encourage students to develop multiple solutions to a problem and then assess each solution in terms of effectiveness and logic. In a computer lab, an online class discussion list, or peer group, for instance, have each student raise a problem, and ask the other students to suggest as many solutions as possible.

20. *Analyzing or Evaluating Actions and Policies.* You urge students to raise questions about the actions or policies of important people. Students ask why a particular action was taken, what purpose it served, whether it accomplished its goal, and whether circumstances changed because of it. Select a topic relevant to your institution or community, and ask students to write analyses appropriate for publication in the school or local paper.

21. *Reading Critically: Clarifying or Critiquing Texts.* Rather than having students recall random information in a text, you have them recall the text's argument and evaluate it for clarity, implications, and assumptions. Students paraphrase information, supporting their understanding with specific references to the document. This kind of critical reading skill helps students see the difference between plagiarism and paraphrasing, and emphasizes the importance of citing sources.

22. *Listening Critically: The Art of Silent Dialogue.* Students become aware that listening can be an active and critical process. They learn to ask questions that clarify their understanding of the speaker's views and orient their own opinions in relation to that of the speaker. Students take notes on each other's presentations and compare notes afterward. Even if you don't assign oral presentations in your class, you can have students attend an outside lecture and critique the presentation in class.

23. *Making Interdisciplinary Connections.* Students recognize that arbitrary academic distinc-

tions between subjects do not limit the connections that can be made between subjects. Students practice analyzing a particular piece of information from a variety of viewpoints, such as historical, sociological, or psychological. Bring in a picture, such as one of a sports brawl, for instance, and ask students to speculate how a psychologist might explain the scene and how that explanation might be different from the one a sociologist, a sports physician, a philosopher, or a poet might give.

24. *Practicing Socratic Discussion: Clarifying and Questioning Beliefs, Theories, or Perspectives.* Classroom activities give students the opportunity to question each other and the material they study, helping them to become more comfortable with being questioned. Your questions provide an example of the effectiveness and thought-provoking nature of inquiry. If this kind of dialogue takes place online in a chat room or threaded discussion, students will have the added opportunity to make a printed transcript of the ideas as they develop.

25. *Reasoning Dialogically: Comparing Perspectives, Interpretations, or Theories.* Reasoning dialogically means reasoning through dialogue. Students discuss different points of view, juxtaposing ideas and theories. Such discussions make students aware of the complexity of an issue. This, too, is easily and productively done online in a moderated forum.

26. *Reasoning Dialectically: Evaluating Perspectives, Interpretations, or Theories.* Reasoning dialectically means reasoning dialogically with the aim of testing the strengths and weaknesses of differing viewpoints. Students argue opposing viewpoints while others evaluate them. You propose evaluative questions such as, Was that a good reason? and What is the other side's response to that objection? Build both descriptive and evaluative questions like these into your peer response assignments.

27. *Comparing and Contrasting Ideals with Actual Practice.* Students examine a text for the presentation of ideals as facts. They then rewrite the misleading portions of the text. Students

also discuss how ideals presented in the text will work in actual practice. Op-ed sections of newspapers contain a rich fund of examples.

28. *Thinking Precisely about Thinking: Using Critical Vocabulary.* You encourage metacognition, using analytical terms such as *relevance, assumption, inference, justify,* and *interpret.* Be sure to explain the meaning of such terms, and provide several examples, both good and bad, to clarify the meaning.

29. *Noting Significant Similarities and Differences.* Students list similarities and differences between two things and use the list to draw conclusions about the relationship between the two. See Chapter 8 (Using Comparisons and Contrasts) in *Focus on Writing.*

30. *Examining or Evaluating Assumptions.* Students identify assumptions in an assigned text and in their own work. They then speculate on the thought process that led to the assumption. Consider assigning double-entry journals to allow students to practice this difficult skill at their own pace.

31. *Distinguishing Relevant from Irrelevant Facts.* When presented with a complicated issue, students identify relevant facts and discard irrelevant information. You assist this process by discussing how each fact helps students arrive at a conclusion. Working through the activities in Chapter 2, section B (Using Evidence to Support Your Paragraph's Main idea), in *Focus on Writing* will help students learn to do this in their writing and their reading.

32. *Making Plausible Inferences, Predictions, or Interpretations.* Students practice making inferences from a wide variety of statements or materials. For example, students are presented with pictures or brief text selections and are asked to predict what will happen next. Students can also discuss inappropriate inferences and why they are inaccurate. Making inferences is an important academic skill that developmental students struggle with. The more examples you can provide, the better.

33. *Evaluating Evidence and Alleged Facts.* You challenge students to support conclusions drawn from written material by citing evidence and making references to specific statements. Challenging students in this way

helps them learn how to agree and disagree with experts in appropriate academic style. Developmental writers, like most of us, tend to believe what they read. The Internet can provide many examples of assertions without proof—or with questionable proof.

34. *Recognizing Contradictions.* Students state opposing views and find points of agreement and points of disagreement. The class then discusses a possible reconciliation between views. You might want to have students brainstorm all the pros and cons of a polarizing issue like abortion or capital punishment and then ask them to write a paragraph describing the common ground they find between the two sides.

35. *Exploring Implications and Consequences.* Students discuss the implications and consequences of their own beliefs. They also draw implications from course material and apply them within other contexts.

Classroom Techniques That Promote Critical Thinking

Dana Flint and Penelope Kinsey, professors of philosophy and psychology, respectively, at Lincoln University, compiled the following list of activities and class instructions for a faculty workshop designed to help instructors develop a classroom environment that enhances critical thinking. You may find the list useful as you plan your class format.

- **Lecture Format.** Instructor provides information on critical thinking and demonstrates skills.

- **Individual Learning.** Student works alone on assignments.

- **Groups:**

  Full Class, Instructor Centered. Instructor leads entire class in discussion and practice about critical thinking.

  Small Group. Instructor meets with each small group and leads discussion and practice.

  Developmental Discussion. Instructor breaks down discussion into four steps—formulate the problem, suggest hypothesis, obtain relevant data, evaluate evidence—and works on them one at a time.

The Inner Circle. Half the class moves into a small circle in the middle of the classroom, with the other half in a larger circle. Inner group discusses a topic; then outer group analyzes the discussion using critical thinking skills.

Student-Centered Discussions. Instructor has students lead discussion, encouraging them to use critical thinking.

Leaderless Discussions. Small groups are given tasks to perform on their own. Instructor may or may not circulate among the groups, listening to their progress.

Buzz Groups. Class is divided into small groups and given time to develop a solution to a particular problem.

Circle of Knowledge. Small groups are asked to come up with answers to a question with many possible answers. One student in each group acts as recorder or note-taker. Group members take turns coming up with answers to the question. This technique is most often used to review information.

Ongoing Leaderless Discussions. Small groups are formed that remain active throughout the course. These groups work on projects and discussions. Instructor may answer questions but does not monitor group progress.

Brainstorming. Small groups are formed, each with a recorder. Group members are asked to identify ideas as quickly as possible.

Case Studies. Small groups are formed, each with a leader and recorder. In the context of one particular event or situation, students answer questions that prompt them to recall facts and develop thinking skills. Leader facilitates the discussion, and recorder keeps track of the group's answers.

Cooperative Learning. Students work in pairs, reading and studying material. One partner summarizes the material while the other corrects errors and elaborates.

Research Grouping. Small groups of students are assigned a topic that requires research. Group leader assigns research tasks to group members and monitors progress.

Jigsaw Method. Small groups are formed. Each group member is assigned different material to learn and then teach to the other group members. Students researching the same topic work together in new groups, to ensure consistency of content. Then they return to their original small groups, and each group member makes his or her presentation, putting the puzzle back together so that the group learns the complete lesson.

Numbered Heads. Four-member teams are given a list of questions. Each team works to make sure its members can answer the questions. Instructor calls on individual team members to answer questions aloud for class.

Think-Pair-Share. A question is addressed to the class as a whole. Students pair off to discuss the question. Pairs then present their response to the class.

- **Other Class Activities.** These include evaluating primary and secondary sources, debating, and role-playing.

- **Out-of-Class Activities.** These include written assignments such as summaries, argumentative essays, critiques of articles and books, comparison and contrasting of two articles, and exams constructed by students.

Critical thinking is a precondition of good writing, and in practice, writing is one of the most effective instruments for clarifying and refining thinking. Although it should not be the main focus of your writing course, helping students develop their critical thinking skills will indeed help them become better writers. *Focus on Writing* encourages this interrelationship by leading students to reflect on their own writing. The text also provides specific sections on collaborative activities that make use of many of the group activities previously listed. Instructors interested in more information on the topic will find a number of useful articles in *Teaching Developmental Writing: Background Readings* (Bernstein, 2007) and on the Internet at **criticalthinking.org**.

WORKS CITED

Bernstein, Susan N. *Teaching Developmental Writing: Background Readings.* 3rd ed. Boston: Bedford/St. Martin's, 2007. Print.

Moore, B. N., and Richard Parker. *Critical Thinking: Evaluating Claims and Arguments in Everyday Life.* 2nd ed. Mountain View: Mayfield, 1989. Print.

Paul, Richard. *Critical Thinking: What Everyone Needs to Survive in a Rapidly Changing World.* Rohnert Park: Sonoma State, 1990. Print.

5

Facilitating Collaboration

Working Together: An Overview

The best answer to the question, "What is the most effective method of teaching?" is that it depends on the goal, the students, the content, and the teacher. But the next best answer is, "Students teaching other students."

—W. McKeachie et al.,
Teaching and Learning in the College Classroom

Collaborative activities in a writing class fall into two basic categories: **peer response groups** (also called *peer editing, peer critique,* or *peer review groups*), in which a small number of students work together to improve the individual written products of each group member, and **collaborative writing**, in which students work together to create one collective project. This chapter addresses both types but focuses mainly on peer response, the most common kind of collaboration in composition courses. At the end of most chapters in *Focus on Writing*, you will find a variety of collaborative activities to choose from.

Collaborative activities, such as the Sample Generic Peer Response Activity on p. 50 in this chapter, can be used throughout the semester and at every stage of the writing process. Groups can brainstorm ideas for essays, try out possible thesis sentences, talk through first drafts before writing them, give constructive criticism for revision, and serve as style editors and even proofreaders. Students can plan together, write together, and correct each other's errors. With developmental writers, though, we believe that the biggest gains occur when stu-

dents critique early drafts for general issues of understanding, organization, and development. We recommend that type of collaboration as the focus of your group activities.

If you are new to group work, be forewarned that simply putting students in a group and giving them forty-five minutes to talk about one another's finished essays is not collaboration, nor is it likely to involve much learning. Collaborative activities, especially with developmental writers, must be carefully structured and address—preferably in writing—all of the following:

- the task
- the rationale for assigning the task
- the time frame
- relevant definitions
- procedures, with examples when possible of what students as individuals are expected to learn and do and what the group as a whole is expected to accomplish
- criteria for success

Group skills required to work effectively with others—listening actively, giving and receiving feedback, disagreeing constructively, reaching consensus—need to be explained, modeled, and practiced. Group size and membership must be monitored carefully. Consider the appropriateness of the task carefully. Some instructors, especially those working with younger students, report that immature students have great difficulty handling peer critique. Using groups effectively will require considerable effort on your part: structuring the task before the activity begins, managing the classroom during the activity, and synthesizing and evaluating the results afterward. Most instructors and researchers agree, however, that this effort is worthwhile.

Why Encourage Collaboration?

> What children can do together today, they can do alone tomorrow.
> —Lev Vygotsky, *Mind and Society*

Collaboration enhances student writing and provides valuable side benefits for both students and instructors. The first and most important reason to devote some part of your class time to group work is that student papers that have been presented and discussed in groups are better than those that have not. They tend to have more specificity of detail, more supporting examples, more transitional and introductory phrases indicating awareness of the audience, and fewer stylistic and grammatical problems. Second, peer review activities encourage revision, making it a natural part of the writing process. Third, group work involves and integrates the four skills of reading, writing, talking, and listening, thereby making students more active and motivated learners. Fourth, students gain an increased metacognitive awareness of the writing process in general and of personal writing strengths and weaknesses in particular. Metacognition, reflecting on one's thinking process and being able to explain that process in words, is an essential step in improving both thinking and writing. The more students know about how their ideas are formed, the more control they have over those ideas. Group involvement also helps students learn to work effectively with others: how to reach group consensus, listen effectively, respect differing views, and draw sound conclusions. It encourages critical thinking as students analyze texts, suggest alternative solutions, and struggle to understand multiple perspectives.

Group work has advantages for the instructor as well. Incorporating peer review in the syllabus can help you manage your paper load because other eyes have the chance to find and correct problems of focus, organization, content, and mechanics before you make your own comments. Moreover, you are no longer the students' sole evaluator and audience. Making use of peer review activities allows you to define your role as helper rather than as arbiter and judge.

Collaborative efforts enable developmental writers to move beyond low self-esteem, lack of motivation, anxiety about writing, poor understanding of the revision process, and the tendency to view error as a sign of deficiency rather than an opportunity to learn. When students are actively involved in every aspect of the writing process, and instructors are freed to direct and coach, the talents of both teacher and learner are used effectively.

Despite its many benefits, group work is not the only way students learn. Don't focus exclusively on group work; instead, structure your classes so that they contain a good mix of activities. Students can learn a great deal about writing from one another, but they also learn from you and from reflecting individually.

Getting Started

A good way to begin (and to stress the importance of peer review while modeling good practice) is to devote the first week of the course to an analysis of student essays from previous classes. On p. 144 of this manual we include three sample essays you can use for such an activity, in case you have not already put together your own set of examples. Whatever texts you use, be sure that the essays show clear differences in quality: one should be very good, one acceptable, and one poor. The goal is to get your students to realize that they in fact do know what good writing is, even if they are not as yet ready to produce or describe it using the vocabulary they will acquire as the semester progresses.

Distribute the three essays in the first class, along with the article they are based on, "Seven Keys to Effective Learning" by Cyril Houle (p. 157). Ask students to take them home, read them, and rank them from best to worst. They should come to the next class prepared to explain and defend their ranking. The point of this exercise is to elicit from the students what they already know, so do not give them detailed suggestions for how to evaluate the three essays.

You might suggest that they make notes on the essays while ranking them so that they can remember later what they liked or didn't like. In the next class, divide students into small groups and assign them the task of reaching a consensus on ranking. While they're doing this, make a grid on the chalkboard, with the essay example numbers across the top and group numbers down the side. Fill in the grid as the groups report their rankings.

Usually there is a clear class consensus, but if there is not one, have the groups discuss their differing opinions until one convinces the other. Once they have decided on the best and worst essay, start with the lowest-ranked essay and ask students what deficiencies they noted. You may have to ask some leading questions at this point to guide their attention to broad elements such as supporting detail and overall thesis because initial comments tend to focus on sentence-level errors. You can also use this opportunity to introduce some of the concepts you will be discussing later, such as thesis or audience, or editing versus revision. Remember, too, to ask about the positive aspects of all the essays so that students get used to the idea of peer critique as fair and constructive criticism, not just fault-finding. Ask students what single most important piece of advice they would give to each writer. As a last step in this activity, have students rank all the criteria of good writing that they have generated, from most to least important, producing a hierarchy of concerns to be used later in their own peer response groups.

This consensus-reaching activity can easily fill the first week of class, although you can streamline it, if time is a problem, by limiting discussion. As a follow-up we distribute the article that the sample essays responded to, asking students to read it and draft their own response for the next class. Being familiar with the topic and the expectations takes a little of the fear away from the first writing assignment. This first draft can then be critiqued in peer groups, using the criteria that the class developed during the previous class period. Another possibility is to collect students' first drafts, write a few positive comments on each, and then select a few good examples to read in the next class. Alternatively, you might ask for a few volunteers to have their papers used in a model peer review session in which you show the class the kinds of comments you would like them all to make in their peer response groups. After feedback from you or from each other, students should take back their drafts to revise once more for submission and grading.

Elements of Successful Group Work

Effective peer response doesn't just happen; it must be taught. Although there are many ways in which groups can be used and structured (see Part Four of this manual for a variety of examples), you will have to make some general decisions for all collaborative activities.

Determining Group Size

Appropriate group size depends somewhat on the task and the length of the class period. The optimum group size is three to five. Fewer than three members does not allow for multiple perspectives. Groups with more than four or five members run the risk of shortchanging some of the participants because most activities require between ten and fifteen minutes per student. (If you prefer larger groups, you can of course stretch an activity over more than one class period.)

Selecting Group Members

Choose groups carefully. Research suggests that heterogeneous groups work best, so it's good to include stronger and weaker students in each group. When students self-select, they tend to produce homogeneous groups, so you will probably want to assign members, even if it's only by counting off, to ensure a random mixture. Allen Loibner of Arkansas State University reports success with his practice of asking students to write a diagnostic essay about their past writing and editing experience. From the responses, he learns how much experience they have and how well they write. He then makes up groups of three, each containing a good, an average, and a poor writer.

Deciding on Your Role

After you have structured the activities, your main task is to remind students constantly what they are doing in the group and why. You will also need to decide whether to sit in on the groups and, if you do, how active a role to play. Some instructors prefer not to sit in on groups at all, lest they inhibit the autonomy of the peer reviewers. Others sit in quietly, moving from group to group and simply monitoring activity for possible later intervention. Still others like to sit in as a participant, especially early in the semester, helping to shape responses and modeling appropriate behavior.

Structuring Group Activities

Another variable to consider is how you want papers to be presented within groups. Should group members

- discuss papers that were read and analyzed at home prior to class?

- read a paper silently in the group and then discuss it or fill in response forms?

- read a paper aloud in the group without passing out copies, to get general reactions?

- read the paper aloud once and then pass out copies for other students to follow along while the author reads it a second time?

Each option has advantages and disadvantages. Reading aloud helps writers hear problems they might not have seen, for instance, but it takes more time in class. Following along on printed copy allows for more detailed discussion, but it can tend to focus group members on mechanical problems rather than on organization and development. Part Four of this manual contains a list of basic advice for students giving and receiving feedback. You may want to distribute this to your students before their first group activity.

If your students have access to email, their collaboration can extend beyond the classroom confines, even beyond the university. Students are able to exchange essays through email after class hours with one another or with students at other institutions. Responses can be structured tightly (with specific questions for students to ask and answer) or loosely (with students giving general reactions to one another via email). Chat rooms offer real-time opportu-

nities for writers to brainstorm, "talk," and ask for advice. Even the informal letters and chat participation will need some monitoring, though, because criticism in cyberspace can easily become harsher than when students are speaking face-to-face.

Getting Students to Take Their Roles Seriously

Especially in the beginning, students tend to complain that (1) they have little to learn from other students, (2) they aren't qualified to find fault with other writers when they're just beginners themselves, and (3) only the instructor's comments count toward the grade anyway. There are a number of ways to respond to these spoken or unspoken concerns and to help students develop a more positive attitude toward peer review. First, be sure you structure and sequence assignments so that you aren't asking group members to do something they can't do. Don't expect them to edit peer essays for style or grammar, for example, before you've focused on those issues in class. Second, be sure that all directions are written down clearly and discussed prior to beginning group work so that everyone is sure of what is expected and has something to refer to if the group gets off track. In general, it is easiest—and most useful—for students simply to point out places where changes might be needed instead of suggesting what those changes should be. Structure your assignments, therefore, so that they ask students to be descriptive (*note whether there are any very short or very long paragraphs*) rather than prescriptive (*indicate what kind of additional examples are needed*).

Third, make student participation in peer review a part of the final grade. You can collect written peer review sheets after each group activity and skim them, giving them a ✓+, ✓, or ✓- and then averaging those grades as a percentage of the final grade. You can also sit in on each group briefly, making any suggestions necessary to help members give specific, constructive feedback and, if necessary, calling members aside to discuss problem behavior. Generally, complaints subside after students have participated in a few activities and realized that the feedback they receive is valuable.

■ Sample Generic Peer Response Activity

Recommended group size: 3–4

Directions: Distribute and discuss the "Advice to Students" on p. 150 of this manual. Then the author reads his or her paper aloud while responders follow along on written copy. The paper is read twice, allowing 1 to 2 minutes of silence after each reading for responders to collect their thoughts.

Feedback from each group member:

1. What was the main point? What were the major subtopics?
2. What questions do you have?
3. Were there any points the author didn't cover that you wish he or she had?
4. Do you agree or disagree with the author's main idea? Discuss your reactions to points made.
5. What did you like best about the paper?

Time for reading and responding to each paper: 10–15 minutes. Repeat the above process until all papers have been critiqued. It is difficult to respond to more than three papers in a 50-minute class period.

The following peer review handout illustrates the kind of general feedback your students could be asked to provide for any writing assignment. It can be used as is or modified to direct student attention to any particular focus that you want them to consider. The general components in this example—size of group, time frame for the activity, specific group tasks, and the process that the group is to follow—should always be spelled out clearly and in printed form.

COMPONENTS OF AN EFFECTIVE GROUP ACTIVITY

☑ It is clearly worded and unambiguous.

☑ It divides the exercise into workable pieces.

☑ It explains to students what they must do and how they should do it.

☑ It matches student needs, goals, and abilities.

☑ It requires consensus.

☑ It stimulates critical thinking.

☑ It takes students together beyond what they know as individuals. (Wiener 136)

Common Concerns

A number of students repeatedly show up on peer response day without their completed drafts. Although unprepared students can't receive feedback on their own writing, they can still give suggestions to others and should be expected to participate actively. Make it clear, both in your syllabus and in class discussion, that coming unprepared will affect students' final grades. You may want to consider a policy specifying that an individual essay's final grade is lowered by some predetermined amount if the paper wasn't reviewed *or* that coming empty-handed on peer review day counts as an absence. The point to stress is that the unprepared students are mainly hurting themselves because they will be, in effect, turning in a first draft for your evaluation rather than a revised paper that has had the benefit of peer comment.

Most of my groups are functioning well, but there is one that just isn't working. Talk with group members and see if they can tell you what is causing the problem. Often groups can work out problems among themselves. If there are ongoing personality clashes, you may want to move one or two people into different groups. When you initially assign groups, it's a good idea to mention that you may be switching people around from time to time so that students will anticipate the possibility. Another possible intervention is to have a well-functioning group model a review session for the rest of the class to watch and discuss.

Several of my students are reluctant to read their own writing in their groups. This often occurs at the beginning of the semester and diminishes as trust is built. You will have to decide if you want to permit students to respond without sharing their own work for a while. Sometimes having another student read the anxious student's paper aloud helps. You can also work individually with that student at first, to build confidence.

Students say they are uncomfortable critiquing someone else's writing. Remind students that all writing, no matter how good, can be improved by peer feedback, so they are doing their colleagues a disfavor if they withhold that help. It's often useful to bring in one of your own manuscripts that someone else has commented on, to show them the arrows, underlinings, crossouts, and comments that decorate it. Peer review is a chance to make better, not to find fault, and it's a practice that all professional writers prize.

I worry that collaboration could prove counterproductive, with poor writers giving bad advice to better writers. If you structure your peer response tasks appropriately, explaining tasks clearly and asking more for descriptive than evaluative feedback, this shouldn't be a problem. Even inexperienced critics can point out sections they didn't understand or didn't like. It is then the writer's option to make changes. Our experience suggests that getting people to accept and respond to the good feedback they've been given is much more of a problem than is students making good essays worse because of bad feedback.

If I emphasize group work in my classes, I'm afraid it might cause my department chair to think I'm not doing my job, resulting in a poor evaluation. This does sometimes happen. Not every chair understands the benefit of group work, and many are still committed to a teacher-centered classroom. Our best advice on this potential problem is that you can make a very strong case for what you're doing by pointing out the advantages noted earlier, showing favorable student evaluations, and most influential of all, providing a sample or two of a student essay that has been substantially improved as a result of peer review.

Beyond Peer Review: Talking Together, Writing Together

We include a variety of samples of peer review group structures in Part Four of this manual. Most of them assume that groups are structured for the purpose of giving written or oral responses to early drafts of written assignments. There are many additional ways beyond using peer response groups to involve students in group work in a composition classroom, however.

Collaboration is quite useful at the beginning of the writing process, easing students past the writer's block that can occur when they try to begin writing before thinking through the topic. After you present an assignment topic, for instance, pairs of students can simply interview each other, discussing the following questions:

- What will the paper be about?

- For whom are you writing it?

- What do you know that you can put in your paper?

- What do you need to know in order to make your paper complete?

Another interesting group activity requires students to write together rather than just talk about or review previously written work. Many group writing tasks can be used to vary the class routine and get students actively involved with the concepts under discussion. (1) Assign a group paragraph, with all members contributing ideas, deciding on organization, and writing and editing a draft. When the groups read their paragraphs aloud, it usually inspires friendly competition as students practice their evaluative skills and explain why their group's paragraph is superior. (2) Provide just the body paragraphs of an essay, and have each group write an introduction and conclusion that draw the ideas together and make an interesting point about them. (3) Ask students to write paragraphs individually on a general theme (e.g., adjusting to college). Then form groups of three, and have each group structure their three separate paragraphs into one coherent essay by finding a common theme to present in a brief introduction and conclusion, deciding which paragraph order works best, and adding transitions to make the composition cohere. You will find that *Focus on Writing* provides many additional creative ideas for collaborative activities in each chapter review.

An instructor who is committed to having students work together can structure collaboration that lasts throughout an entire essay cycle. A basic plan (adapted from Johnson, Johnson, and Smith 16–19) might run as follows:

1. The instructor assigns students to pairs, with a stronger and weaker student in each pair, and has them write individual compositions.

2. Student A describes to Student B what he or she is planning to write. Student B listens carefully, asks questions, and outlines Student A's composition. The written outline is given to Student A.

3. This procedure is reversed, with Student B describing what he or she is going to write about and Student A completing a written outline.

4. The students individually research the material they need to write their compositions, keeping an eye out for material useful to their partner.

5. The two students work together to write the first paragraph of each composition to ensure that they have a clear start on their papers.

6. The students complete their papers individually.

7. The students review each other's completed drafts, making suggestions for revision according to peer review instructions provided by the teacher.

8. The students revise their compositions according to the suggested revisions.

9. The two students reread each other's compositions, proofread for grammar and mechanics, and sign their names to each (indicating that they have done their best to guarantee there are no errors in the composition).

Tips for Successful Collaboration in Developmental Writing Classes

- Train your students in the skills they will need, and model those skills consistently through your own oral and written comments. Students get a confusing message if, for example, you instruct peer groups to ignore grammar and mechanics and concentrate on larger issues, but you then comment only on grammar and mechanics when you evaluate the resulting essay.

- Devote the bulk of your time and energy to activities in which beginning writers can provide the most helpful peer feedback: giving general reader responses to first drafts.

- Structure your assignments clearly and always provide detailed written instructions so that students have something to refer to as the group task proceeds.

- Get to know your students' attitudes toward correcting writing because their attitudes and their previous writing class experiences will shape their responses. You might assign an early essay about prior writing experiences and teacher reactions. You can then use that in discussing appropriate peer response.

- Be sensitive to student fears. You may want to wait until class members get to know one another before assigning them to groups. Alternatively, you may want to ask peer response groups for only positive or descriptive feedback until students are more prepared to accept criticism from one another.

- Don't take over student groups. If you do sit in on groups, participate carefully, remembering that your voice should be just one of many, not the single authority.

- Assign an appropriate percentage of a student's final course grade to peer editing work, and remind students periodically that their involvement in collaborative activity will affect their grade.

- Obtain student feedback on how well groups are functioning. You can do this through conferences, written evaluations, and informal surveys. Monitor progress throughout the semester, and be willing to intervene and change group membership when necessary. One way to check is to ask students periodically to write comments about the strengths and weaknesses of their group.

If you run into problems, consult the extensive literature on collaborative writing. The articles in Chapter 9 (Collaborative Learning) of *Teaching Developmental Writing: Background Readings* (Bernstein, 2007) offer a good place to start.

WORKS CITED

Bernstein, Susan N. *Teaching Developmental Writing: Background Readings*. 3rd ed. Boston: Bedford/St. Martin's, 2007. Print.

Johnson, David W., Roger T. Johnson, and Karl A. Smith. *Active Learning: Cooperation in the College Classroom*. Edina: Interaction, 1991. Print.

McKeachie, W., P. Pintrich, L. Yi-Guang, and D. Smith. *Teaching and Learning in the College Classroom: A Review of the Research Literature*. Ann Arbor: Regents of the U of Michigan, 1986. Print.

Vygotsky, Lev. *Mind and Society*. Cambridge: Harvard UP, 1978. Print.

Wiener, Harvey. "Collaborative Learning in the Classroom: A Guide to Evaluation." *College English* 48 (Jan. 1986): 52–61. Print. Rpt. in *The Writing Teacher's Sourcebook*. 3rd ed. Eds. Gary Tate, Edward P. J. Corbett, Nancy Myers. New York: Oxford, 1994. 132–40. Print.

6

Assessing Student Writing

As an instructor, you are responsible for devising an appropriate method by which to evaluate student progress and for clearly communicating your evaluation throughout the semester by means of written responses and grades. This chapter addresses the two interconnected responsibilities separately, beginning with advice on how to respond effectively and fairly.

Responding

Responding to student writing may be your most important duty as a writing instructor. It is certainly one of the most time-consuming teaching chores and probably the one you like least. In this section we discuss the importance of commenting and give some practical advice and examples that may help you go about this task efficiently and effectively. Part Four contains sample response and evaluation forms.

Why Comment?

You respond to student papers for a variety of reasons. As their primary audience, you have a responsibility to let students know if they have achieved their communication goal. As an experienced writer, you are able to suggest techniques for improvement. As a coach, you must motivate students to care enough about their writing that they are willing to continue revising. And, of course, at some point you will probably want to explain a final grade.

For basic writers, the most important comments are those received while the work is in progress. As you respond to your students' papers, keep in mind the following guidelines.

- **Be positive.** Developmental writers need to be encouraged to write and take risks. Papers returned only with error notations and recommendations for change are counterproductive, reinforcing students' negative perception that they can never "get it right." If they read comments at all, students tend to search out the positive remarks, ignoring ones that discourage them. If your written comments produce a smile, albeit slight, and a "So, I'm getting a *little* better" remark after the student reads through them, you'll know you're on the right track.

- **Be specific to text and assignment.** You don't provide much guidance to the student struggling to produce an acceptable summary if, for example, your sole comment is that the summary left out some important main points while including a number of unimportant details. Instead, phrase your comment so as to help the student find the underlying structure. (For instance: *Mills points out three main reasons that people work. Be sure to include all three, but when writing a short summary like this, leave out the examples Mills gives to show that these reasons are true.*)

- **Provide suggestions and questions rather than labels.** As Nancy Sommers writes, students need *strategies*, not *rules* (148–56). For example, they know that they must support assertions. What they often don't know is just what an assertion is, or where the support is lacking, or why a different kind of example would be more effective. Rather than simply writing *SUPPORT!* in red letters in the margin with an arrow pointing to an undefined section of the text, you should provide the kind of response that causes students to add that support naturally. (For instance: *I was interested in your comment that you have always been afraid of writing. What kind of experiences caused this fear? Can you explain a few? Do you think the fear is still reasonable today, given your experiences? Are there any kinds of writing that you do enjoy?*)

- **Be concise.** Don't scribble more in the margins of a student's paper than the student has produced between those margins. Be selective. Developmental writers, who are often fearful writers and weak readers, are easily overwhelmed, even when all your comments are positively stated and helpful. A concise and descriptive end comment, focusing on the main thing(s) the student could do to improve this draft—or to improve future papers if this is a final submission—generally produces better results than do notes written all over the text that the student may or may not read and may or may not understand. The main reason for any comment is to direct students toward what should happen next.

- **Be consistent in terminology.** If you use the term *thesis* in your classroom discussion, don't comment that the student's *main theme* was unclear. If you've been discussing *transitions*, don't suggest that the student add more *linking* words. Simplify your response vocabulary as much as possible, and keep it consistent with that of your lectures and textbook.

- **Be unambiguous.** Vague directives such as *shorten* or *lengthen* or *add detail* result in unproductive worrying about the degree of change necessary. If you mean that the student should add another paragraph giving a personal example, say exactly that. If you mean that the second paragraph gives more reasons than are necessary and the student should leave out all but the two or three most important ones, say exactly that. If you

mean that a brief personal example to explain some claim would be useful, say exactly that. Be sure the students are spending time thinking about how to make their next draft better and not speculating about what your comment means. Your responses should draw out the student's undeveloped meaning, not impose your own.

Who Should Comment?

THE INSTRUCTOR. You, of course, will provide both formative and summative comments, helping students revise effectively and also internalize standards and techniques. Most of your time and effort should go into the formative comments while a paper is in the process of revision, and they should be limited to those aspects of the paper that are important at that particular stage. Resist the urge to discuss every possible area of improvement on every draft.

OTHER STUDENTS. As shown in Chapter 5 of this manual, other students can provide valuable feedback during peer review through written or oral comments or a combination of both. Peer feedback is probably most valuable at early stages of the writing process, but many instructors report successful use of peer response throughout the entire cycle, from idea generation through proofreading.

THE WRITER. An important source of feedback that instructors sometimes overlook is the writers themselves. Ask students to include a note at the end of their drafts pointing out parts that they were proud of, along with problem areas for which they are seeking advice. Have students keep journals in which they analyze the strengths and weaknesses of each written assignment, comment on the feedback they received from other students and from you, and set specific goals for the next assignment. Some instructors ask students to keep editing logs. Writing instructor Christel Taylor described an editing log like this in a posting on a basic writing listserv.

> I have students keep an editing log. They hate it at first because I have them copy their errors as I've marked them on final drafts, label the error, find the section in the handbook to help them correct it, and revise the sentence (or group of sentences). I think this activity is effective, partly because they do hate it. After they've done the first couple editing log installments, they start to look for their

errors before I see the final draft, simply so they won't have to go to all that work again.

The more actively writers evaluate their own work, the more independently they will apply these standards to future efforts.

What Should You Comment On, and When Should You Do It?

Although the content of your comments will depend on the focus and goals of your course, a general principle to keep in mind is that an instructor should respond to one set of issues at a time. It's confusing to the students and a waste of your time to comment extensively on grammar or mechanics on a first draft. Limit early remarks to global issues of content and organization. Let the students know you aren't marking errors at this point. Problematic sections might well be left out of the next version or be corrected automatically as the writer gains clarity about what he or she wants to express. At most, you might want to make a general statement on a paper about the need to pay attention when revising for correctness, formality, or any other issue that has caught your eye.

A note about error: Even on a final draft, it is not necessary to point out every grammatical error and correct every stylistic problem. It is not your job to edit the students' papers—that's their task. The most useful thing you can do for developmental writing students is help them get an idea of the relative frequency and severity of their typical errors so that they can determine where to focus their attention as they revise and proofread. If your course is designed so that students work together through different grammar chapters of *Focus on Writing*, one option is to comment on problems only after you have covered them in class. This way, students gradually become aware of all basic issues of correctness—but only as they gain the ability to identify and correct each problem through class practice. If you prefer to address grammar and style only as needed for individual students, it is still important to give comments that help students judge what is more and less important, perhaps setting specific goals in your end comments. For instance: *As you revise, pay particular attention to subject-verb agreement. You tended here to drop the final -s on verbs, writing "she ask" rather than* "she asks." *Check your handbook, and be sure to proofread carefully for final -s before you submit the next version.*

Where Do You Comment?

The three typical places to comment on student texts are in the margins, between the lines, and at the end.

Marginal and interlinear comments should be kept to a minimum. On an early draft, marginal notes might include questions, expressions of approval or agreement (sometimes just an exclamation mark or a "yes"), or suggestions about additional information needed at a specific location. Interlinear comments work best when you are suggesting different wording, underlining a sentence or phrase with a wavy line and writing an alternative above it. Your major response should come in your remarks at the end of the paper, focusing student attention on the one or two main recommendations you are making. If you have inserted a number of brief comments throughout the text, the endnote is the place to summarize these, arranging them in manageable order and recommending a strategy for improvement. Start this comment with a positive remark or two, and don't subordinate the positive to a more negative statement. Consider, for example, an endnote such as this: *I really liked all the specific details you included in this essay. They helped me understand why you say your grandmother was such an important role model to you. Now you need to work on the order in which you present those details to make the description even more effective.* It is more encouraging to a student than one like this: *Although I liked all the specific details and could understand why your grandmother was such an important role model, I was confused by the organization of ideas. Please work on organization.*

The Commenting feature on word processors and other kinds of writing software such as Interchange, Connect, CommonSpace, and Bedford/St. Martin's Comment allows you to say as much as you want wherever you want without appropriating the student's text. Your comments show up as a superscript number or highlighted area that the student can click on to open or print out if desired. Be sure, if you choose this means of responding, that students understand how to open the comments and that they have the necessary software at home or in a convenient lab. For classes that meet in a computer lab, a good way to familiarize students with the process is to require them to use the Commenting feature in their peer review activities.

How Do You Comment?

There is no best way to respond to student papers. Instructors have developed numerous personal methods to match the needs and constraints of their own teaching environment. Even the standard red pen is often set aside in favor of less "strident" colors (such as green or purple) or penciled responses, which have the twin benefits of not proclaiming your criticisms as harshly and of allowing you to erase a comment when you need to. We discussed earlier the most common means of responding: remarks written directly on student papers. Other options are described in the following paragraphs.

STANDARDIZED FORMS. Using prepared forms, often with checklists or rankings for different features, helps you give consistent feedback and speeds up the process of grading. We've included a few samples in Part Four. Such checklists, though, can lead to "rubber stamp" responses that are not very effective, especially in the formative stage of evaluation. They are most useful to explain a final draft evaluation and should be used along with a written note at the end.

MINIMAL MARKING. This system, developed by Richard Haswell (600–4), is designed for use in grading final drafts. The instructor comments as usual on the paper as a whole. Surface errors, however (e.g., spelling, punctuation, capitalization, grammar), are left unmarked within the text of the student essays. Each mistake is indicated simply by a check in the margin of the line in which it occurs. Two checks in a margin would indicate two errors on that line. After commenting on other issues, the instructor records the number of checks both at the end of the student's paper and in the gradebook. Papers are then returned fifteen minutes before the end of class, and students are given time to search for, circle, and correct their errors by writing the corrections on the paper itself. When corrected papers are passed in, the instructor reviews the student corrections, fixes any that are undiscovered or miscorrected, and

returns the paper with the final grade. (The grade for any assignment is not recorded until the student has attempted to find and fix the errors.) Haswell estimates that students can correct up to 60 or 70 percent of their own errors, saving the instructor time, helping to develop better proofreading habits, and most important, freeing the instructor to comment on more important issues of content, organization, and style. If you want to be more directive, you can highlight the error within the sentence, drawing it to the writer's attention.

ELECTRONIC COMMENTING. With the increase in Internet access and sophistication of commenting software, instructors have exciting new ways to respond to their students. The major concern here is that technology problems not come between you and the student. If you're going to comment by email or insert responses in student files, be sure you have trained the class thoroughly on how to retrieve your comments.

AUDIOTAPE. Sometimes older technology can still be useful. One way to provide more extensive feedback than can be squeezed onto a one-inch margin is to record your comments on a tape supplied by the student. This alternative to face-to-face conferencing and to expensive computer technology can work perfectly well with a commuting population, especially one of low-income students who might not have easy access to more expensive equipment. Taping also is an option for learning-disabled students who prefer auditory to visual processing. With the increasing popularity of MP3 format, teachers now have the option of recording their comments digitally, directly to the hard drive with a USB microphone. They can also use an inexpensive digital voice recorder like Olympus that compresses the sound file when it is downloaded and that provides a free downloadable player.

CONFERENCES. In the ideal world, all feedback would be given one-on-one so that you could clarify your comments and students could ask questions. Although schedules—both yours and the students'—often make face-to-face meetings difficult to arrange, we urge you to try to set up such meetings when possible, especially early in the semester. You may want to "trade" some class time for individual office hours by replacing classes one week with a series of fifteen-minute conferences. Because conference time is always limited, use it wisely. Have a clear idea of what to accomplish. You may want to give a form to the students to prepare in advance, asking them to write down their main idea, how they organized the assignment, what they liked best about it, and in what areas they especially want your advice.

No matter what means you choose for communicating your ideas to students, keep in mind that your comments should be positive in tone but realistic in message. Don't write only enthusiastic praise about the creativity of an essay's contents throughout the early drafts and then assign that paper a failing grade at the end because of poor mechanics. Your task is to be sure students understand, as they work through each stage of the assignment, whether they are meeting your expectations and what they still need to do.

Grading

Grading is difficult, and grading developmental writers is more difficult still. These students enter your course with many barriers between them and success, and a sizable number will not be able to overcome all those barriers despite their good effort and your good teaching. The most you can do is be sure that your class is structured so as to give students every chance to succeed, with clearly presented criteria and expectations, well-structured and sequenced assignments, and a fair, consistent grading policy.

Establishing Standards

It's often problematic for instructors who are new to teaching or to a particular institution to decide on standards. What constitutes an A as opposed to a B? What is passing? What is failing? If there are departmental policies written down, or benchmark papers on file, this is a good place to start. Another option is to talk with an experienced composition instructor about how he or she determines grades. Experienced teachers will generally be happy to share their ideas and will often have papers that they have commented on and graded that you can review. You might well also consider asking these colleagues to look at some sample papers after you have graded your first set of assignments, to see if they have any advice about what

you said or how you graded. Don't think that it's an imposition. Most instructors are pleased to be asked and find the discussion useful.

THE IMPORTANCE OF STATING CLEAR STANDARDS. Set out clearly in your syllabus how, when, and why the students will be graded. Be sure to include the percentage of the final grade assigned to each activity. Consider weighting the written assignments done in the second half of the semester more heavily than those done in the beginning. In fact, consider withholding grades on early assignments, just giving descriptive feedback instead. This prevents students from getting frustrated by repeated failing grades and giving up prematurely.

The following breakdown of percentages of the final grade allows students to see exactly how they will be graded.

■ Course grading

15%	Participation
10%	One in-class paragraph. Higher grade of two in-class paragraphs
30%	Three essays @ 10% each
10%	Two quizzes @ 5% each
5%	Journal
30%	Portfolio of two best revised writings and cover letter

The following box elaborates on the percentage breakdown. If you do not wish to assign letter grades regularly, you must clearly spell out your method of assessing students.

■ Grading

P, P-, and NP are the three grades you will see on assignments, quizzes, practice paragraphs, and so on. P means that satisfactory progress has been demonstrated; P- means that some satisfactory and some nonsatisfactory progress has been demonstrated; NP means that satisfactory progress has not yet been demonstrated. P and NP are the only grade options for your two long essays and your in-class final. The long essays will demonstrate sufficient mastery or lack of it;

there is no in-between. Your department final will be graded by a panel of English Department faculty. They will advise me as to whether they find that your essay demonstrates skill sufficient for you to proceed to English 101. This is an advisory grade, not the determination for your proceeding to English 101. I will use all your grades and my assessment of your writing-skill level to make that decision.

WHEN STUDENTS DON'T MEET STANDARDS. Handing back a failing essay, especially when you know the student has worked as hard as possible on it, is tough. There's not much you can do at that point except let the student know that you appreciate the effort expended and that effort is a necessary but not sufficient feature of good writing. One can't write a successful essay without effort, but effort alone doesn't always guarantee a successful outcome. Give the student one clear goal to work on for the next assignment. Be sure to mention resources or techniques that could be helpful in reaching that goal.

Many instructors prefer to assign an unsatisfactory essay the grade of R (meaning "needs revision") rather than F. We grade essays A, B, C, or R, and we tell students that any essay assigned an R must be revised according to the written feedback and returned the following week. Students may revise essays as many times as necessary to bring the grade up to passing, as long as they resubmit the paper no later than one week after receiving it. This prevents students from waiting until the final week and turning in five or six essays. It also ensures that the learning that comes from revision will not be postponed until it's too late to do any good. Students attach the original draft with instructor's comments to the new one so that we can easily see what the problem was and simply note on the revision whether it addressed our concerns successfully or whether additional work is needed to remove the R.

Portfolios

One means of grading student effort over the course of the semester, a way that gives them every opportunity to succeed, is to require students to assemble portfolios of their writing for your review — or in some departments, for review by one or more outside evaluators. Portfolio use promotes the following:

- **Revision**: Students continue to revise assignments right up to the end of the term.

- **Critical thinking**: Students develop both the criteria for selecting documents to be placed in their portfolios and the metacognitive skills needed to present their work to outside readers.

- **Collaborative learning**: Students work together on revision tasks.

- **Real-world writing strategies**: Students write to an audience other than their own teacher.

Some instructors assign grades to individual papers before they are placed in the portfolio. Others do not, grading the portfolio holistically after it has been completely assembled. Either way, the instructor works as a coach throughout the semester, giving constructive feedback on how to improve each assignment and helping students put together a sampling of their best efforts by the end of the course. Portfolio use is an excellent way to ensure that you are grading fairly by evaluating a complete picture of the student's writing skills. Whether or not portfolio use is a departmental practice at your institution, you might want to consider some modification of the concept for your course. Nedra Reynolds's *Portfolio Keeping: A Guide for Students* and *Portfolio Teaching: A Guide for Instructors* provide excellent brief guides to portfolio creation and assessment.

Student Contracts

Another method for involving students actively in the grading process is to structure your grading system around contracts. This involves developing clear criteria, sometimes with student input and sometimes by the instructor alone, explaining what must be done to earn each possible final course grade. Criteria can be quantitative (describing the number of assignments that must be submitted to earn each letter grade), qualitative (describing the qualities an essay must have to earn each letter grade), or both (the number of essays with a specific set of qualities for each letter grade). The hard work for the instructor occurs up front in this system, but once detailed criteria have been established, student arguments about grading are minimal.

WORKS CITED

Haswell, Richard. "Minimal Marking." *College English* 45 (1983): 600–4. Print.

Reynolds, Nedra. *Portfolio Keeping: A Guide for Students*. Boston: Bedford/St. Martin's, 2000. Print.

——. *Portfolio Teaching: A Guide for Instructors*. Boston: Bedford/St. Martin's, 2000. Print.

Sommers, Nancy. "Responding to Student Writing." *College Composition and Communication* 33 (1982): 148–56. Print.

Taylor, Christel. "Re: Textbooks." Online Posting. 10 May 1999. Conference on Basic Writing Listserv. 31 July 2007. www.asu.edu/clas/english/composition/cbw/listserv.html.

PART TWO
Addressing Student Needs

7

Working with Developmental Writing Students

Any generalization about developmental writers must, by definition, fail to provide an accurate description of the students in your particular class. The following profile, therefore, is meant simply to give you an idea of some types of students you may encounter. Once your class gets under way, you will quickly get to know your own students and appreciate their individuality.

Be prepared for a classroom filled with students with a wide range of academic backgrounds, cultures, ages, preferred learning styles, life experiences, socioeconomic statuses, abilities, and attitudes toward self, others, and higher education. One of your greatest challenges is to deal with these differences.

Common Traits of Developmental Writing Students

Amid this diversity, certain characteristics are likely to show up frequently. Your students will be first-generation college students, be married and/or parents, have demanding but not necessarily rewarding jobs, be commuting and/or attending school part-time, have dropped out of earlier educational settings, speak English as a second language, or speak a nonstandard dialect of English. Additionally, they will tend to be highly gregarious and social, more oral than verbal, ambivalent about learning because of negative past experiences, and in need of an overview before learning details.

They may exhibit nonacademic interests, pragmatic educational goals, and an expectation of failure in academic settings. They are typically less fluent, prone to more surface errors in their writing, and in possession of a narrower range of writing options than is the usual nondevelopmental college writer. At the beginning of the semester, they may not have achieved the cognitive maturity needed to complete the kinds of synthesis/analysis tasks academic writing demands.

They probably will not plan their writing extensively and will demonstrate editing practices hampered by (1) confusion about rules of grammar, (2) selective perception, and (3) egocentricity. They will not make much distinction between editing and proofreading and will doubt their ability to do either. Thus, they will tend to produce prose that makes sense to them but that doesn't address audience needs. They will be more likely than the average college student to have a learning disability. Their learning style may not be compatible with traditional instructional methods. Their self-confidence will often be unreasonably low or unjustifiably high.[1]

What does this mean to you and your use of *Focus on Writing*? In the words of Mina Shaughnessy, teaching clearly *has* to make a difference (Tate 181). That's both the challenge and the reward ahead.

Working Successfully with Developmental Writers

Capitalize on Their Strengths

The characteristics just noted, which might seem overwhelmingly negative at first glance, can be sources of strength. Nontraditional students in particular possess a wealth of life experiences and strong opinions that can make their essays and classroom discussion sparkle. The cultural diversity in a developmental writing classroom informs debate and provides a rich source of opportunity for students to learn to write for different audiences. And although real-life demands — jobs, childcare, family — can pull students away from their homework, those demands can also motivate students to excel in order to change careers, gain a promotion, or provide a better role model for their children. Students already in the workforce know the value of good communication skills and should be able to appreciate the goals of the class, especially if those goals are presented in a real-life context. Instead of "Why do we have to learn this?" you may hear, "Why didn't anyone ever teach me this before?"

Understand Their Attitudes and Problems

One of the most important things you can do for your students is to help them recognize and overcome negative perceptions that interfere with their ability to perform satisfactorily in class. Be alert for signs of *fear*, and realize that a developmental writing student may fear success as well as failure, consciously or unconsciously wanting to avoid the life changes that might accompany academic achievement. Both kinds of fear often manifest as a tendency toward procrastination. A clear policy identifying your penalty for late assignments, coupled with a grading policy that allows revisions for higher grades, can provide students with the structure they need while lowering anxiety levels. If possible, postpone giving any letter grades at all, working early in the semester to stimulate fluency and develop good editing habits. Once students have learned to see themselves as writers, they are more ready to accept and use constructive criticism.

If *procrastination* seems to be a problem for some of your students, try talking over the common reasons for procrastinating: feeling overwhelmed by too many details, overestimating the amount of time needed, preferring to be doing something else, hoping the task will eventually go away, fearing failure, fearing success, and enjoying the adrenaline rush that comes with just beating a deadline. The following list of suggested ways for dealing with procrastination can form the basis of a good group discussion, journal entry, or in-class writing task.

- Keep a log of how time is actually spent.
- Make use of small chunks of time rather than waiting for a long uninterrupted stretch.
- Set interim deadlines and give yourself rewards as each is met.
- Eliminate distractions.
- Have all materials accessible.
- Have someone remind you periodically about the deadline.
- Delegate tasks when possible.
- Relax during scheduled leisure time.

Writer's block is another common complaint in developmental classes. Consider bringing it up as a topic of discussion in an early class. What is writer's block? When does it happen? Why does it happen? How can it be lessened, if not totally avoided? Learning that other people find writing frustrating and get stuck now and then is often all the encouragement students need. You can assure students that writer's block in its true form is a psychological condition that completely prevents the act of writing. What they are experiencing, instead, is most likely a sense of unreadiness, a result of skipping some phase of the writing process. You might also direct students to sources such as Purdue University's Online Writing Lab (OWL) at **owl.english.purdue.edu**. Its tips on overcoming writer's block are set up in a helpful if/then format, asking students to consider what might have caused the problem: starting in without preliminary planning, not liking the topic, not understanding the assignment, anxiety, perfectionism, or fear of grading. The OWL then offers coping strategies: spending time freewriting or brainstorming before trying to write the draft, finding a new topic or personalizing the boring one, thinking of the first draft as a practice run that will be revised and improved later, or forcing oneself to write without censoring.

If you or your colleagues have tips for moving beyond writer's block, it's helpful to share them. Consider the following examples:

- Begin in the middle.
- Talk through the first draft, using a tape recorder.
- Freewrite with the computer monitor turned off.
- Break down the assignment into pieces and give yourself a reward at the completion of each piece.

Practical advice for worried but conscientious students is simply to stop the unproductive worrying, move on to something else, and return to the task later in a better frame of mind.

Consider that you and your course, no matter how well meaning, are but the latest in a series of what may have been *negative experiences* throughout the typical developmental writer's academic life. It is helpful to have students articulate—orally or in writing—their most unpleasant experiences with writing. Students can forge bonds with one another while commiserating about problems they have had with writing and writing instructors. As you listen or read, you will get a better understanding of potential student problems, reactions, and worries.

A discussion of their ideas about writing can be illuminating to both you and your students. Consider asking students to come up with *myths* they have heard about writing by seeing how many ways they can finish the sentence "Writing is . . ." or "A good writer is someone who . . ." or "When I write, I . . . ." They will probably volunteer ideas such as "Writers are born, not made"; "For a good writer, writing is easy"; "Once a paper is written, making changes will probably only make it worse." Discussing these notions can dispel negative myths and lead students to see writing as a process that they can master with practice.

Speaking of practice, many developmental writers struggle because they simply *lack practice*. Due to the attitudes and problems explained above, some students have given up by the time

they reach your class. You might remind them that learning any skill takes practice. Try viewing yourself as a coach leading practice.

- Have students discuss or write about skills they have had to practice to learn.
- At each class meeting, ask students how many times they practiced writing since the last class meeting.
- Point out to students that the grammar exercises in *Focus on Writing* are called Practice[s].

Clarify Your Ideas on the Importance of Grammar and Error

Perhaps the most controversial word in developmental writing scholarship is *error*, followed closely by *grammar*. Before planning your class, give some thought to where you fit into the "great grammar debate": what you believe grammar is, how you think one acquires it, and how those beliefs inform your teaching. Most scholars today accept the fact that good grammar is not the same as good writing and that the teaching of formal grammar by itself does nothing to improve students' writing skills and little to improve their grammatical usage. Nonetheless, the waters are murky with political, sociological, psychological, and pedagogical issues—whether students have a right to their own language, whether the instructor's job is to help students change to fit into a new discourse community or to work on expanding that community so that more students fit in, whether good grammar is a prerequisite for complex thinking, and whether good writing will eventually produce grammar to match.

Focus on Writing has been composed with sensitivity and respect for developmental writing students' ability but in the firm conviction that guided practice with grammar and mechanics, when done in the context of writing, can help students write better and increase their mastery of the basics of Standard Written English. Adult students rarely question the need for such practice and for learning or relearning the occasional rule. When the question of relevance does come up, you can discuss Mina Shaughnessy's notion of grammatical error as static or white noise, something that makes the reader work harder than necessary to understand what is being said (11–13). Because the writer's job is to deliver the message so that a reader can comprehend it accurately with a minimal expenditure of energy, nonstandard grammar (requiring energy expenditure on the part of the reader without offering anything in exchange) is not a good bargain.

Your challenges are to figure out how to deal with your students' grammatical errors productively without being discouraging and to motivate the students while pointing out if, when, and why their efforts do not succeed. Don't get consumed with the hunt for errors. Mike Rose points out, "Error marks the place where education begins" (189). It's essential that you seek creativity, strength, well-phrased thoughts, new ideas, and logical arguments in your students' work, even if you sometimes have to listen hard for these merits behind the static of mechanical error. As Rosemary Deen reminds us, "What kills teaching is pursuing error and weakness in others; what enables teaching is releasing students' energy by defining their success" (qtd. in Tate, Corbett, and Myers 55).

Changing unproductive grammar habits is a tough job, and there's no use pretending otherwise. Part of respecting your students involves giving them a realistic appreciation of the difficulty of the task ahead. Be prepared for morale to break down when students reach the point at which they start asking why they can understand rules, answer workbook exercises correctly, and correct their peers' errors yet still produce papers of their own filled with faulty mechanics. Directing students' attention to the writing tips in each chapter of *Focus on Writing* or providing your own tips on revising and proofreading can help. It is also comforting to explain to your students that as they gain new knowledge and try out new skills, other features of their writing may temporarily fall apart. Such backsliding is a normal part of growth.

If you sense at some point that your students are beginning to demonstrate an unproductive concern for grammar per se, focusing on mechanical correctness before making sure they actually have something to say, you can help them adjust their perspective a bit by sharing Langston Hughes's thoughts on the issue of "Grammar and Goodness":

> "I agree that the sentiment of your poem is correct," I said. "But I cannot vouch for the grammar."

"If I get the sense right," answered Simple, "the grammar can take care of itself. There are plenty of Jim Crowers who speak grammar, but do evil. I have not had enough schooling to put words together right—but I know some white folks who have went to school forty years and do not do right. I figure it is better to do right than to write right, is it not?"

"You have something there," I said. "Do keep on making up your poems if you want to. At least they rhyme."

"They make sense, too, don't they?" asked Simple.

"I think they do," I answered.

"They does," said Simple.

"They do," I corrected.

"They sure does," said Simple. (Hughes 181–82)

Set a Climate Conducive to Learning

Maximizing the physical and psychological environment is the first task of any teacher, and it's an especially important task for teachers of developmental writing students.

PHYSICAL ENVIRONMENT. You may not have much control over the physical environment, but anything you can do to increase the comfort of students will be helpful. Remember that your students may have worked a full day (or night) before coming to class. Can they see the chalkboard? Can they see each other? Can they move around? Is the temperature cool enough to keep them awake? If you can't change the room conditions, it's useful to acknowledge them and be willing to make whatever adjustments are possible.

PSYCHOLOGICAL ENVIRONMENT. Whether or not you can maximize the physical environment, you can indeed establish a psychological environment that encourages learning. According to most research on adult learning, adults work best in an atmosphere of mutual respect and mutual responsibility, one that is supportive, friendly, and collaborative. Although discipline is more often an issue with younger students, these "traditional" students, too, respond well in an environment where they are recognized as adults. An interesting challenge is raised by the fact that developmental writing students regardless of age often display dualistic thinking—"Things are either right or they're wrong, and I want the teacher, the authority, to tell me which is which"—while still proclaiming their own independence. It's important to be aware of these contradictory impulses and plan how to accommodate one need while understanding the other.

New information should be set in context so that the *why* and not just the *what* is apparent. Humor can break the ice, but sarcasm can be misperceived, especially by ESL students. Because developmental students are often reluctant to ask questions and expose gaps in their knowledge, it's important that you become comfortable with silence and allow enough time for a timid student to formulate a question or an answer.

In addition to your role as an empathetic and patient instructor, you will be expected to be a mentor: a source of support, challenge, and vision. In this capacity, your role is to affirm the validity of the students' present experience, challenge them to move beyond it, and help them to develop a clear vision of where they are headed (Daloz 212). This means

- listening patiently and actively
- providing clear structure in class and assignments
- stating and repeating positive expectations
- challenging negative ideas
- sharing ideas from your personal/educational/ professional experience
- setting interesting, achievable goals
- insisting on high standards
- holding up a nonjudgmental mirror to their actions

Model Appropriate Behaviors

As instructors, we need to set a good example, displaying the kinds of intellectual and social behavior we expect of our students.

When you develop your individual assignments, daily lesson plans, and course syllabi, therefore, be sure they reflect the organization and clarity you hope to see in your students' writing. Spell out formatting requirements or preferences. Apply to both your actions and your assignments the time-worn but effective maxim "Tell 'em what you're going to do, do it, and then tell 'em what you did." Beginning a class, discussion, or assignment with a general overview of what's to come helps students understand the context and gives them a framework on which to hang their new knowledge. Summarizing at the end—even better, asking students to summarize—encourages retention. And remember, *Can you explain to the rest of the class what we've just gone over?* is almost always a more productive question than *Does anyone have any questions about what we just discussed?*

Be conscious, too, of the need to go over written assignments orally so that students who learn best verbally are accommodated. Let students know how much time you expect an assignment to take so that they can plan their time effectively and measure their progress against an average. Listen patiently and courteously; display the kind of civil behavior you expect in the classroom. Be alert to confusion and problems unexpressed. One quick and easy method for finding out what your students have and have not learned from the day's lesson is to set aside five minutes at the end of class and ask students to write a sentence or two completing the phrases "The most important thing I learned today was . . ." and "The one thing I hope we will spend more time on is. . . ." Point out resources that students, especially the overwhelmed students most in need, might overlook. You can start with the resources available in their text. Read through "A Note to Students" together, and then look through a sample chapter. Discuss the text's organization: the table of contents and index; the Highlight boxes, Grammar in Context boxes, checklists (Self-Assessment checklists, TEST checklists, and Review checklists); the differences between Flashback and Revising and Editing exercises; where to find more practices online at *Exercise Central*; where the answers to textbook exercises are to be found and how best to use them; and the information to be found in the appendixes. Discuss, too, how students' notebooks should be organized.

You should also make your students aware of the support resources offered on your campus: distribute a schedule of writing center hours, direct students to computer laboratories, discuss staff and resource availability, be aware of what kind of testing is available for students who might be learning disabled, and keep handy the names and phone numbers of counselors who can help students with academic or psychological issues. If you have a course or departmental Web site with student resources, give students the URL and consider spending a class period in the computer lab showing them what help is available online.

Your behavior and concern will show the student that he or she is not alone and that your class is not a place where only the fit survive. It is a supportive learning community that will only be as successful as each of its members is.

Help Students Develop Metacognition

Good writers generally understand their own strengths and weaknesses as writers. This allows them to address new writing tasks effectively, efficiently, and confidently. The more you encourage student writers to think about *how* they think and *how* they write at each stage of the writing process, the more they will be able to pinpoint individual problem areas and make wise choices about where and when to compensate. Writing will then begin to seem a much more manageable task. If you assign essay topics, in-class discussions, and journal questions that require students to think about what parts of the writing process they did well and where they struggled, asking them each time to come up with plans for making the next effort more successful, students will gradually become aware of their productive and nonproductive habits.

Developmental writing students often have unusual ideas about "writerly" behavior. You might make a handout of the following list of differences (Walvoord and Smith 7) between skilled and unskilled writers and ask what your students think of each comparison.

**BEHAVIORAL DIFFERENCES BETWEEN
SKILLED AND UNSKILLED WRITERS**

Skilled/Successful Writers	Unskilled/Unsuccessful Writers
1. conceive of the writing problem in its complexity, including issues of audience, purpose, context	1. conceive of the writing problem narrowly, primarily in terms of topic
2. shape writing to the needs of the audience	2. have little concept of the audience
3. are committed to the writing	3. care little about the writing
4. are less easily satisfied with first drafts, think of revision as finding the line of argument, revise extensively at the level of structure and content	4. are more easily satisfied with first drafts, think of revision as changing words or as crossing out and throwing away, revise only at the level of single words or sentences
5. are able to pay selective attention to various aspects of the writing task, depending on the stage of the writing process	5. often try to do everything perfectly on the first draft, get stuck on single word choices or on punctuation, even at early stages when good writers ignore punctuation and concentrate on getting ideas down on paper

Once your students start to see themselves as writers, their self-confidence will begin to grow. They begin to believe that they really might have a place in the academic community. It is no easy task, as writers like Mike Rose (*Lives on the Boundary*) and Richard Rodriguez (*Hunger of Memory*) have powerfully shown. Helping students to develop their metacognitive awareness of the act of writing is an important first step.

Choose Useful Evaluation Strategies

Chapter 6 of this manual contains detailed information about evaluating student writing. Following, however, are general recommendations to consider as you shape your course. First, because revision is a skill that developmental writers generally lack, it is important to develop a grading strategy that promotes substantive revising. One way to do this is simply to comment on initial submissions, delaying a letter grade until the paper has gone through a number of revisions. Another approach is to allow graded papers to be revised and resubmitted for a new grade, which then either supersedes the old grade or is averaged together with all revisions for an overall assignment grade.

Regardless of the grading policy you choose, be aware of the need for positive feedback. Some research has suggested that positive comments may have a more salutary effect on student writing than other kinds of feedback do. Developmental writers especially need to feel that at least some part of their writing effort has been successful. Don't forget, in the maze of surface error and awkward syntax that awaits you, to find and appreciate a nice turn of phrase, a clear thesis, a well-structured argument, a fully developed paragraph. Low grades can be damaging both to fragile egos and to your attempts to help students take control of their own work. As Jerry Farber reminds us,

"You can tell students anything you want about 'taking responsibility' and 'thinking for yourself.' The grading system you employ—a middle finger extended before them—is always more eloquent still" (qtd. in Tate, Corbett, and Myers 215).

Set Expectations for Discipline

While discipline is often less a problem in a developmental writing classroom than in a basic freshman composition course, that is not always the case. Be prepared to encounter students who resent being placed in a "remedial" class. Some may be bored and resistant, and some may have emotional problems. You will certainly have students who are tired and distracted by events at work or home. It is important, therefore, to set the tone early for what you will and will not tolerate. Make explicit—in your written syllabus and in class discussion—your policies regarding lateness, absence, and entering and leaving the room once class has started. If you are having a problem with discipline, reevaluate your lesson plans. Is there a way to accomplish the same goals while enabling students to play a more active role? Students who are actively involved in tasks they consider meaningful have little time for off-task behavior.

The Rewards of Teaching a Developmental Writing Class

The preceding discussion has focused more on problems than on rewards. Working with developmental writers does take effort, sometimes a greater effort than you feel able to make. To maintain perspective on those days when you are contemplating mounds of student papers, all of which seem to display the same deficiencies you've spent the last month of class working to eliminate, it helps to remind yourself of the positives.

First, more than many other teaching experiences, a developmental writing class affords you the opportunity to see tangible improvement, to watch students move from chaos to competence. Second, you are in a position to make a difference that will dramatically expand someone's life

and future choices. The student who comes back a semester or two later proudly brandishing an A paper from another instructor and saying he couldn't have done it without you, and the student who shows you her positive job evaluation citing improvement in writing skills and announces her promotion, are reminders that the hard work—yours and theirs—was worth it. They *did* learn. Most important, in a developmental writing classroom your students will not be the only ones learning. Perhaps your greatest reward is the opportunity you will have to learn from your students—from their life experiences, their cultures, their questions, their challenges, and the motivation they provide for you to revisit and revise your own teaching ideas.

NOTE

[1]For a comprehensive overview of developmental writers and writing instruction, see Theresa Enos, ed., *A Sourcebook for Basic Writing Teachers.* New York: Random House, 1987; and Gary Tate, Edward P. J. Corbett, and Nancy Myers, eds., *The Writing Teacher's Sourcebook*, 4th ed. New York: Oxford UP, 1999.

WORKS CITED

Daloz, Laurent A. *Effective Teaching and Mentoring: Realizing the Transformational Power of Adult Learning Experiences.* San Francisco: Jossey-Bass, 1986. Print.

Hughes, Langston. "Grammar and Goodness." *Simple Stakes a Claim.* New York: Rinehart, 1957. Print.

Rodriguez, Richard. *Hunger of Memory: The Education of Richard Rodriguez.* Boston: Godine, 1982. Print.

Rose, Mike. *Lives on the Boundary: A Moving Account of the Struggles and Achievements of America's Educational Underclass.* New York: Penguin, 1989. Print.

Shaughnessy, Mina P. *Errors and Expectations: A Guide for the Teacher of Basic Writing.* New York: Oxford UP, 1977. Print.

Tate, Gary, ed. *Teaching Composition: 12 Bibliographical Essays.* Fort Worth: Texas Christian UP, 1987. Print.

Tate, Gary, Edward P. J. Corbett, and Nancy Myers, eds. *The Writing Teacher's Sourcebook.* 4th ed. New York: Oxford UP, 1999. Print.

Walvoord, Barbara, and Hoke Smith. "Coaching the Process of Writing." *New Directions for Teaching and Learning: Teaching Writing in All Disciplines.* Ed. C. W. Griffin. San Francisco: Jossey-Bass, 1982. Print.

8

Accommodating Students with Learning Disabilities

Some students are placed into developmental writing sections because of undiagnosed learning disabilities. Dealing appropriately with the needs of such students can be a challenge. Only within the last fifteen or twenty years has the public education system become aware of learning disabilities. A large number of students with learning disabilities remain unidentified and continue to struggle. Many students who have difficulty with writing may have no idea that they are simply "wired" differently and need to learn compensating strategies to keep up with the rest of the class.

Understanding Learning Disabilities

Learning disabilities[1] are a complex and diverse group of disorders that affect the student's ability to acquire and use information. It's important for instructors to understand that a learning disability does not necessarily correlate with a person's intellect. In fact, one of the key indicators of a learning disability is that a person's performance is significantly below that predicted by their intelligence level. Students with undiagnosed learning disabilities often think of themselves as stupid or dense, when in fact they are not. You can help such students understand and use strategies to compensate for their particular disorder.

Types of Learning Disabilities

Learning disabilities tend to fall into five categories: academic, which includes dyslexia and

dysgraphia; language; attention deficit disorder (ADD); perceptual motor; and social perceptual.

1. Academic Learning Disability. The student will have a particular problem learning one or more fundamental academic subjects (e.g., math) or some aspect of reading. Students may also be able to comprehend what they read but have difficulty, for example, with phonics.

2. Language Learning Disability. Students may have difficulty either understanding what people are saying to them (receptive language) or saying what they want to say (expressive language). Students may have a combination of problems. A student with a receptive language disorder may not understand a lecture but will be able to work through a book of grammar exercises. A student with an expressive language disorder may have trouble asking the instructor for assistance or coming up with something to write about. Note that these disorders can be very mild or barely noticeable in everyday life, but they can present a lot of difficulty when the student is faced with a language-intense challenge such as assignments in a developmental writing course.

3. Attention Deficit Disorder (ADD). A number of adults have ADD in some form, although it is often thought to affect children only. This disorder makes it difficult for the student to focus on the instructor and screen out distractions. Changing seats, calling on a distracted student periodically in class, and, in some cases, supplying medication have all been used to address ADD.

4. Perceptual Motor Disability. This disorder makes it difficult for a student to use pen and paper, to choose the right computer keys, or to take notes accurately from a chalkboard. Handwriting is usually illegible.

5. Social Perceptual Disorder. Students with social perceptual issues usually have trouble picking up social cues from their classmates. Subtlety and hinting won't work with these students. If you have a student with this disorder, it is especially important to be concrete and direct about your expectations.

Special Concerns: Dyslexia and Dysgraphia

Two academic learning disorders—dyslexia and dysgraphia—strongly affect the student's ability to write.

DYSLEXIA. Most of us think of backward letters when we think of dyslexia, but there are more serious problems than simply switching the letters *d* and *b*. These reversals also happen at the sentence level (*to go the store* for *go to the store*) and at the conceptual level (the student might start with the "middle" part of what she wanted to say, then end with an unfinished sentence, the "start" of the concept she intended to express).

Students who have dyslexia tend to have trouble

- writing legibly
- writing in a straight line
- keeping their place on the page
- accessing long-term memory

They might also have visual problems that cause the letters to dance around on the page.

DYSGRAPHIA. Dysgraphia includes any serious problem with writing, including those related to spelling, coherence and organization, copying down what one sees, and being able to write down ideas at all. A student with a form of dysgraphia probably has a hard time with the complicated process of writing. This student tends to

- take a very long time to write a sentence or even a word
- complain that she knows what she wants to say but can't seem to get it down on paper

- have poor handwriting
- write in fragments
- write incoherently (sentences have no particular order)
- write sentences with little syntactic complexity
- do very poorly on timed essay tests or exams
- have difficulty copying text from the chalkboard or copying down lecture notes given orally

Accommodating Identified Learning Disabilities

Sometimes students arrive with a full understanding of their learning disabilities and can explain what kinds of help they need. Accommodations can range from something as simple as allowing a student extra time to finish tests, to modifying the course material (providing audiotaped versions, assignments printed in large type, etc.). Under the Americans with Disabilities Act, reasonable accommodations must be provided to people with disabilities. If a requested accommodation seems unreasonable or inappropriately time-consuming to you, discuss it with the student and an administrator, and see if the need can be addressed through some other means. Your university may have free tutoring or writing labs that can offer support beyond what you are able to provide.

Using Technological Aids

Students with learning disabilities often have sloppy handwriting and are unable to spell words correctly. Individuals with difficulties in these areas may ask to work on a computer. By all means, grant the request if possible. Some learning disabled students are never going to be able to spell correctly, and no amount of practice will significantly improve the look of their handwriting. Allow the use of the computer and move on to more attainable writing goals.

You, too, can get a great deal of help from technology, especially in the form of Internet resources. Muskingum College offers a learning strategies database at **muskingum.edu/~cal/ database/** in which students can click on the problem they are experiencing, such as "Attention and Learning," "Reading Comprehension," or "Encoding and Retrieval." They can then follow links to background information and specific coping strategies.

Recognizing Signs of Unidentified Learning Disabilities

As mentioned earlier, some students have an undiagnosed learning disability and have been frustrated within traditional classroom settings. An alert instructor may be able to steer such students toward means of identifying learning disabilities and help them develop compensating strategies.

Developmental writers often exhibit many symptoms of learning disability, so how do you know if someone actually has a disability? Symptoms usually cluster in one category and seem out of character with the rest of the student's performance. A student who always has the right answer when called on in class and who does well on paper-and-pencil quizzes, but who has serious problems in organizing an essay, may have a learning disability.

Another clue is the degree to which the student experiences the problem. Does the problem afflict most of your students or just a particular student? Students often express frustration about some aspect of their performance. A student once complained to us that she could never understand articles that we gave the class to read. She said, "I read it and read it, but it just doesn't sink in." She probably has a mild form of a reading comprehension disorder. We suggested some compensation strategies, such as having someone else read the articles aloud to her, highlighting important thoughts one paragraph at a time, and reviewing her understanding of the article with a classmate. These seemed to work for her. Had the problem persisted, we would have suggested that she be tested for learning disabilities and counseled on other compensation strategies.

Following is a list of symptoms of writing-related learning disabilities, grouped by skill area.

READING

- confusion of similar words, problems with multisyllabic words
- slow reading rate
- difficulty retaining, comprehending, remembering

- difficulty identifying important themes or points
- skipping words or lines of printed materials
- difficulty reading for long periods

WRITING

- poor grammar, omitted words, difficulty with sentence structure
- frequent but inconsistent spelling errors
- difficulty copying from overhead projector, chalkboard
- poor spacing, capitals, and punctuation; poorly formed letters
- difficulty planning and organizing a topic and putting thoughts on paper
- difficulty proofreading and revising
- long and rambling or very short compositions
- monotonous sentence structure
- illogically sequenced sentences
- writing and printing mixed in the same document
- very slow writing
- writing off the lines
- difficulty with expressive, creative language

SUMMARIZING

- inability to summarize from an organizer chart
- not knowing how or where to begin
- inability to find the main idea
- inability to separate the main idea from the supporting details
- inability to see connections between points
- inability to link reading to prior knowledge
- inability to understand context clues in the text

REVISING

- difficulty when asked to scan or discuss what is written
- difficulty identifying errors in own writing
- inability to use a dictionary successfully to check for errors
- using various spellings of the same word
- inability to understand or use grammatically correct sentence structure

STUDY/ORGANIZATION SKILLS

- poor organization and time management
- difficulty following directions
- poor organization of written materials

- late submission of assignments
- slowness to start tasks
- inefficient use of library and reference materials

OTHER

- difficulty reading facial expressions and body language
- inappropriate, impulsive behavior
- difficulty grasping subtlety
- spatial problems (cannot navigate in a small classroom or on trips)
- tendency to "overload" quickly and then "shut down"
- susceptibility to distractions
- difficulty sustaining attention
- hyper- or hypo-activity

It is important to remember, though, that not all students who exhibit such behaviors have actual learning disabilities. Lack of experience in an academic classroom, a mismatch between learning and teaching styles, lack of effective study skills, external problems with family or health, and native language or dialect interference are just a few of the factors that could lead a student to exhibit behaviors mimicking learning disabilities.

Coping with a Suspected Learning Disability

If you suspect a learning disability, you may want to conduct an informal assessment of the student prior to recommending formal testing. Take care not to exaggerate the problem. Describe your concern as an attempt to identify the student's learning style rather than saying that you think the student may have a learning disability. Approach the student one-on-one. If you believe she has difficulty understanding text, you may want to have her read some text and then explain it. You can also ask the student the questions in the list that follows. According to Hollybeth Kulick, a student who answers "yes" to six or more of these questions should be encouraged to get formal assessment for reading difficulties.

1. Are you a slow reader?

2. Do your eyes feel as if they are floating in your head when you read, or do the letters bounce around the page?

3. When you are reading from a distance, do the letters seem to disappear?

4. Have you been aware that you reverse letters, or was it pointed out to you by a teacher?

5. Do you have difficulty remembering what you have read ten minutes after you have read it?

6. Do you have difficulty pronouncing words when reading?

7. Do you have difficulty putting your thoughts down on paper when writing?

8. Do you find that you cannot finish reading during class when the rest of the class has finished?

Once a learning disability has been identified or suspected, suggest that the student use the following strategies to compensate for the disability. Indeed, many of the strategies in the following discussion, which come from Colorado State University's online writing program, will be useful for any developmental writer.

Planning

There are several different ways a student can plan a paper, including freewriting, brainstorming, and clustering (see Chapter 1, Step 1, Planning, section C, in *Focus on Writing* for a description of these strategies). Have the student try several of these strategies to see which one works best. When the student has found a strategy that works for her, have her refer to her notes or diagram and do some freewriting (if the student has difficulty with freewriting, have her make a list instead); encourage her not to worry about what she includes in her text at this point. She will be able to decide what to include or exclude later.

Next, have the student read through what she has written so far and decide what might be included and excluded from her essay. Have her then compose a new way to approach the essay and separate her plan into an introduction, a body, and a conclusion. Together, go over the content of each.

Drafting

Now it is time for the student to translate her chart into a draft. Some students will benefit from creating a linear outline before drafting, and others will benefit more from a "pictorial" outline.

One technique to recommend to all developmental writing students with organizational problems is to write each idea or piece of information on an index card. Then the student rearranges the cards into a logical order. From that order, the student develops an outline and writes the draft. This is an effective strategy for students who are overwhelmed by seemingly huge writing tasks.

Some students, once they have constructed a detailed outline, find drafting to be the easiest part of writing. However, most students with learning disabilities have a very difficult time drafting. They may need to freewrite again and then use a strategy such as cutting up the draft and pasting it back together. Others will just need to write many drafts.

Reviewing

The last phase with which the student will need special assistance is reviewing. Students may benefit from keeping a "drafting diary" in which they record revision questions such as "Do my thoughts follow each other logically and make sense?" and "Does each sentence say what I want it to say?" and "Have I left out any important information?" Most students with learning disabilities should work with you to create an editing/proofreading checklist that they can use throughout their academic career. (See p. 168 in this manual for an example of a typical sentence-level editing checklist. *Focus on Writing* also provides a number of self-assessment checklists you and your students can work from.)

In addition, some students might benefit from reading their essays into a tape recorder.

They can then listen to the essays to find inconsistencies, errors, lack of coherence, and so on. If the equipment is available, speech synthesizers are also useful "hearing" aids.

Last, offer your students this helpful mnemonic device to remind them of the important steps in editing:

SCOPE

S—Spelling: Is the spelling correct?

C—Capitalization: Are the first words of sentences, proper names, and proper nouns capitalized?

O—Order of words: Are the words in the right order?

P—Punctuation: Does each sentence end with a period, question mark, or exclamation mark? Are commas and apostrophes placed where needed?

E—Express complete thought: Is each sentence complete? Does each sentence have a subject and a predicate?

These activities solidify the writing process for students, encouraging them not to skip any steps.

NOTE

[1] Much of the following information was taken from two sources: Colorado State University's Online Writing Lab, **writing/colostate.edu/references/teaching/ldteach/index.cfm**, and Gary Fisher and Rhoda Cummings, *When Your Child Has LD* (Minneapolis: Free Spirit, 1995).

WORKS CITED

Colorado State University's Online Writing Lab. **writing/colostate.edu/references/teaching/ldteach/index.cfm**.

Kulick, Hollybeth. *Telltale Signs of a Learning Disability.* Denver: Blue Spectrum Press, 1980. Print.

9

Working with ESL and Second-Dialect Students

As Chapter 7 of this manual points out, developmental writing classrooms are always diverse. Mainstreaming efforts and budgetary or placement limitations frequently increase instructional challenges by adding nonnative and second-dialect speakers to this already diverse student mix. Just like native speakers, ESL and second-dialect students come in all ages, bringing a variety of personal and professional goals; an assortment of personality types, learning styles, study habits, and motivations; and a range of external problems and support systems.

To make things even more complex, the characteristics of those within the ESL subgroup itself differ widely, depending on a number of factors. How close to the structure of their native language will students find the structure of English? Are they used to an alphabetic or nonalphabetic writing system? Are they literate in their native language? How much tolerance do they have for the kind of trial and error that language learning requires? Are they immigrants making a new home in the United States and seeking to integrate themselves into the culture, international students planning to return to their native countries after their education is complete, or refugees uncertain of the future and conflicted about their place in both countries? What kinds of writing instruction and assignments, if any, are they used to having in school? How experienced are they with the forms and conventions of written English? How fluent are they with spoken English and vocab-

ulary? Are they proud of or embarrassed by their native language, their culture, their dialect? If English is their native language, how strongly has it been influenced by the language of nonnative relatives and friends?

Because there is no one-size-fits-all description of second-language or second-dialect students, there can be no one "right" way to meet all of the varying instructional needs of these students. The goal of this chapter, therefore, is simply to discuss a number of issues in hope that some of the questions or approaches presented will prove useful in your own particular context.

Approaches to ESL Instruction

Philosophies of ESL instruction and philosophies of writing pedagogy have been mutually influential. The accompanying table outlines some major approaches and their resulting pedagogical practices.

Each of the approaches presented in the table has both advantages and limitations. You'll probably find yourself borrowing from all, mixing and matching to meet the needs of your students, your evolving philosophy of instruction, and the constraints of your local setting. Whatever your approach, however, keep in mind one basic principle that is stressed throughout the research. ESL students will typically need more of everything: more time to produce their writing, more instructions on how to write, more

■ Pedagogical Approach	■ Classroom Focus
Audiolingual	Practice drills for improving grammar
Writing as a process	Revising through multiple drafts
English for academic purposes	Writing tasks that approximate real-world situations, emphasis on socializing students into academic discourse community
Contrastive rhetoric	Considering similarities and differences between native language and English to see how these might impede and/or improve English writing skills
Error analysis	Looking for patterns of error and diagnosing reasons/solutions
Freirean (also called participatory or liberatory education) process	Drawing writing/reading topics from students' real-world needs and interests; students gain control over their world as they learn to control their communication process
Whole language	Assuming that language is learned through interaction with speakers, writers, and readers; classrooms as learning communities
Language experience	Making use of verbal skills by having students talk about personal experiences and then use this transcribed speech as reading material
Writing and publishing	Brainstorming, drafting, sharing, conferring about, editing, and finally publishing students' own writing
Competency-based education	Assessing students' needs, selecting a group of specific competencies based on needs assessment, targeting instruction to those selected competencies, and evaluating progress toward achievement

models to read, more practice in reading and writing, and more kinds of feedback, given at more stages of the writing process.

General Teaching Tips

Luckily, many of the practices that can help make your writing class more effective with nonnative speakers work equally well with other students. The recommendations that follow, while drawn from ESL pedagogy, will enhance any developmental writing classroom, regardless of the students' linguistic histories.

- **Get to know your students.** This advice holds for any student, but it is especially important for a student whose body language, class response patterns, and school experiences were shaped by a culture different from yours. Consider having students fill out a self-survey that could then be used as the basis of class discussion or for a writing assignment. For additional ideas, see Yu Ren Dong's description of the writing autobiography assignment she uses with her students at Queens College, CUNY (Bernstein 370–80).

- **Model activities clearly.** Show students how to highlight texts effectively, take notes in margins, and turn headings into questions so that they read with a purpose. Demonstrate writing strategies like brainstorming or editing, and classroom activities such as peer review.

- **Encourage reading of all kinds.** Point your students to your library's newspaper and periodical section, the Internet, and the campus bookstore.

- **Encourage questions, critical attitudes, and risk taking.**

- **Build email and journal assignments into your syllabus** where possible. Give students the chance to practice writing in nonthreatening, nongraded situations and to explore ideas about their reading. The double-entry journal, for instance, in which students copy selections from reading assignments in one column and write their reactions (questions, notes about applications and significance, etc.) in the other, is a good tool for helping students see the value of writing as discovery.

- **Make the "shape" of a class period clear.** Explain goals in the beginning, preview the structure you will be using to reach those goals, outline main ideas to be covered, indicate clearly when you get to those main ideas ("You might want to write this down..."), repeat important points without waiting for requests, and explain difficult vocabulary in simpler terms.

- **Use audiovisual aids** whenever possible to preview, illustrate, and/or review, so that information students might miss during your spoken presentation can be picked up through other means.

- **Be aware of your assumptions** about how students "should" act, and question whether cultural differences might explain deviations from this "norm."

- **Expect backsliding.** As students try new tasks or work in new contexts, their language skills will frequently seem to fall apart. Reassure them that this cognitive overload will lessen as they become comfortable with each new task.

- **Limit classwide, formal grammar instruction** to those features that can be explained clearly and understood easily, and that follow general rules. Focus your class on *writing*, not on language correctness. Reserve any needed instruction on the more idiosyncratic parts of English grammar, like preposition usage, for individual conferences with students in whose writings the problems occur.

Special Considerations for Teaching a Mixed Writing Class

Although all students tend to benefit from the kinds of teaching techniques described in the preceding section, some important issues require special attention when you are teaching a developmental writing class that contains a mix of native and nonnative speakers.

Encourage class participation. Make your expectations for classroom behavior explicit. Many international students come from educational systems in which they were expected only to listen. Assure students, for instance, that you expect them to ask questions. Explain how and when this can be done. (Are they free to interrupt while you're speaking? Should they raise their hand first or just speak?) Be aware of the need for frequent and varied comprehension checks. Pause longer than you ordinarily would after asking whether anyone has questions. ESL students may need the extra time to be sure they have understood the question, to formulate their answer, or just to gather the courage to respond. When possible, give students time to think through their questions and comments in writing before presenting them orally. Consider setting aside a few minutes at the end or beginning of class during which students write on note cards their main question, the main thing they've learned, or both. You can collect the cards and respond to them in the next class period or use them as the basis of small group discussions. You can also maximize student participation by creating a class email discussion forum where students can ask and answer questions at their own pace.

Watch your language. You may be used to making your classroom comfortable and conducive to learning by adopting a colloquial, informal conversational style. Although such speech can work well with second-dialect students, bridging the gap between their home speech and academic discourse, it can, paradoxically, be harder for ESL students to understand and adjust to, since many international students are more at ease with the formal English they learned in their home countries. Be conscious of your delivery in general; speak clearly, slowly, and audibly. Check with students frequently to be sure they are following your presentation.

Remember the importance of affect. Although educational growth in general often occurs when students are forced out of their comfort zone, second-language learning seems to require a feeling of safety and comfort. Students must know that it's all right to take risks, that failing is a necessary part of learning, that errors are signs of growth. They need to know that you value their native language, culture, and dialect, and that you are seeking only to give them additional choices with your instruction, not telling them the "right" way to express themselves. Take time to talk with them, one-on-one if possible, early in the term in order to establish a personal connection. Then continue to show your interest in their cultures throughout the term by checking with them about any unexpressed needs or such things as the suitability of assignment topics.

Be aware of attitudes students may bring with them. Recognize that the different kinds of students in your classroom will come with different feelings about language learning and may need different kinds of attention. Consider the accompanying table and how these features might affect student performance. What other differences could you add?

Structure assignments clearly. Consider all aspects of your assignments carefully: rhetorical modes, context, wording, and number and length. For instance, ESL students may find the kinds of personal narratives often assigned in developmental writing classes harder than more formal assignments. They are not used to producing that kind of writing in school, and their vocabulary may be more suited to academic and work writing than personal description. It may also be harder for them to write about things that occurred in their native countries (such as childhood events) which they experienced in their native language, than things (such as academic tasks) that they have experienced more recently and in English. Furthermore, students in college with particular career goals may find personal-exploration writing of little use in preparing for real-world writing. This is not to

■ Potential Differences	■ ESL Students	■ Second-Dialect Students
Feelings about home language/dialect	Generally source of pride.	May be source of embarrassment.
Sense of self	Often feel part of mainstream culture of native country, now just temporarily isolated.	Often feel permanently marginalized, out of mainstream.
Past experience with teachers	Often positive: Teachers see language problems as natural part of growth.	Often negative: Teachers see language problems as result of carelessness, laziness, intellectual deficiencies.
Editing for grammar and correctness by having student read draft aloud	Doesn't work: Students can't hear errors in patterns they haven't learned.	Does work: Students frequently correct errors automatically as they speak.
Clarifying ideas by having teacher summarize in own words what teacher thinks student meant	Doesn't work: Students may have problems understanding oral summaries as well as a tendency to accept whatever teacher says as right, even if teacher has misunderstood their meaning.	Does work: Students get a model for how to express their ideas differently.
Audience awareness	Difficult: Audience is always a stranger.	Less difficult: Underlying response patterns are known; students just need to be prompted to consider audience.

say that such assignments should not be used, only that you may need to explain and justify them to an ESL population.

Whatever mode of writing you expect, remember that audience awareness is a major problem for an ESL writer who may not have internalized the conventions of the various genres. What kind of material is needed to prove a point to an American reader? What points need to be proven? What are the reader's expectations with respect to content, structure, and tone? Practice, by itself, won't make perfect; students need guided exposure to samples of a range of responses before they can begin to internalize structures and expectations. ESL students will benefit from explicit directions and models. It is often helpful to ask students from different cultures what a good narrative or description or a good persuasive paragraph consists of in their culture, so that you can discuss contrasts and thus expand their options (and your awareness).

Watch for cultural differences. Obviously, the list of possible misunderstandings could be a long one, from body language issues (Why does my student never look at me when we're speaking?), to classroom management (Is this student not participating out of a lack of understanding, a lack of interest, a different idea about the role of student versus teacher?), to topics for assignments (What kinds of issues are appropriate or inappropriate, easy or hard, for my students to write about?). If you see some behavior that doesn't fit your idea of good classroom practice, such as inappropriate responses or unproductive behavior in groups, try to find out the actual cause; don't just assume one. Also, watch out for conflicts, whether voiced or not, that may arise when ESL students consider their non-ESL classmates to be their intellectual inferiors or when second-dialect students feel disrespected by students whose primary dialect is closer to standard written English. Be alert to any "us/them" divisions.

Clarify the writing process. Many students will not have been exposed to the concept of the writing process and may resist the idea. Explain your reasons for requiring freewriting or a sequence of revisions; tell students both how and why such things are done. You might explain the process by having the class work through Tarvers's five drafting sessions (Ferris and Hedgcock 112):

1. Zero draft

2. Shaping draft: focus on organization, audience, and voice

3. Style draft: focus on paragraphing, syntax, and diction

4. Editing draft: focus on grammar, mechanics, and formatting

5. Final draft: submit for evaluation

At each of the five steps, give specific advice on the kinds of activities and thinking required. When working on the shaping draft, for instance, you might have a group discussion about audience awareness, using questions like the following for small-group discussions.

QUESTIONS FOR AUDIENCE ANALYSIS

- How old is the audience?
- What is the economic or social condition of the audience?
- What is the educational status of the audience?
- What values and beliefs would be common to an audience of this age?
- What general philosophies of government or politics does the audience hold?
- What economic or social values is the audience likely to hold?
- What value does the audience place on education, religion, work?
- Which of these values — economic, social, political, educational — is most important to the audience? Least important?
- What patterns of thought do audience members expect? Will they want data? Are certain authorities more convincing than others? How much explanation, illustration, or definition will I need?
- What kinds of issues most frequently make audiences angry or defensive?

Source: Lindemann 90–91.

Working through this kind of detailed analysis as a class or in small groups will help nonnative students become more aware of general audience expectations.

Rethink peer review activities. Because peer review helps students internalize a sense of reader response, it is extremely useful for ESL students. However, the process must be carefully thought through if it is to be effective. If you typically have students read drafts aloud and then get oral feedback—which is often recommended to get students to focus on global and style issues rather than issues of mechanical correctness—consider whether all students' oral comprehension skills are advanced enough for this technique. Perhaps you will need to ask the author to read aloud while others follow on a printed copy. Will it be difficult for native speakers to understand an ESL student's spoken English? If so, perhaps you will want to have students read texts silently before responding. Might reading-comprehension skill levels prevent some students from keeping up with a peer review activity in which they read and respond immediately? If so, you might consider having drafts emailed to students prior to class, or turned in during one class period and discussed during the following one, so students can read drafts and respond at their own speed. You can then use class periods for discussion only. When you set up the groups, assign roles (facilitator, recorder, reporter), and rotate the assignments.

Whatever system you use, structure the process clearly, specifying both the kind of writing you are looking for and the role of the reviewers. If left to their own standards, students whose native culture encourages more formal and circuitous arguments might, for instance, give unhelpful advice to a writer. Explain *in written directions* what reviewers should be looking for, and why. Similarly, be sure the reviewers know that their role is to give constructive criticism. In many cultures, the purpose of a group project is to reach consensus, not to present individual critiques, so students may need direction and encouragement before they feel free to disagree or to present their own opinions.

For examples of peer review questionnaires designed for specific kinds of assignments, see p. 147 in this manual. Also, see Chapter 5 in this manual for additional information on the general topic of collaboration.

Rethink your commenting practices. If you typically decorate student papers with lots of interlinear and marginal comments, you may want to try a different system. Reading hand-writing in a foreign language can be difficult. Typing up a longer end comment on a separate sheet of paper may improve the odds of students' understanding your responses. Also, ESL students are often unfamiliar with our common editing symbols, so be sure to point out the list facing the inside back cover of *Focus on Writing* or distribute your own list, including examples of edited text, early in the term. Remind students of the symbols throughout the term as you introduce new grammar rules and begin to point out problems in student papers. One other caution to keep in mind is that students might not be used to the kind of indirect comments that U.S. writing teachers often employ, such as asking questions and giving personal responses. Thus they may be upset that you aren't giving them more direct advice on what to change and how to change it. Be sure to spend some time discussing the difference between commenting and correcting, and why you do what you do.

There is one final issue to consider: going against accepted wisdom, many ESL instructors recommend commenting on patterns of grammar error even during early drafts. This does not mean marking every error on an early draft, or marking only grammatical problems and ignoring more global issues. However, if you see recurring language problems, it is appropriate to mention them as part of your end comment even on a preliminary draft, perhaps highlighting one or two as examples, so that the student can attend to them. See Chapter 6 in this manual for additional advice on evaluating and responding to student writing. You will find a variety of books available if you want to brush up on terminology and rules for English grammar, most notably Constance Weaver's *Grammar for Teachers* (Urbana, IL: NCTE, 1979), her *Teaching Grammar in Context* (Portsmouth, NH: Boynton, 1996), and Marianne Celce-Murcia and Diane Larsen-Freeman's *The Grammar Book: An ESL/EFL Teacher's Course* (Boston: Heinle and Heinle, 1999).

Review your grading philosophy. As you consider how to grade a nonnative speaker fairly, it may help to distinguish between errors that are simply the equivalent of a foreign accent in that student's writing and ones that are serious, stigmatizing, and frequent. Address the latter; don't penalize the former. Remember, too, how unequal the playing field is for ESL and second-dialect students. Do what you can, within the limits of your own particular system, to even it out. Some teachers allow more time for writing, both in class and outside, even if that means cutting down on the number of assignments required; others allow nonnative students to start an in-class exam early. Of course, as with native speakers of English who demonstrate serious writing issues, you may not be able to address all of a nonnative writer's needs within your class. The important thing is to make this assessment as early as possible and then to counsel the student on available options. The student may want to consider a more basic ESL class focusing on spoken language or may want to obtain outside help from tutors, writing labs, and/or online resources. The Internet can be a wonderful source of additional practice and advice for the ESL student and instructor. See the following section, "Using the Internet," for specific ESL-related suggestions.

Be proactive about preventing plagiarism. Different cultures have vastly different conventions about what sources to cite, as well as when and how to cite them. Plagiarism, always a complicated issue for developmental writers, can be even more of a minefield for ESL students. Some cultures, for instance, teach that incorporating another author's words into one's own writing is a sign of respect, both for the author and for the reader who, as an educated person, is assumed to know the source. It is important to show examples of texts that cite sources correctly, to discuss the process, to practice in class with samples, and to require multiple drafts so you can give corrective feedback early in the process.

Using the Internet: Expanding Classroom Options

One final recommendation is to expand your textbook and your classroom by making use of technology. The Internet offers three general kinds of resources to ESL students and teachers:

1. new communication tools like email, chat rooms, and student discussion lists

2. the opportunity to publish and access class materials from a class home page

3. Web resources for academic research and personal enrichment and entertainment.

Using email, students can practice direct and authentic communication with all sorts of people for all sorts of purposes. Accessing the Internet expands the kinds of writing prompts available to teachers. Now you can ask students to write a business proposal to a corporation they researched and visited online; to describe a picture they "saw" at the Louvre; to give directions for getting from one place to another, complete with subway stops and road maps; to review a movie that they don't have to leave their dorm room to see; to compare the coverage of a news event in their hometown newspaper to its coverage in the *New York Times*; to post their thoughts in a class forum; or to write a biography of someone from sources in an online archive.

If you teach your class in a writing lab, you have all the options mentioned in Chapter 3 of this manual. Even if you are teaching in a traditional classroom, you might consider pointing your ESL students toward the kinds of options that your school's student labs offer: a chance to keep in contact with friends at home, a chance to make new friends all over the world while practicing English writing skills, a chance to practice grammar and mechanics at online sources such as *Focus on Writing*'s *Exercise Central*, a chance to do research for other school courses, and a chance to practice reading authentic English on any topic of interest. Consider providing on your personal or course home page a group of useful links that students can use to get started if they are new to the Internet. Following are just a few of the available Web sites that contain resources of interest to both you and your students.

- **rong-chang.com/main.htm** Links to a wealth of ESL learning materials, from proverbs of the day to "Chat with Alice," a robot that uses artificial intelligence to carry on a conversation.

- **eslcafe.com** Dave's ESL Cafe, billed as the "Internet's meeting place for ESL and EFL teachers and students from around the world." It contains chat rooms, student forums, and teacher forums, along with many other resources, from explanations of slang to pictures for use as writing prompts.

- **ncela.gwu.edu/** A government-funded Department of Education site for the National Clearinghouse for English Language Acquisition and Language Instruction Educational

Programs. It is maintained by the DOE's Office of English Language Acquisition, Language Enhancement, and Academic Achievement for Limited English Proficient Students, and it provides information on research, statistics, practices, policies, and more.

- **owl.english.purdue.edu/owl** The Purdue OWL (Online Writing Lab) home page, with an ESL menu that offers handouts, quizzes, email lists, MUDs and MOOs, games, and links to many other sites.

- **cc.kyoto-su.ac.jp/~trobb/slinfo.html** An international listing of EFL/ESL student discussion lists, established in 1994 to provide a forum for cross-cultural discussion and writing practice for students around the world. Clear directions are offered for how to register and subscribe, whether as a class or an individual.

- **tesl-ej.org** The site of *TESL-EJ*, the online journal for teaching English as a second or foreign language.

WORKS CITED

Bernstein, Susan N. *Teaching Developmental Writing: Background Readings.* 3rd ed. Boston: Bedford/St. Martin's, 2007. Print.

Ferris, Dana, and John S. Hedgcock. *Teaching ESL Composition: Purpose, Process, and Practice.* Mahwah, NJ: Lawrence Erlbaum, 1998. Print.

Lindemann, Erika. *A Rhetoric for Writing Teachers.* New York: Oxford, 1982. Print.

ADDITIONAL RECOMMENDATIONS

Fox, Helen. *Listening to the World: Cultural Issues in Academic Writing.* Urbana, IL: NCTE, 1994. Print.

Hedgcock, John S. *Teaching ESL Composition: Purpose, Process, and Practice.* Mahwah, NJ: Lawrence Erlbaum, 1998. Print.

Leki, Ilona. *Understanding ESL Writers: A Guide for Teachers.* Portsmouth, NH: Boynton/Cook, 1992. Print.

10

Accommodating Learning Styles

Try this exercise: Start a class discussion by drawing a series of concentric circles on the board and then, moving from the largest to progressively smaller circles, label each in order:

1. Everything that is known about good writing

2. What *I* know about all that is known

3. What *I* choose to teach out of all that I know

4. What *you* hear out of what I teach

5. What *you* retain and apply out of what you hear

The challenge for students and instructor is to find ways to expand the smallest circle so that it fills as much of the next larger circle as possible—in other words, to maximize student retention. A prime way for you to approach this challenge is by considering how best to accommodate your students' varied learning styles.

Why Are Learning Styles and Learning Preferences Important?

As writing instructors, we focus on one goal: improving our students' writing skills. We all know the importance of choosing appropriate texts, making clear assignments, and devising fair evaluation methods. Sometimes, however, we overlook factors that at first glance have little to do with whether a student learns how to write a clear thesis or avoid comma splices. A brief look at the research on the many factors that influence student learning may suggest new approaches in the classroom and how or why to apply them. A general understanding of learning styles can help you teach more effectively in a multicultural classroom and can help you remember that any one student is unlikely to learn in the same way as the students sitting next to him—and still more unlikely to learn in the same way you do. Even though a specialized knowledge of psychological type is not required for effective teaching, it *is* important to realize that we tend to teach in ways that feel comfortable to us. These ways may not be equally appropriate to our students.

What Kinds of Factors Vary from Learner to Learner?

Learning Preferences

One aspect of learning you might want to consider is how students differ in their learning preferences. Such preferences have been classified by Dunn and Dunn into five categories:

- **Immediate Environment.** Does a student prefer quiet or noise, bright or dim lighting, warmth or coolness, seating around a table or in a row? In testing situations, especially, it is important to make sure students are in the environment most conducive to good writing. A small gesture like allowing a student to listen to his favorite music on a headset while working on an in-class writing assignment or allowing a student who likes solitude to move her desk into a corner of the room to take a test can go a long way toward making sure your students are showing you their best work.

- **Emotionality.** How is a student motivated, and what makes him or her persist when discouraged—internal or external factors? Inner-directedness has been shown to correlate with higher achievement: students find pleasure in setting and meeting their own goals rather than just working to please the instructor. When students follow *Focus on Writing*'s structure, creating some text of their own, returning to it in flashbacks, and finally revising and editing it, they are learning a most useful lesson in taking control of their own learning process and seeing the tangible rewards this can bring.

- **Sociological Preferences.** Do students prefer studying alone or with peers? Do they want an authoritative or collegial teacher? Are they comforted or bored by a consistent routine? *Focus on Writing* provides a wide variety of learning activities, and each section ends with a selection of activities specifically appealing to collaborative learners.

- **Physiological Characteristics.** Do students learn best by hearing, seeing, or doing? Do they learn best in the morning, afternoon, or evening? What amount of stimulation is effective; what amount is counterproductive? What are you doing to get all of your students' senses involved? Are you allowing students to read their work aloud to others who listen while looking at printed versions? Do you write main points on the chalkboard or use overheads while explaining concepts so that visual learners can be accommodated at the same time that auditory learners' needs are met?

- **Psychological Processing Inclinations.** Do students need to see the big picture before understanding the details, or must they become familiar with individual pieces before grasping the whole? Are they deductive or inductive reasoners? Remind students to use the Focus boxes and Review Checklist boxes in *Focus on Writing* to help them understand the different chapter concepts.

Although you can't accommodate all preferences in all activities, keeping these categories in mind while you plan your classes will prompt you to (1) include diagrams, pictures, or PowerPoint slides for the visual learners, for instance, and (2) provide hands-on tasks that involve group work and physical motion for the kinesthetic learners, while (3) accommodating the needs of auditory learners by reading written assignments aloud and remembering to save adequate time for in-class questions and answers.

Personality Types

Another factor to consider is the effect of your students' personality types on how they learn. The Myers-Briggs Type Indicator, a system of personality typing developed by Katherine C. Briggs and Isabel Briggs Myers, based on the work of Carl Jung, suggests four basic personality types. Each student in your classroom will fall somewhere on a continuum of four different factors:

- **Attitude toward Life.** Are the students more *introverted* or more *extroverted*, focused more on people or ideas?

- **Way of Perceiving.** Do they understand best what they have taken in through their five senses (*sensing*), or do they make meaning through unconscious connections (*intuiting*) between abstract ideas?

- **Way of Judging.** Do they rely primarily on *thinking* and logic in their decision making, or do they rely on their *feelings* based on personal or social values?

- **Way of Dealing with the World.** Do they process external events by *judging* them or simply by *perceiving*?

Much research has been done on the effects of personality type on academic achievement. Keeping these four dualities in mind can be helpful as you plan your class activities. An extrovert, for instance, prefers to see examples first, whereas an introvert prefers to learn the rule initially. Therefore, if you are discussing sentence style, you might engage your extrovert students by starting out with examples of good (or poor) sentences drawn from student work, using those as a springboard for discussion of stylistic principles. You can engage introverts by having them read through an explanation as a homework assignment before coming into class to work on specific examples. Thinking types might work best on assignments built around logical order, with a numbered series of tasks to perform. Feeling types might prefer to have the outcome specified but be allowed to discover their own path toward that outcome. Sensing types excel in tasks that require practical skills, making sure that assignments are complete and effectively presented. Intuitive types can provide leadership to groups working under broad, general guidelines. It is important, therefore, to be sure you are providing a balance of tasks in order to draw on everyone's strengths, for it is safe to assume that the students in any classroom will display all these personality types.

Information Processing

Students process information in various ways, according to learning style expert David Kolb, whether they prefer to learn from:

- concrete experience
- reflective observation
- abstract conceptualization
- active experimentation

This learning preference is easily measured and could provide some interesting data for class discussion, but we point it out mainly as a consciousness raiser. Are there any adjustments you might make to your syllabus so that you accommodate each of these preferences at some point? Are you providing a variety of opportunities for students to do, think, dream, and practice?

Instructional Methods

Yet another area of research, spearheaded by Reichman and Grasha, focuses on teaching styles, classifying student preferences for different instructional methods. The categories that have emerged are as follows:

- **Dependent thinkers,** who prefer teacher-directed, structured classes with explicit assignments

- **Collaborative learners,** who like discussion-oriented group projects with lots of social interaction
- **Independent learners,** who prefer to influence the content and structure of their own learning, using the teacher primarily as a resource

Again, the question to ask is whether your class activities favor one group over the other.

Kinds of Intelligence

One final classification theory worth considering is the concept of "multiple intelligences" advanced by Howard Gardner. Important especially in K–12 pedagogy, Gardner's theory reminds us that individuals have many kinds of intelligence: linguistic, logical-mathematical, spatial, musical, bodily-kinesthetic, interpersonal, and intrapersonal. The students in your classes will show different degrees of aptitudes in each of these areas, and a well-rounded education encourages growth in all seven. Even within your writing class, which focuses primarily on building linguistic skills, you may find it beneficial to keep in mind the seven kinds of competencies when planning the range of assignments. Did you remember to include tasks that require interpersonal skills—working in groups and writing group reports, for instance? If a student is having trouble constructing a logical paragraph, could you ask him to present his ideas in a diagram first? Would it make subject-verb agreement clearer to students with strong spatial skills if you stood two of them in front of the class to be your subject and verb and then let them be moved apart by a group of students acting as a prepositional phrase, showing that the movement doesn't affect the original agreement? How can you make creative use of your students' varied strengths to help them learn?

An Internet search using the term *learning styles*, the last name of the individual theorist you are interested in, or both, will quickly lead you to numerous online explanations and self-test instruments such as those at **colorado.edu/cewww/Fac101/success5.htm** or **chaminade.org/inspire/learnstl.htm**. These Web sites can provide valuable material for class discussions, group work, essay topics, or simply recommended reading.

Where Does All This Fit into Your Teaching?

Once you begin thinking about learning style applications, you will probably begin to rethink your pedagogy. How you present material in class may change if reflection reveals that you have been teaching in a style that suits just one kind of learner. The advice you give students on how to study may change, as you learn more about their personality types and learning preferences. The formats you use to assess competency may change. You may vary your assessment tools to match different learning styles — offering group grades for social learners and portfolios and logs for reflective analyzers, asking for peer and self evaluations, and assigning creative as well as analytical writing tasks. The applications of this awareness are bounded only by the limits of your own creativity.

BRIEF BIBLIOGRAPHY OF LEARNING STYLE MEASUREMENT INSTRUMENTS DISCUSSED IN CHAPTER 10

Bernstein, Susan N. *Teaching Developmental Writing: Background Readings.* Boston: Bedford/ St. Martin's, 2001. Print.

Dunn, R., K. Dunn, and G. E. Price. *Learning Style Inventory.* Lawrence: Price Systems, Inc., 1989. Print.

———. *Productivity Environmental Preference Survey Manual.* Lawrence: Price Systems, 1989. Print.

Dunn, R., and Dunn, K. *Teaching Elementary Students through Their Individual Learning Styles: Practical Approaches for Grades 3–6.* Boston: Allyn and Bacon, 1992. Print.

Gardner, H. *Multiple Intelligences: The Theory in Practice.* New York: Basic, 1993. Print.

Kolb, D. A. *Learning Style Inventory: Technical Manual.* Boston: McBer, 1976. Print.

"Learning Style Inventory." Adapted from *Barsch Learning Style Inventory* by Jeffrey Barsch, Ed.D., and *Sensory Modality Checklist* by Nancy A. Haynie. personal.psu.edu/bxb11/LSI.htm.

Myers, Isabel B. *Manual: A Guide to the Development and Use of the Myers-Briggs Type Indicator.* Palo Alto: Consulting Psychologists, 1985. Print.

Reichman, S. W., and A. F. Grasha. "A Rational Approach to Developing and Assessing the Construct Validity of a Student Learning Styles Scale Instrument." *Journal of Psychology* 87 (1974): 213–23. Print.

PART THREE

Teaching Focus on Writing: A Chapter-by-Chapter Guide

Please refer to Chapter 1 of this manual for an overview of *Focus on Writing*. Following are chapter-specific notes to help you make effective use of the text.

UNIT 1: Writing Paragraphs

The first part of the text guides students through the writing process. While you can mix and match many chapters in the text to build your semester according to your course objectives (see sample class schedules in Chapter 1 of this manual), it is recommended that you begin by introducing students to writing as not only an important life skill, but also as a process that can be learned. Use the many opportunities in Unit One to build student confidence through repeated practice.

Chapter 1: Understanding the Writing Process

Chapter 1 introduces the writing process in the context of paragraph development. It covers planning, organizing, drafting, and revising and editing. We recommend that you assign this chapter as homework reading early in the semester and then spend a number of early class periods practicing and discussing the various components. By the end of the chapter, the student will have planned, organized, drafted, and completed the initial revision of a paragraph. Exercises in the text move students back and forth between (1) analyzing a typical student's writing as he or she works through the various stages and (2) practicing each step on their own, either individually or in small groups. Developmental writers tend to see writing as a "once and done" activity, not a series of recurring steps, so you will probably need to persuade students of the value of spending time on anything other than what they will consider actual "writing" (i.e., drafting). You might spend one class period showing how a writer would work through the whole process, asking the class to provide the content while you model the text creation and revision at the chalkboard or using an overhead projector or computer. Once students accept the fact that each stage leads to

a better final product, they can spend the next several class periods developing their own paragraphs and discussing their problems and achievements.

STEP 1: Planning

A. UNDERSTANDING PARAGRAPH STRUCTURE Let students know that paragraphs are a "basic unit of writing" and make sure they understand the difference between a topic sentence and supporting sentences. Remind students that learning how to write effective paragraphs allows them to build stronger critical thinking and writing skills. Also, writing a paragraph is a necessary step toward writing an essay.

Some developmental writers are unfamiliar with the physical format of a paragraph. As you discuss the important content elements of a paragraph (a topic sentence that states the main idea, sentences that support the main idea, and a concluding statement), it can be helpful to also point out formatting features (typical length, indentation, space between sentences). You can do this using a paragraph in the textbook or on an overhead.

B. FOCUSING ON YOUR ASSIGNMENT, PURPOSE, AND AUDIENCE One way to help students internalize the importance of planning their writing is to ask them to turn in a cover page for each assignment with the following categories filled in. Help the students fill in each section as they reach that stage of their first assignment, and then require a similar cover sheet for all assignments:

Name: (your name)

Date: (date you turn in the assignment)

   Date resubmitted (if applicable)

Purpose: (what you are expected to do in this assigment. Should start with *To . . .* followed by a verb such as *explain, convince, describe, compare.*)

Audience: (person or persons to whom you are writing)

Topic: (general topic expressed in a few words)

Title: (the title you create for the assignment, with all main words capitalized)

Thesis: (the main idea of your paragraph, expressed as a complete sentence)

C. Finding Ideas Some students have had little, if any, practice using the kinds of invention strategies discussed in Chapter 1 of *Focus on Writing*. It is helpful when covering these strategies to discuss learning styles (see Chapter 10 of this manual). You might explain, for instance, that clustering helps people who understand concepts best when they see them presented graphically, whereas listing does the same thing for linear thinkers. Point out, too, that sometimes writer's block occurs because students start drafting without first thinking about the topic and coming up with possible ideas. If you want students to use any of these strategies, be sure to set aside class time for them to discuss what worked and what didn't. Most students are not likely to figure out new strategies on their own. If you're teaching in a computer lab, have the students practice free-writing with the monitor off. Called *invisible freewriting*, this technique is often liberating for students who get stuck because they continually go back to correct what they just wrote. Invisible freewriting also frees poor typists from looking up and down from keyboard to monitor.

D. Identifying Your Main Idea and Writing a Topic Sentence. One way to help students grasp the difference between a topic and a topic sentence is to have them read several paragraphs, identifying each paragraph's main idea, locating its topic sentence, and demonstrating that each topic sentence does not merely state the topic but expresses the main idea. Show students how a well-articulated topic sentence can help them write a well-organized paragraph.

STEP 2: Organizing

E. Choosing Supporting Points. Help students connect the concept of support with the criteria for an effective topic sentence outlined in the previous section. Students should understand that a paragraph's topic, topic sentence, and support are intimately related: a good topic sentence makes some statement that needs to be supported, and supporting points developed during the prewriting stage help writers clarify their topic and draft an effective topic sentence.

F. Arranging Your Supporting Points Have the class generate ideas on a topic to which they will all be able to contribute (e.g., "problems I have with writing" or "how my life has changed since I enrolled in school"), and then discuss how the organization of a paragraph on the topic would differ if it used a chronological structure, went from least to most important, or went from most to least. Discuss which type of organization students prefer and why. Emphasize the fact that creating brief outlines before starting the first draft will make the organizational structure clear and ensure that the sentences follow a logical progression.

STEP 3: Drafting

G. Drafting Your Paragraph Be sure to give some length parameters; otherwise, some students will write two or three sentences and others two or three pages. Acknowledge that writing without worrying about wording, grammar, and spelling can be difficult for writers who like to craft each word perfectly before going on to the next, but encourage all students to postpone their "perfectionism" until they are proofreading, when it will be most useful. Rather than stopping to choose the perfect word, suggest that they circle or underline words and phrases that they will want to change later.

H. TESTing Your Paragraph. This section introduces a mnemonic to help students write effective paragraphs that include a topic sentence, evidence, a summary statement, and transitions. These elements are explained in further detail in Chapter 2 of the text.

STEP 4: Revising and Editing

I. Revising Your Paragraph. Students may be unfamiliar with the distinction between revising and editing. Remind the class that *revision* can be broken into *re* and *vision* and that you want them literally to try to *re-see* their writing. Stella's example provides a useful class discussion topic. Discuss with students what kinds of changes she made and if/how these changes improved the draft. If time permits, encourage students to set their drafts aside awhile before trying to revise. You may need to establish a feedback system that encourages substantial rewriting, at least until students are convinced of the benefits of true revision.

J. Editing Your Paragraph. Many students try to edit too early in the writing process, or they do not edit at all. To build up editing skills, consider requiring an editing worksheet for each assigned writing on which students must (1) copy any errors that you have indicated on their final drafts, (2) label the errors (sentence fragment, verb error, etc.), and (3) make the correction, explaining how they decided what the correct answer was: what section of the text they turned to, which handout they looked at, and/or what other resources they used.

Once students have read and discussed the concepts of editing and revising, you can introduce the concept of peer review. The Self-Assessment Checklist on pp. 22–23 of the text provides a good list of questions for students to apply to their own first drafts in peer-response groups.

Chapter 2: TESTing Your Paragraphs

Chapter 2 has the students examine the paragraph they drafted in Chapter 1 using the word **TEST** (**T**opic sentence, **E**vidence, **S**ummary statement, and **T**ransitions) to guide them.

A. USING A TOPIC SENTENCE TO UNIFY YOUR PARAGRAPH. To demonstrate to students how topic sentences unify paragraphs, offer them additional examples. Then ask them why the first sentence—rather than any of the others—in the paragraph is, in fact, the topic sentence. For additional practice with identifying topic sentences and organizing paragraphs coherently, Practices 2-1, 2-2, and 2-3 work well as group or individual activities. In Practice 2-1, some students may find it easier to locate the paragraph's topic sentence by reading the paragraph aloud; if students are working in groups, encourage them to read the paragraph both silently and aloud and then discuss why a particular sentence expresses the main idea of the paragraph or why it does not. In Practice 2-4, students must write their own sentences to support the provided topic sentences. Point out that an effective topic sentence connects to every other sentence in the paragraph: if each sentence were to stand alone, the topic sentence would be the only clear, definitive, and declaratory statement, and the others would be informational or detail-oriented in content and supportive of the topic sentence.

B. USING EVIDENCE TO SUPPORT YOUR PARAGRAPH'S MAIN IDEA. In discussing paragraph development, it is helpful to acknowledge that academic paragraphs tend to be longer than the paragraphs students are used to seeing on the job or in the newspaper. Remind students that the typical academic reader is skeptical, looking at what's been said and muttering, "Oh yeah? Prove it to me." Students often turn in paragraphs that we compare to empty sandwiches—just one slice of topic sentence on top and another slice of conclusion on the bottom, leaving out the "meat" of the explanation. In addition to Practice 2-6, which provides a good group activity, you can raise awareness of the need for adequate development by presenting exaggerated two-sentence paragraph "sandwiches" such as "I have learned a lot in this class already. It is clearly going to be useful in many ways," and assigning groups of students to put five or six sentences of detail in between. Then ask the groups to read their paragraphs aloud for class comment and evaluation.

C. USING A SUMMARY STATEMENT TO REINFORCE YOUR PARAGRAPH'S UNITY. Some students may already have studied this concept under a different name: clincher, conclusion, restatement of the topic sentence. Assure students that, whatever they call it, the last sentence of the paragraph should remind readers what their paragraph is about, reiterating their topic sentence and further unifying their paragraph.

D. USING TRANSITIONS TO ADD COHERENCE TO YOUR PARAGRAPH. Appropriate use of transitional expressions can be difficult for developmental writing students to master, with respect to both meaning and punctuation. You may want to assign 16C, Using Transitional Words and Phrases, at the same time you introduce transitions. If students are working in a computer lab, you can have them Save their paragraph, then use Cut and Paste to move the sentences into a different order, and see if a partner can figure out how to put the sentences back in the original order, checking carefully to see if punctuation is used correctly as well.

UNIT 2: Patterns of Paragraph Development

Chapters 3 to 11 acquaint students with nine different patterns of idea development. Students learn to recognize and construct paragraphs organized around exemplification, narration, description, process, cause and effect, comparison and contrast, classification, definition, and argument.

Chapter 3: Using Exemplification

Chapter 3 focuses on exemplification paragraphs, teaching students the importance of using appropriate and specific examples. Practices 3-1 and 3-2 are good options for group activities. You may want to have the class brainstorm a list of supporting examples for a topic and then assign different groups the task of writing a paragraph in different ways: from general to specific, from specific to general, in chronological order, from most to least important, and from least to most important. Have groups read their paragraphs and discuss with the class which ones seem to work best and why. Give students examples of everyday writing tasks that call for exemplification. For example, in a letter to the local paper, students might give examples of quality-of-life improvements that need to be made in their neighborhood.

Chapter 37 provides two examples of exemplification essays, "Don't Call me a Hot Tamale" by Judith Ortiz Cofer, p. 636, and "Volunteer Workers of the World Unite" by Nicols Fox, p. 640.

Chapter 4: Using Narration

Chapter 4 introduces narrative paragraphs, emphasizing the need for transitional words. Caution students not to overuse transitions, however; logical connections between sentences can be made apparent by the content of the sentences and by the repetition of terms. Not every sentence has to start with a transitional expression. Give students examples of writing tasks that call for narration. For example, in a complaint letter, they might summarize, in chronological order, the problems they had with a particular product.

Chapter 37 provides two examples of narration essays, "Orange Crush" by Yiyun Li, p. 643, and "Pick One" by David Matthews, p. 646.

Chapter 5: Using Description

Chapter 5 emphasizes the importance of vivid description. The introduction encourages students to organize specific details of what they have seen, heard, smelled, tasted, or touched in spatial order. Remind students that descriptive details should cluster around a single focus — the dominant impression that the writer wants to make with the word picture. Give some examples that help students see the difference between a list of unrelated details and a group of details centered on one theme. Determining the topic sentence or dominant impression helps the writer decide which details to include and which to leave out. A good way to make this point is to have students brainstorm a list of all the possible details they might include if they were asked to describe their university or college. Then, ask which details they would include in descriptive paragraphs built around different topic sentences, such as "You meet all kinds of people at [name of university]," "A walk around the campus at [name of university] is filled with surprises," or "Attending [name of university] changes you in every way."

Chapter 37 provides two examples of description essays, "An American in Mexico" by Alex Expinoza, p. 650, and "A Fable for Tomorrow" by Rachel Carson, p. 653.

Chapter 6: Using Process

Chapter 6 presents the concepts of process explanation (helping readers understand a process) and process instructions (helping readers perform that process). A grammar problem that often arises during work on this chapter is an illogical shift: this occurs when a writer mixes commands with third-person declarative sentences, writing first *about* and then *to* someone (e.g., "When applying for a job, applicants must complete all forms. Take the forms to the receptionist."). Be alert for this problem, and remind students that they can't mix commands and regular sentences in this way because the reader will perceive the command as an illogical shift, or worse, a sentence fragment. Give students examples of everyday writing tasks that call for outlining a process. For example, they might write a set of instructions telling their family members or roommates what to do in case of a fire.

Chapter 37 provides two sample process essays, "Mummy Arts" by Adam Goodheart, p. 656, and "My Grandmother's Dumpling" by Amy Ma, p. 659.

Chapter 7: Using Cause and Effect

Chapter 7 introduces the basics of cause-and-effect analysis. Some developmental writers struggle with distinguishing *cause* from *effect*. Diagramming a causal chain on the board may help them see that while all events may be related, they can still isolate and analyze a specific event's causes (events to the left on the chain) or effects (events to the right on the chain). Be sure to point out to students the difference between the words *affect* (a verb) and *effect* (a noun).

Chapter 37 contains two examples of cause-and-effect essays, "The Poncho Bearer" by John Schwartz, p. 667, and "At the Heart of a Historic Movement" by John Hartmire, p. 670.

Chapter 8: Using Comparison and Contrast

Chapter 8 describes the two organizational principles of comparison-and-contrast writing: telling everything about the first subject and then everything about the second (AAABBB) or discussing the two subjects point by point (ABABAB). If students use the first schema, be sure that they decide in advance what features they will be comparing and then present the same topics in the same order for each of the subjects. The main thing to stress is the importance of planning and finding the most important characteristics to discuss, not just the first ones that come to mind. Also emphasize that readers should ultimately be able to see whether the subjects of comparison are more alike or more different. The writer will need to include opening and closing sentences in the paragraph that make it clear why the comparison was made. Forming students into single-sex groups and having them write paragraphs in which they compare and contrast men and women can be an enjoyable (although potentially rowdy) way to practice this rhetorical mode. Assign some groups the AAABBB schema and others the ABABAB so that afterward the class can discuss which method seemed to work better and why. Give students examples of everyday writing tasks that call for comparison and contrast. For example, students might write a paragraph comparing the qualifications of two people applying for the same job at their workplace. Chapter 37 provides two examples of comparison and contrast essays, "My Two Lives" by Jhumpa Lahiri, p. 674, and "The Transaction" by William Zinsser, p. 678.

Chapter 9: Using Classification

Chapter 9 introduces a difficult but important skill: classification, or the ability to break a general topic into relevant and logical categories. This skill is the basis of effective organization for all the rhetorical modes. It is also necessary in producing the forecasting type of thesis statement: "My life has differed from my mother's life in the kinds of opportunities we each had, the kinds of preparation we were given to take advantage of those opportunities, and the outcomes of the opportunities we chose to accept." This chapter is a good place to review general organizational methods (presenting things in order of importance, specificity, etc.) because deciding on the classification categories is only the first step; the next step is determining the most effective order in which to present those categories. Give students examples of everyday writing tasks that call for classification. For example, for a local library's book sale, they might write a flyer classifying books according to subject and grade level.

Chapter 37 provides two examples of classification, "But What Do You Mean?" by Deborah Tannen, p. 681, and "The Dog Ate My Disk, and Other Tales of Woe" by Carolyn Foster Segal, p. 689.

Chapter 10: Using Definition

Chapter 10 focuses on definitions, explaining what something is (the class) and what it is not (the differentiation). Be sure to alert students to avoid the "According to Webster" cliché; explain that topics such as those explored in the paragraphs in this chapter require the writers to come up with their own definitions, which should be more interesting and more persuasive than those of a dictionary. Defining an idea is a way to establish credibility with the readers, persuading them that you know what you are talking about. Give students examples of everyday writing tasks that call for definition. For a study group at their place of worship, for example, students might write short definitions of terms such as morality, goodness, and repentance.

Chapter 37 provides two examples of definition essays, "The Wife-Beater" by Gayle Rosenwald Smith, p. 693, and "Triskaidekaphobia" by Paul Hoffman, p. 696.

Chapter 11: Using Argument

Chapter 11 provides a brief overview of argument, explaining how to persuade a reader by using facts, examples, and expert references. This is the most complicated kind of writing your students will do. Emphasize the importance of analyzing the audience before deciding what to say and how to say it. One approach is to have groups write persuasive paragraphs on the same theme to different audiences (e.g., a paragraph arguing that grades should be abolished—written to (1) the student body, (2) the writing instructor, and (3) the university president). Brainstorm all the possible reasons with which one might support such an argument, and then have the different groups choose the reasons that would be most persuasive to their particular audience. Groups will have to decide what kind of supporting evidence their audience would find most relevant and what tone to adopt. Warn students not simply to repeat a claim in other words but to support it with evidence, and watch for examples as you read their drafts.

Another exercise that promotes total student involvement is to give groups the task of persuading you that they understand how to write arguments better than all the other groups, so their group should be excused from the written homework assignment for that chapter. Be sure to give each group the opportunity to critique their classmates' arguments according to the qualities of effective argument you have covered.

One aspect of argument that developmental writers often find difficult is acknowledging that there are at least two sides to any issue. Remind them that it is important to show the reader that they have considered all sides of an issue before taking a stand. One way to do this is to point out the positive parts of the opposing view before going on to explain why their view is better. It is useful to practice this in class, having students write brief, three- to five-sentence introductory paragraphs on controversial themes, following this format: "I believe . . . Others have argued that . . . However, . . ." Give students examples of everyday writing tasks that call for argumentation. For example, in a letter to the local school board, students might argue against raising class size in the elementary school.

Chapter 37 provides three examples of argument essays: "Don't Hang Up, That's My Mom Calling" by Bobbi Buchanan, p. 702, "For Most People, College Is a Waste of Time" by Charles Murray, p. 704, and "Impounded Fathers" by Edwidge Danticat, p. 708.

UNIT 3: Writing Essays

Chapters 12 and 13 guide students through the basic structure of an essay, the steps of the writing process, and techniques for creating effective introductions and conclusions. Chapter 14 helps students see how the patterns of development introduced in Chapters 3 to 11 may be applied to essays.

Chapter 12: Writing an Essay

Chapter 12 shifts the focus from single paragraphs to longer compositions. Students learn to understand essay structure, choose a topic, generate ideas to support that topic, select a thesis, organize main points to support the thesis, write the first draft, and revise and edit the completed essay.

Understanding the difference between topic and thesis can be difficult. Remind the students that a thesis sentence, unlike a title or topic, is a complete sentence that explains both what the essay is about (the topic) and the main point the essay will make about that topic (the thesis). Once students understand the principle, ask volunteers to give their own thesis sentence for the assignment they are working on or for one they have just completed. If you have not previously addressed the various idea-generating techniques referred to in the chapter—freewriting and brainstorming—now is the time to discuss their importance and have students practice them in class.

If you are just introducing the concept of peer review at this point, Jared's essay on p. 179 provides a useful example. The class can discuss it first as an example of basic essay structure: thesis, support, conclusion. Then, together or in small groups, they can work through a peer response activity, describing and evaluating what Jared wrote according to your written guidelines and making recommendations for change. Groups can then compare their suggestions to Jared's final version to see if they anticipated changes he made and to determine what advice they would give for further improvement. (See Part Four in this manual for sample peer response guidelines.)

Chapter 13: Writing Introductions and Conclusions

Chapter 13 summarizes the do's and don'ts of introductions and conclusions. For visual learners, it is helpful to portray the typical introduction as an upside-down triangle: a general statement of topic or background narrowed down at the end of the paragraph to a statement of thesis. Remind your students, in terms of increasing specificity, of the difference among topics, titles, and thesis sentences. Students often succumb to writer's block after working on this chapter, worrying about creating the perfect introduction before they know what the essay is going to say. Encourage them to write the introduction after they've written the body of the essay; or, if they can't bring themselves to work out of sequence, suggest that they start with a "placeholder" introductory sentence ("This essay will show . . ."), which they can replace once they have a better idea what their main point is going to be. Use this opportunity to emphasize the fact that "In this essay I will . . ." introductions and "In conclusion, I have . . ." endings are not acceptable for the finished product.

To help them understand the process, you can ask students to write a paragraph for homework introducing themselves to the rest of the class. In the next class period, assign students randomly to groups of three with the task of forming their three separate paragraphs into one united essay by adding an introduction and concluding paragraph and making any necessary changes for consistency and transition.

Chapter 14: Patterns of Essay Development

Chapter 14 connects what students have learned about patterns of development in Chapters 3 to 11 with what they have learned about essays in Chapters 12 and 13. The chapter addresses each pattern of development in turn, offering students (1) help in identifying when the pattern is called for in an assignment; (2) options for

organizing an essay in the pattern; (3) a list of transitions commonly used in the pattern; (4) a model student essay in the pattern; (5) possible topics for an essay in the pattern; and (6) a Self-Assessment Checklist for an essay in the pattern.

You may want to pair sections of this chapters with the related paragraph chapters; or you may work through all the paragraph modes, addressing essays later in the semester (or not at all). Regardless of the approach you choose, it should demonstrate the correspondence between topic sentence and thesis, between supporting ideas and body paragraphs, and between clincher sentences and conclusions. All the rules for one apply equally to the other.

REVISING AND EDITING YOUR WRITING

UNIT 4: Writing Sentences

Chapters 15 to 20 are designed to help students edit at the sentence and word level. They introduce a variety of sentence structures, beginning with a breakdown of the basic parts of simple sentences and moving on to increasingly sophisticated editing choices.

Chapter 15: Writing Simple Sentences

Chapter 15 reviews the basic building blocks of a simple sentence: subject, prepositional phrase, and verb. Depending on the level of your students' ability, you may review these concepts in class or just refer students to them as needed. We recommend working through at least a few of the exercises with the whole class because the rest of the grammar chapters are based on this fundamental knowledge. Students will not be able to understand or apply rules of subject-verb agreement, for instance, if they can't identify the words that are supposed to agree. Prepositional phrases, linking verbs, and participles are concepts that generally need some identification and explanation.

Chapter 16: Writing Compound Sentences

Chapter 16 is deceptively simple, showing how two sentences of equal importance can be joined by using coordinating conjunctions, semicolons, or semicolons plus a transitional word or phrase. A sophisticated understanding of written English is required, though, to make distinctions between sentences such as "The woman came to the meeting, but she didn't stay long" and "The woman came to the meeting but didn't stay long," not to mention "The woman came to the meeting; however, she didn't stay long."

A. USING COORDINATING CONJUNCTIONS Remind students that there are only seven words in this category, and they are all three letters or less. Try using the mnemonic FANBOYS (*For, And, Nor, But, Or, Yet, So*) in your class to help students retain this list of coordinating conjunctions. Remind them, too, that they do not always need to add a comma when they see the word *and* in a sentence; it is only needed when there is a subject-verb unit on both sides of the *and*.

B. USING SEMICOLONS Semicolons, like coordinating conjunctions, can only link elements of equal weight. The main point to stress when working through 16B is that a semicolon is the equivalent of a period, not a comma.

C. USING TRANSITIONAL WORDS AND PHRASES Conjunctive adverbs and other transitional expressions are the main cause of run-ons and comma splices; students find it difficult to keep the list of conjunctive adverbs in this section separate from the list of subordinating conjunctions in section 17B. Emphasize the difference, offer lots of opportunities to practice, and always remind students to proofread their own writing carefully to make sure they haven't mixed the punctuation inadvertently.

Chapter 17: Writing Complex Sentences

Chapter 17 introduces subordination into the mix: ideas linked by subordinating conjunctions and relative pronouns. Students generally have little difficulty identifying fragments as such when they are presented as isolated examples, but they tend to overlook incorrect punctuation when editing their own papers.

A. IDENTIFYING COMPLEX SENTENCES Practices 17-1 and 17-2 are helpful in showing students what constitutes an independent or dependent clause. Try doing these exercises aloud as a class or in small groups. Many students will be able to label the clauses as independent or dependent based on how each sounds: independent clauses flow from a beginning point to an ending point, while dependent clauses have an abrupt and incomplete-sounding ending. You can also ask students to cast votes on whether each item is

independent or dependent. Then tally the votes and discuss why the students voted the way they did. Asking the students to explain how they voted will provide you with insight into how the students are applying the grammar they have learned. It will also help you gauge the students' comfort level with the material.

B. USING SUBORDINATING CONJUNCTIONS A test to decide if a word is a subordinating conjunction or a conjunctive adverb involves checking whether the word can be moved around in the sentence. If it can be moved, it is a conjunctive adverb.

EXAMPLE: The conjunctive adverb *however* can be moved from the beginning to the middle or the end of a sentence, and the sentence still makes sense.

> I finished my meal. *However*, he was still eating.
> He, *however*, was still eating.
> He was still eating, *however*.

In contrast, *although*, a subordinate conjunction, can't move around; it has to be the first word of its clause.

> I finished my meal, *although* he was still eating.

> "He *although* was still eating" or "He was still eating *although*" will not work without sounding awkward or changing the meaning.

C. USING RELATIVE PRONOUNS Remind students that *who* and *which* will generally not be the first word of a sentence unless the sentence is a question.

| Okay: | He got a new computer. Which brand did he buy? |
| Not okay: | He got a new computer. Which is still sitting in the carton. |

Chapter 18: Writing Varied Sentences

Chapter 18 is a concise and useful guide to sentence combining, giving practice on varying sentence structures, beginnings, lengths, and styles. Students will benefit from working through all the exercises, both alone and in groups.

A. VARYING SENTENCE TYPES You may need to point out that exclamation marks are used sparingly in academic writing so that students don't think this section is advocating equal portions of each type of sentence.

B. VARYING SENTENCE OPENINGS Students often complain, "My writing is boring. All my sentences sound the same; I think I'm using too many *I*s." Often, it is not the use of first-person pronouns that is the problem. The fact that all sentences begin with the subject is what makes the paper seem monotonous. Section B of Chapter 18 gives options for opening sentences with adverbs and prepositional phrases so that they flow more smoothly.

C. Combining Sentences We recommend requiring students to write out the exercises in section C and using class time to read and discuss the results. Sentence-combining exercises offer one of the few short-term ways of improving students' grammatical skills as well as enhancing their writing style. Seeing, writing, and hearing the new forms can help them internalize the unfamiliar structures.

D. Varying Sentence Length As you work on helping students gain control of increasingly longer syntactical units, emphasize that an essay in which every sentence is lengthy and complex is no better than an essay in which every sentence is short. The former type of essay is, in fact, less effective because it's usually more difficult to understand.

Chapter 19: Using Parallelism

Chapter 19 introduces the concept that related ideas can be presented most effectively by using parallel structure. Remind students that the way they start a sentence makes an implied promise to the reader. If they switch directions mid-sentence, they've broken this promise and probably confused the message. The best way to edit papers for parallel construction is to read them out loud or listen while someone else reads them, noting any place the reader stumbles.

A. Recognizing Parallel Structure To help students grasp the pattern, read the exercises out loud, exaggerating the break in rhythm.

B. Using Parallel Structure Stress that students should not worry about issues such as parallelism during early draft writing. Discuss this chapter only in the context of late-stage editing.

Chapter 20: Using Words Effectively

Chapter 20 provides tips on editing for specificity, brevity, formality, originality, and sensitivity. It is probably most effective when used to reinforce and explain a wording change you are recommending on a student's paper, rather than as a general class activity.

A. Using Specific Words Suggest to students that they keep a list of vague words such as *some*, *very*, *good*, and *nice* by their computer and use the Find command to replace or leave out these words in their final drafts.

B. Using Concise Language Students used to the "bureaucratese" of the workplace will often argue vehemently that concise expressions such as "At my job" sound elementary and "At my place of employment" has a much more formal academic tone. There are more important arguments to win with basic writers, so this is not an area in which to spend much time. However, you might try at least to plant a seed for future instructors to nourish.

C. Avoiding Slang An in-class discussion about slang and how often it changes can be enough to convince students that it has no place in academic writing. The class could also brainstorm a list of current slang expressions, and students could keep a copy of the list as a reminder to avoid those expressions in their writing.

D. Avoiding Clichés Instead of labeling an expression a cliché, it is easier on fragile egos just to underline it with a wavy line and ask if the writer can find another way of expressing the same idea.

E. Using Similes and Metaphors If you address this issue in an all-class discussion, encourage moderation because forced comparisons tend to turn into clichés and detract from, rather than enhance, the effect of the writing. The description involved in the peer response activity in Chapter 5 of this manual provides a natural means of stimulating students to express their ideas in similes and metaphors.

F. Avoiding Sexist Language In trying to avoid sexist language, students often produce noun/pronoun disagreements. Many instructors accept constructions such as "everyone . . . they"; but if you don't, you will need to warn against this as a very common and tempting error.

UNIT 5: Solving Common Sentence Problems

The five chapters in this unit give students practice in understanding, locating, and correcting sentence structure errors that typically result from developmental writers' lack of familiarity with written (as opposed to spoken) language and their lack of experience in composing complex "academic" sentences. Point out to your class that once they've mastered this unit, especially Chapters 21 to 23, much of the red ink with which other well-meaning instructors decorate their papers will disappear.

If student mistakes were simply a question of confusing two punctuation marks, it would be simple to teach students to put a period or semicolon, rather than a comma, between two independent clauses separated by conjunctive adverbs. However, most developmental writers will arrive in your class lacking an internalized sense of what makes a clause "independent." Memorizing a rule is easy; understanding the underlying grammatical structure from which that rule was derived is not. You and your students will probably be returning to these five chapters throughout the semester.

Depending on the level of ability in your class, you may have skipped Chapter 15, Writing Simple Sentences. Remind the students about it when you begin Unit Five so that they can backpedal a bit if necessary. Consider assigning Chapter 15 to some students on an as-needed basis, perhaps scheduling an office hour to go over any problems. Encourage students who have chronic problems with sentence structure to write short, simple sentences, explaining that instructors would prefer an essay comprised entirely of short sentences to one filled with run-ons. Once students internalize the basic structure of a sentence, they can move on to combining sentences, adding dependent clauses, and so forth.

Chapter 21: Run-Ons

This chapter begins by defining terms and giving students a chance to test their understanding by labeling sentences *correct, fused,* or *comma splice.* The chapter then presents five means of fixing sentence errors, with a Focus box highlighting one of the most common errors: using a comma rather than a semicolon or period when a conjunctive adverb links two complete ideas. Sentence and paragraph exercises follow, leading to an essay-length editing practice in the Chapter Review.

A. RECOGNIZING RUN-ONS After students have practiced identifying problems in the chapter exercises, assign them to groups and have the groups do the same type of work with any writing assignment students are currently working on. This will provide a good selection of examples as you work through the rest of the chapter.

B. CORRECTING RUN-ONS The semicolon tends to cause particular difficulties, perhaps because students haven't used or seen it frequently. Stress that it acts like a period (i.e., it ends a complete thought) rather than a comma. Explain that if they can't put a period somewhere, they can't use a semicolon, either. Easier yet, suggest to students who frequently misuse semicolons that they ignore it and instead concentrate on the choice between comma and period. It's usually easier to distinguish when to use those two marks.

Be prepared for some chaos if you are going over practice exercises in class for which correct answers may vary, as is the case for most exercises in this unit. Students will want to know whether their own versions are correct rather than hear just one possible right approach. You'll probably find that the class exercises take much longer than planned.

After you discuss and practice the five different ways of correcting run-ons, you may want to distribute a handout listing coordinating conjunctions, subordinating conjunctions, and common conjunctive adverbs/transitional words, along with correct punctuation for each. Students can use this brief guide to proofread their work. Seeing the different categories of words contrasted in one location helps students remember the differences and provides a convenient, quick reference guide to use when proofreading.

Three other supplements—*Exercise Central, Diagnostic and Mastery Tests to Accompany FOCUS ON WRITING,* and *Supplemental Exercises to Accompany FOCUS ON WRITING*—contain additional practice exercises you may want to assign as homework or in-class group work. Examples from students' own writing can also provide material for group editing.

Chapter 22: Sentence Fragments

This chapter follows the same format as the preceding one. It begins with a definition of the problem, asking students to show they understand the definition by identifying types of fragments in exercises; then it describes four different types of fragments, with recommendations for how to correct each type.

Identifying Sentence Fragments

DIRECTIONS: Read through the following ten examples, and be prepared to explain which are fragments, which are complete sentences, and why.

1. Spinning out of control on the icy road.

2. The car spinning out of control on the icy road.

3. Since the car was spinning out of control on the icy road.

4. Although my car was covered with snow which the snow plow had piled up when it tried to clean the street.

5. The snow that had drifted in front of my driveway overnight.

6. The city official who would not take my call.

7. It made me furious.

8. Which made me furious.

9. Stop your plowing!

10. There is only one solution to winter. Moving to Florida.

A. Recognizing Fragments A quick way to determine which constructions present particular difficulties for your students is to make up a handout using examples of all the different kinds of fragments in this chapter. Mix in some complete sentences and have your students form groups to decide what's missing in the sentences they correctly identify as fragments. Then you need to focus only on the sections of Chapter 22 that address general problems. See our handout on p. 99.

B. Missing-Subject Fragments While most students can identify this type of fragment in isolation, they sometimes find it more difficult within their own writing. One technique to suggest is reading backwards—from last sentence to first sentence—as this helps make missing-subject fragments more obvious.

C. Phrase Fragments An easy way to dramatize the information missing in fragments like the ones in the aforementioned handout is to walk up to a student as if you were just starting a conversation and say something like, "Hi, Tom. Such as staying up an hour later." Students easily see that something important is missing. They can use this "walk-up" test to help identify sentence fragments in their own writing. Remind students, however, that pronouns are acceptable as subjects. This is a concept many students have trouble with, arguing that "It is lying on the desk" can't be a complete thought because the reader doesn't know *what* was lying on the desk. Contrasting that structure with a true fragment such as "Lying on the desk" may help them see the difference. You'll frequently have to remind your students that a pronoun is a legitimate subject. Remind them to proofread their papers for pronouns like *it* or *this* and to check the punctuation in front of each one; clauses containing these pronouns are prime candidates for comma splices. If students are using computers, show them how to use the Search/Find command to locate all occurrences of these problem words.

D. Incomplete-Verb Fragments Reiterate for students that the most common helping verbs are forms of *to have* and *to be*.

E. Dependent Clause Fragments Remind students that one of the best ways to catch fragments of this type is to take them out of context by proofreading their papers from the end to the beginning.

Chapter 23: Subject-Verb Agreement

Chapter 23 explains the concept of agreement. Sections B, C, D, E, F, and G introduce problem areas that complicate agreement: compound subjects, irregular verbs, intervening words, collective noun subjects, indefinite pronoun subjects, and inverted word order.

Because this chapter focuses attention on dialect versus Standard English, you may want to address that distinction in class discussion or in individual conferences. We often simply mention the maxim that whether a form is considered dialect or standard depends on who controls the army and navy, acknowledging it as a political rather than linguistic issue.

A. Understanding Subject-Verb Agreement For students who understand best when they see underlying patterns, it may be helpful to conjugate the present tense of a few common verbs on the board. Draw a circle around the -*s* or -*es* ending in the third person. Point out that this is the only place where the verb breaks the pattern of not having any ending and that it is the most common place for errors to occur. Visual learners may benefit from diagrams like the following:

> **Subject: no -*s*   Verb has -*s***
>
> The book . . . say**s**
>
> The book**s** . . . say
>
> **Subject has -*s*   Verb: no -*s***

Point out the special problem caused by verbs, such as *ask* or *insist*, that contain an *s* sound in the stem. Because the final *s* of a form like *asks* is sometimes omitted in speech, your students must make a special effort to remember to write it.

If your class meets in a computer lab, one easy and effective exercise is to compose a paragraph using first-person present tense sentences and then have the students use the Replace command on their word processor to replace each occurrence of the pronoun *I* with their own name or the name of a friend. (You can even have them change the font color for the name to make it stand out more.) When they give the Replace All command, the paragraph is filled with subject-verb disagreements that they can correct individually or in a small group.

B. Compound Subjects Agreement when subjects are linked by *or* often causes difficulty. You might simply tell students to make the verb for any subject linked with *or* agree with the part of the subject closest to the verb. If they have learned basic agreement, they'll produce it correctly. Save your time for practicing forms that do not follow logical patterns.

C. Be, Have, and Do When you introduce the irregular verbs, note that an *s* still marks the singular verb (*has, does, is*); the irregularity is only in the stem, not in the ending.

D. Words between Subject and Verb Developmental writers may need some practice in identifying prepositions and prepositional phrases. Only then can they work on identifying subjects and verbs in more complicated sentences that include prepositional phrases. A useful technique for helping students make sure they're matching the true subject with the verb is to have them name the verb first and then ask who or what is performing the action. Examples such as "The computers in that room are not working" help them get the pattern. What isn't working? It's the computers, clearly, not the room. This is a construction in which grammar works against what the ear hears as correct, so it's a pattern that needs extra practice.

E. Collective Noun Subjects Making a list on the board of the singular and plural forms of these words can help students see that *team* is singular while *teams* is plural, and so on.

F. Indefinite Pronoun Subjects The main difficulty here occurs with the two singular pronouns that are counterintuitive: *everybody* and *everyone*. These are commonly misused in spoken English, so students may argue that they "sound right." Remind students, especially nonnative speakers, that any indefinite pronoun that ends in *-one*, *-thing*, or *-body* is singular.

G. Verbs before Subjects Students can check what the verb should agree with by rephrasing the sentence: "Where is the Bering Strait?" becomes "The Bering Strait is where?" "There are ten computers in the writing center" becomes "Ten computers are in the writing center." This makes it easier to determine who or what is performing the action.

Chapter 24: Illogical Shifts

Chapter 24 addresses verb tense consistency, pronoun choice and agreement, direct versus indirect discourse, and passive versus active voice. This chapter is more complicated for developmental writers than the first three chapters in the unit because it moves them from right or wrong scenarios to one with shades of correctness. Depending on the level of your students, you may want to pick and choose among the concepts, referring students to them as needed but not spending class time on practice. Sections C, D, and E in Chapter 28 contain additional information on these topics.

A. Shifts in Tense ESL students will be more likely than native English speakers to have trouble with this section. Chapter 30 offers additional help.

B. Shifts in Person Because the second-person pronoun *you* is the one most often misused by developmental writing students, who are more used to informal speech than to formal academic writing, it is useful to practice eliminating second-person references from sentences. A simple rule for students to follow is not to use *you* in a sentence unless they are speaking directly to a known reader. In other words, advise them not to say, "I think you need a college education to get a good job," but rather "Getting a good job requires a college education" or "I need a college education to get a good job." Suggest that students use the Search/Find command on their computer as they're proofreading to highlight each second-person pronoun and determine whether it is used appropriately.

Another good exercise is to have students rewrite the same paragraph from three different points of view—first, second, and third person—so that they develop a feel for each.

C. Shifts in Voice Active versus passive constructions probably rank low on a developmental writing instructor's list of worries. You may not want to spend much time on this other than making the general statement that a sentence such as "I hit the ball" works better than "The ball was hit by myself." We have found that students often bring the issue up independently, asking what it means when they're told by the grammar-check function that they have a "passive construction." Students generally have more important writing problems, and you might want to have them at least deselect "check for passive" in their Spelling and Grammar Options if you can't convince them to ignore the grammar checker completely. (For more discussion on the use of grammar and spell checkers, see Chapter 3 of this manual, Using Technology in the Classroom.)

Chapter 25: Dangling and Misplaced Modifiers

Chapter 25 presents the concepts of present and past participle modifiers, how to vary sentence style by using modifiers, and how to spot and correct inappropriately placed modifiers. Chapter 18, section C, introduced this idea in the context of achieving sentence variety.

Students will probably find this chapter somewhat difficult because it introduces them to complex structures they may not produce naturally in their own writing. It is probably best to present modifiers as a way to combine ideas and develop a varied style, rather than as a serious grammar problem. Explain to students that modifiers are just extras, not part of the main sentence, so they are set off by commas as an aid for the reader. It is helpful at this point to contrast pairs of sentences, one beginning with a participial phrase followed by a comma and one in which the subject is a gerund that is not separated from the rest of the sentence by a comma:

> *Using a computer,* I solved my spelling problems.

> *Using a computer helped* me solve my spelling problems.

The old Groucho Marxism, "I shot an elephant in my pajamas; how it got in my pajamas I'll never know," usually works well to get across the general idea of misplaced modifiers. One common "dangling" construction students tend to produce is a sentence like "As a conscientious student, my homework is always finished before it's due." Remind your students that their *as*'s shouldn't dangle any more than their participles should.

UNIT 6: Understanding Basic Grammar

Chapters 26 to 30 focus on the basic parts of speech — nouns, verbs, pronouns, adjectives, and adverbs — and on the grammatical issues that accompany them, such as irregular verbs, plural nouns, and noun-pronoun agreement. The unit also includes a chapter specifically for ESL students. A good writing assignment for this unit is to have small groups produce paragraphs or brief essays describing how they felt on the first day of class, using as many different verbs as they can in their description.

Chapter 26: Verbs: Past Tense

Chapter 26 introduces the simple past for both regular and irregular verbs. Chapter 23 discusses the first part of the verb system: the present tense. You may want to review that chapter briefly before moving on to the past tense endings.

A. REGULAR VERBS The main difficulty here confronts students in whose dialects the -*d* ending on past tense verbs is dropped. If you are working in a computer classroom, one easy way to dramatize the difference between present and past tense endings is to give the students a paragraph in the present tense, beginning with "Today I . . ." and then ask them to change the "Today" to "Yesterday" and make the verb ending changes that would logically follow. You may want to assign extra practice from *Exercise Central* to those students who need to develop an ear for the past tense ending.

B. IRREGULAR VERBS Irregular verbs that don't change forms in the past, such as *cut* or *cost*, often tempt students to add an –*ed*; point out the temptation so students are aware of it. Going over the list of irregulars in class with books closed, giving the present and asking for the past, is a quick way to let students know which, if any, forms aren't automatically produced correctly. Students don't need to memorize the whole list, just the few that don't sound natural to them. You might also point out typical spelling problems, such as *choose/chose* and *lead/led*.

C. PROBLEM VERBS: BE Remind students that the rule they learned in the present tense about –*s* marking the singular verb holds true here, too.

D. PROBLEM VERBS: CAN/COULD AND WILL/WOULD You will probably want to refer to this section only if a student is making errors consistently; otherwise, you may create unnecessary confusion by singling out these particular verbs.

Chapter 27: Verbs: Past Participles

Chapter 27 moves students on to the present perfect tense of both regular and irregular verbs. Participial adjectives are also covered. Students tend either to automatically produce these forms correctly (except perhaps for problems with verbs such as *lie/lay* or *sit/set*) or to need repeated practice to develop a feel for the forms that are not part of their spoken dialect. You may find that this chapter is more useful on an individual, as-needed basis than in whole-group activities.

A. Regular Past Participles Have students exaggerate the articulation of the *–ed* endings if you do these exercises as an oral class activity; it serves to raise their awareness. Remind students to watch for the past tense forms in their reading, too, to develop their proofreading skills. Spend extra time on sentences in which the participle is followed by *to* (e.g., *asked to/used to*), because the *–ed* ending isn't generally heard in such constructions and is therefore easy to overlook when writing.

B. Irregular Past Participles Although it seems elementary, spending a few minutes going through the three principal parts—giving the base form in a short sentence ("I awake at 7") and then asking the class to give the past ("Yesterday I awoke . . .") and the past participle ("Every day this week I have . . .")—will let you and your students know which, if any, of the verbs are problematic and will narrow down the amount of material they have to work on individually.

C. The Present Perfect Tense It has been our experience that tense distinctions are extremely difficult even for native speakers to consider in the abstract. Rather than cause even more confusion, you may want to go over sections C and D individually with students whose writing has shown problems, and then only in the context of a particular piece of writing.

D. The Past Perfect Tense See previous comment.

E. Past Participles as Adjectives This presents a particular problem for students speaking African American Vernacular English. You may want to develop a file of typical student errors to have available for extra practice when needed. Requiring students to write in corrections for all verb-ending errors on papers they have submitted helps to raise their awareness of this issue.

Chapter 28: Nouns and Pronouns

Chapter 28 starts with the basics of identifying nouns and distinguishing between common and proper nouns. It then discusses plural formations, issues involving pronouns, and antecedents: agreement, case, and special types.

A. Identifying Nouns Students will probably know the concepts if not the terminology.

B. Forming Plural Nouns Encourage students to use spell checkers, which point out incorrect plural formations. However, you should point out that a spell checker won't pick up a missing plural *–s*.

C. Identifying Pronouns and **D. Pronoun-Antecedent Agreement** If you have covered Chapter 24, Illogical Shifts, you may have introduced this concept already. If not, you may want to assign 24C now. The major problem is the tendency to use *they* as an all-purpose pronoun rather than restricting it to plurals.

E. Special Problems with Agreement The rule for subjects joined by *and* is that two nouns joined by *and* are always plural and so require a plural pronoun. Nouns joined by *or* may be singular or plural, but the pronoun should agree with the part of the subject that follows *or*. Remind students that they learned this principle when you addressed subject-verb agreement in 23B. Avoiding vague pronoun reference is a rule easily understood but difficult to internalize. One way to check is to have students use the Search/Find command on their word processor to identify all instances of *they, it,* and *this* so that they can check to see whether there is a clear referent and whether singulars and plurals are used correctly.

F. Pronoun Case Rather than teaching rules and terminology, just show students how to drop the first half of a compound subject or object to check for correct case. "He gave it to I" doesn't sound right, at least to native speakers; "He gave it to her and I" is not correct either. Less important points about pronoun case in comparisons and use of *who* versus *whom* are probably not worth spending class time on. Direct students to the written explanations to reinforce editing suggestions.

G. SPECIAL PROBLEMS WITH CASE You may find that this section is more useful on an individual, as-needed basis than in whole-group activities.

H. REFLEXIVE PRONOUNS If you address this section with your students, you might want to point out — by example, not as a rule with terminology — the common error of using an intensive pronoun without the personal pronoun, as in "He gave it to myself."

Chapter 29: Adjectives and Adverbs

This chapter provides basic definitions of adjectives (including the demonstrative adjectives *this, that, these,* and *those*) and adverbs, along with rules for forming comparative and superlative forms. One important point to be made, whether or not you use this chapter in class, is the need for writing to contain a variety of modifiers, not just the utilitarian *good, bad, very nice* descriptors. Refer students to 20A.

Chapter 30: Grammar and Usage for ESL Writers

This chapter has been included as a general reference for instructors who want to provide additional help to nonnative writers in their classes. It contains explanations and exercises for specific problem areas that you can assign for reading and drill on an individual basis when you notice those patterns of error in student papers. Chapter 30 addresses the following issues that often occur in the work of ESL students:

A. SUBJECTS IN SENTENCES

B. PLURAL NOUNS

C. COUNT AND NONCOUNT NOUNS

D. DETERMINERS WITH COUNT AND NONCOUNT NOUNS

E. ARTICLES

F. NEGATIVE STATEMENTS AND QUESTIONS

G. VERB TENSE

H. STATIVE VERBS

I. MODAL AUXILIARIES

J. GERUNDS

K. PLACING MODIFIERS IN ORDER

L. CHOOSING PREPOSITIONS

M. PREPOSITIONS IN FAMILIAR EXPRESSIONS

N. PREPOSITIONS IN PHRASAL VERBS

Additionally, Chapter 9 of this manual, Working with ESL and Second-Dialect Students, presents information and resources dealing with ESL issues.

UNIT 7: Understanding Punctuation, Mechanics, and Spelling

Chapters 31 to 35 provide rules and practice exercises to help students review basic punctuation, spelling, capitalization, and commonly confused words. You may not want to devote class time to general presentations of the content of these chapters, but you should be sure that students know that this section exists and what it includes. Remind them that the answers to odd-numbered exercises are at the end of the book, so they can practice and check their own progress. Class time is too valuable to spend much of it on grammar issues that students can practice on their own, but you might consider setting time aside to discuss any questions students still have after completing and checking the exercises you do assign.

Chapter 31: Using Commas

Commas are probably the most frequently misused punctuation because of their many roles in the sentence. This chapter helps categorize major uses: between elements in a series; to set off introductory phrases, conjunctive adverbs, and transitional expressions; with appositives; to set off nonrestrictive clauses; and in dates and addresses. Remember that more comma errors result when students insert unnecessary commas than when they omit necessary ones. You should also emphasize the Review Checklist box in *Focus on Writing:* if a comma doesn't fit in one of these categories, it is probably not needed. Be sure to review the basic rules students will already have learned about commas in connection with avoiding comma splices, fragments, and run-ons, along with the new rules in this chapter. As a review exercise, assign groups of students the task of listing all the comma do's and don'ts that they can think of, with examples for each category. See which group can remember the most.

If you are teaching in a computer classroom, consider using the macro function in your word processor to provide students with a simple program that enables them to hit one key and automatically change the color of all their commas (or any other punctuation they are proofreading for) to red so that they stand out clearly for proofreading.

In general, students will improve the mechanics of their writing more readily by working with their own sentences than by working on grammar drills. Such activities as keeping editing logs, learning proofreading techniques, and sharpening editing skills through participation in peer response groups are the best ways to make sure that students not only know but apply the various rules presented in Unit Seven. If individual students are making numerous comma errors, try to help them determine whether their faulty mechanics result from a lack of knowledge, a lack of time, a lack of editing skills, or some combination, because the method of intervention will depend on the cause of the problem.

This chapter can be approached productively as a source of sentence-combining activities, helping students expand their syntactical options by trying out new sentence patterns such as appositives or nonrestrictive clauses.

A. Commas in a Series Point out for special attention the writing tip on p. 544 that reminds students to use a comma before the coordinating conjunction in a series.

B. Commas with Introductory Phrases and Transitional Words and Phrases Confusion may arise because students have learned to associate conjunctive adverbs and transitionals with semicolons in Chapters 16 and 21. Be sure to show the difference in sentence pairs:

He asked me to go to the movies on Friday; **unfortunately,** I already had a date.

He asked me to go to the movies on Friday. I already, **unfortunately,** had a date.

This section also provides a good chance to review the basics of locating the subject. Explain to students that the comma is used for the convenience of the reader, to show that the introductory material is finished and the main subject-verb unit will follow. See 15A for additional practice.

C. Commas with Appositives Because appositives are structures that developmental writers will not often produce on their own, practice in creating and moving appositives around

in a sentence will help students develop a more sophisticated writing style. Practice these exercises in class, being sure to ask students what other locations they could move the phrases to and still have a correct sentence. Also, remind students that a common punctuation error is omitting the second of the pair of commas. An appositive placed in the middle of a sentence must be set off by commas on both sides.

D. Commas with Nonrestrictive Clauses A simplified way to present the restrictive/nonrestrictive issue is to say that generally students should not use a comma before *that*.

E. Commas in Dates and Addresses Help students see that years and states or country names act like appositives, and like appositives, they require a comma both before and after.

F. Unnecessary Commas The rule here is "When in doubt, leave it out," rather than the "Use a comma whenever you pause for a breath" rule that students sometimes apply.

Chapter 32: Using Apostrophes

Chapter 32 summarizes rules for using apostrophes in contractions and possessives; it also presents common misuses such as plurals and possessive pronouns. Because the apostrophe is strictly a print convention, it causes considerable confusion to students with limited reading backgrounds. Our experience has been that discussing this chapter in class tends to cause more errors than it corrects, at least initially, because students suddenly begin to feel they must add an apostrophe to any word that ends in -*s*. If students tend to leave off the possessive marker completely ("the boy hat"), you might assign the exercises in Chapter 32 to help them develop an ear for the construction, pointing out the need for the apostrophe as well as the *s* when writing.

A. Apostrophes in Contractions If students set their spell-check options to correct for formal style, all contractions will be flagged as possible errors. This is a good proofreading aid, whether or not students choose to leave the contractions in their text.

B. Apostrophes in Possessives Don't spend more time on this section than it merits. Give your students some idea of the hierarchy of grammar error. You and they will use time more effectively by concentrating on avoiding those errors that distract readers most. An occasional missed or misplaced apostrophe is generally not one of these.

C. INCORRECT USE OF APOSTROPHES Stress that most reasons for adding an *-s* to a word—plural nouns, singular verbs—do not involve apostrophes. A rule of thumb is: when in doubt, leave it out.

Chapter 33: Using Other Punctuation Marks

Chapter 33 advises students on the correct use of semicolons, colons, dashes, and parentheses. You may have already introduced the semicolon to join two simple sentences in Chapters 16 and 21. The semicolon's second use—separating items in a series—is introduced here. The use of colons, dashes, and parentheses is not common in the writing of most developmental students, so you may prefer to use this chapter only as reference for those students who need it.

Chapter 34: Understanding Mechanics

Chapter 34 presents general principles of capitalization and punctuation, applies them to quotations and titles, and concludes with brief advice on when and how to use hyphens, abbreviations, and numbers. Students will need to use the information in this chapter if you ask them to include direct quotations in their narrative writing or to cite sources, such as in an assignment that requires them to summarize and respond to a journal article. Practice 34-3 provides useful practice in setting up quotations; it is a good exercise to discuss in class or in small groups, asking students to come up with a few versions for each sentence.

Our experience has been that students make more errors capitalizing words improperly than by leaving out necessary capitalization, so we warn them of this and explain that when they're proofreading for capitalization they should be able to fit any capitalized word into one of the categories discussed in 34A; if not, it should remain lowercase.

Chapter 35: Understanding Spelling

Chapter 35 includes useful advice on how to improve spelling skills and proofread for spelling errors. Although you may not want to devote class time to discussing general rules, in light of the fact that English spelling rules seem always to have more exceptions than not, the nine steps for becoming a better speller presented in 35A provide important advice to all writers. We recommend discussing them when you first work on proofreading and reminding students of the advice periodically. Require students who frequently turn in papers with misspellings to keep—and submit to you now and then—a list of their spelling errors. Encourage all students to keep such a list near their computer or typewriter for reference. Section 35E, Commonly Confused Words, provides material for good warm-up exercises. Start each class by going over the difference between a few of the terms; then have students check any writing they do that day to be sure they have used the terms correctly.

BECOMING A CRITICAL READER

Since reading and writing are interrelated processes, many developmental writing courses have a stated or implied goal of improving students' reading abilities. Unit Eight, Reading Essays, contains carefully selected material to help students reach this goal. Chapter 36, Reading Critically, teaches students the questions they must ask in order to read texts effectively. Chapter 37, Readings for Writers, provides a series of examples from professional writers that help students practice their critical reading skills and increase their understanding of the different patterns of essay development presented in this text. The two appendices—Strategies for College Success and Using Research in Your Writing—offer information that will help students in all their college courses.

UNIT 8: Reading Essays

Chapter 36: Reading Critically

Ineffective reading can be attributed to many things, including physical difficulties such as visual problems, learning disabilities that interfere with information processing, problems with language comprehension, and simple lack of experience in reading critically for meaning. As a writing instructor, you will have neither the time nor the expertise to address most of these problems, but you should be acquainted with the support services your institution offers so that you can refer students appropriately when necessary. This chapter mainly addresses students who have not had much experience in analyzing academic reading material. It offers tips on how to prepare, how to find meaning, and how to respond to reading passages.

A. PREVIEWING When students read, they are entering into a conversation with the writer. As with any conversation, they need to be involved in deciding where the conversation is headed and why they are involved in it. Perhaps the most valuable skill you can help your class develop is how to skim for general ideas. Most inexperienced students read slowly and painfully, word by word, worrying about questions of individual fact and thereby losing sight of overall ideas, not to mention losing time and interest as the process drags on.

B. HIGHLIGHTING and **C. ANNOTATING** Some students will not write in their books because they want to be able to sell them at the end of the semester. You may want to address this issue with the class in terms of general academic survival skills. Require at least that students photocopy the selections you are working with so that they can practice highlighting and annotating. Watch also for the other extreme: students who come in with everything but an isolated sentence or two highlighted. It's helpful to model the activity; word processors have highlighting features that are useful for this purpose. If your classroom is equipped with a computer and projector, type a passage into the computer and then read through it with the class, deciding when, where, and why to mark it up.

D. OUTLINING The outlining activity presented here as a useful reading technique can be applied to students' own writing as well. One good way to help them check organization and focus is to require a "backward outline" of a first draft that lists the main point and subpoints of each paragraph after the draft has been written.

E. SUMMARIZING This activity can also be applied to student writing. Peer groups could be asked to write a brief summary of other group members' essays, giving readers practice in finding main points, key supporting ideas, and examples.

F. WRITING A RESPONSE PARAGRAPH This activity can be applied usefully to student writing. Peer response groups could be asked to write a brief response paragraph to other group members' essays, giving the readers practice in finding main points and the writers a variety of reader response reactions.

Chapter 37: Readings for Writers

Nineteen essays by professional writers are grouped according to the nine patterns of essay development discussed in Chapter 14. These readings serve as models for each of the patterns of development; they also offer opportunities for students to practice critical reading skills. Questions at the end of each selection involve students in identifying the writer's ideas and analyzing how the writer communicates those ideas through stylistic, rhetorical, and organizational choices. Additional Writing Practice questions guide students in creating texts in the featured pattern of development. Though instructors will use these selections in many different ways, we include here brief suggested responses to the questions posed in the text.

EXEMPLIFICATION

"Don't Call Me a Hot Tamale" (p. 636)

Judith Ortiz Cofer vividly illustrates the discomfort she feels when—as a Puerto Rican woman in mainstream America—she is mistaken for a "sexual firebrand." In paragraph 7, she describes the "sloppy, overeager kiss" she received from her date at her first formal dance. In paragraphs 1 and 8–10, she narrates two occasions on which men have approached her in public, passionately regaling her with songs that embody the stereotype of Latinas as "Hot Tamales." In part, she explains, these unwanted overtures are the result of a clothing miscommunication: in Puerto Rico, colorful, flashy dress is not necessarily a come-on, but non-Hispanic men often read such attire as a sexual signal. Cofer says she tries to get her audience to look beyond these stereotypes through "the stories I tell" and "the dreams and fears I examine in my work" (12).

Focus on Meaning

1. Cofer means that the stereotype of Latinas as "Hot Tamales" is pervasive.
2. Cofer grew up within both mainstream American culture and Puerto Rican culture. This is because while living in New Jersey, Cofer's family created a microcosm of island life.

3. On Career Day, Cofer and her Puerto Rican girlfriends were seen as "vulgar" by the other students and criticized by their teachers for "wearing everything at once" (5).

4. Cofer explains that Latinas choose bold colors because they are accustomed to the flashy colors of tropical foliage and because their culture does not view bold colors as a sexual signal.

5. In Puerto Rico, flashy clothing is considered "attractive"; in America, it is considered a come-on. This difference causes American men to mistake Cofer for a "Hot Tamale."

6. Cofer considers herself "one of the lucky ones" because she is not destined to constantly struggle against stereotypes. Instead, her education allows her to use words and stories to replace stereotypes.

7. Cofer tries to counter the stereotypes she encounters by sharing her work with American audiences. In this way, she hopes to replace stereotypes with "a more interesting set of realities" (12).

Focus on Strategy

1. The anecdote can be seen as an effective opening strategy because it is surprising and because it encapsulates the "Hot Tamale" stereotype that is the subject of Cofer's essay. However, students may differ in their evaluations of its effectiveness depending on their age, background, culture, and acquaintance with *West Side Story*. You can use this range of evaluations in a discussion of audience needs.

2. Cofer explains concepts that would be familiar to Latinas, such as machismo.

3. Answers will vary. The poem echoes the emotions Cofer expresses in the essay: first, her desire to be understood and respected, and second, her frustration at being misunderstood and disrespected. In the poem, she expresses this frustration through her comical lowered expectations of God (she merely hopes that "He be bilingual"). A restatement of the thesis would not communicate these emotions as powerfully as the poem does.

Focus on the Pattern

1. Answers will vary, but students may say that Cofer does provide enough examples to convince readers of the pervasiveness of the "Hot Tamale" stereotype. In paragraph 1, she tells of a drunken young man who sang "Maria" to her in a London bus. In paragraph 5, she describes the reactions of her teachers and classmates, who considered her and her Puerto Rican girlfriends overdressed for Career Day. In paragraph 7, she describes her first formal dance, at which she received a sloppy kiss and a comment that made her feel like a ripening fruit or vegetable. In paragraphs 8–10, she describes an encounter in a "classy, metropolitan hotel" with middle-aged man who regaled her with a dirty song. Researchers suggest that women are more persuaded by personal experience, whereas men prefer facts and authority. Do responses from your class confirm or contradict this suggestion?

2. The other phrases Cofer uses to introduce examples are "I learned this lesson at my first formal dance . . ." (7) and "I recently stayed at a classy, metropolitan hotel. . . ." (8).

Focus on Critical Thinking

1. If you would like students to explore this issue more fully, consider assigning Writing Practice 2.

2. In paragraph 7, Cofer defines a "Hot Tamale" as "a sexual firebrand." Students may not know that a firebrand is an agitator—someone who provokes action. As students examine the term, suggest that they consider *hot* and *tamale* individually, and then examine the effect of linking the two words.

3. Encourage students to respond to this question by considering their experience and examining their stereotypes.

4. Rather than using stories to push her audiences "past the particulars" (12) of her ethnic heritage, Cofer might address the stereotypes of Latinas more directly, by bringing them to people's attention and then countering them (much as she does in this essay).

5. Cofer does generalize, such as when she says "our Anglo schoolmates and their mothers" found the young Puerto Rican girls' clothes "too 'mature' and flashy" (3). (Most likely, not all of Cofer's Anglo schoolmates and their mothers viewed her clothes that way.) However, for the most part, her specific examples keep the essay free of generalizations that could be viewed as stereotyping.

Writing Practice

1. You may use this assignment as an opportunity to discuss purpose and audience. How should a proposal to a television network differ from an essay for a composition class? How should it be organized? Will a television executive prefer that the proposal be concise or detailed? What level of formality will he or she expect?

2. Before assigning this writing practice, you may wish to engage in a classroom discussion about the benefits of assimilation versus the virtues of being true to one's heritage.

3. Focus students' attention on the need to provide *specific* examples by reminding them of the anecdotes Cofer uses in "Don't Call Me a Hot Tamale."

"Volunteer Workers of the World, Unite" (p. 640)

Nicols Fox describes what she calls the "Great Labor Transfer" as consumers being given responsibility for serving themselves—for example, by busing their own fast-food tables, pumping their own gas, and finding their own food on supermarket shelves. Disgusted with companies who expect their customers to do the companies' work, she declares—with some humor, but also real frustration—that there will be a consumer revolution someday, or else consumers will "simply collapse with exhaustion" (42).

Focus on Meaning

1. Fox first noticed the trend her essay discusses in the 1970s, when her children made sure she bused her table in a fast-food restaurant.

2. The Great Labor Transfer, as Fox describes it, was a transfer of work from employees to consumers. In many contexts—fast-food restaurants, supermarkets, and gas stations—consumers began serving themselves. Fox explains the phenomenon this way: striving to make their businesses ever more efficient, companies discovered that consumers were willing to do the work that companies had previously paid employees to do.

3. Since the beginning of the Great Labor Transfer, there has been no end to the tasks that customers have been asked to take on. Thus, the potential transfer of labor seems "unlimited."

4. According to Fox, companies told consumers that they would have more "freedom," "choices," or "convenience" if they took on the additional work (8).

5. For employers, the "consumer as worker" demands nothing and creates no headaches, requiring "not just no pay, but no health insurance, no taxes, no forms, no personal days, no sexual harassment lawsuits . . ." (9).

6. According to Fox, the "greatest labor transfer" is the touch-tone "voice mail" system.

Focus on Strategy

1. Fox does not hide her contempt of the companies behind the Great Labor Transfer . The most direct statement of Fox's opinion occurs in paragraph 15: "For my part I'm frustrated, irritated, and exhausted."

2. On the one hand, Fox does seem to expect her readers both to be aware of the trend she describes and to object to it, as she does. Several times she includes readers by using the pronoun *we*, making them seem outraged, too. For example, in paragraph 12, she asks: "What on earth are we doing and who's making us do it?" On the other hand, Fox's coinage of the phrase "Great Labor Transfer" and her careful detailing of the trend make it clear that she is creating a new concept, even if it is created out of experiences that are familiar to readers.

3. "What on earth are we doing and who's making us do it?" (12). We consumers are serving ourselves, instead of demanding that we be served by employees, and we are doing it voluntarily, in part because we have bought into the idea that serving ourselves gives us more freedom, choice, and convenience. "So where does this leave us economically?" (13). Economically, it leaves us well off. We are more productive because of it.

4. In paragraph 14, Fox seems only half-serious when she predicts that consumers will either refuse, revolt, or collapse with exhaustion in response to companies' ever-increasing demands. The last prediction—that consumers will collapse with exhaustion—is an exaggeration, and its presence suggests that Fox's other predictions are intended not so much to forecast the future as to emphasize Fox's disgust with the status quo and her desire for change.

Focus on the Pattern

1. Consumers were found to be willing to bus their own tables in fast-food restaurants (1); dial numbers without the help of an operator (5); find their own food in a supermarket (6); service their own cars (7); attend to their own medical needs (10); and act as receptionists for businesses, using "voice mail" systems (11).
2. In these paragraphs, Fox illustrates how consumers have been fooled into serving themselves at service stations (7), and hospitals (10) and on the phone (11).

Focus on Critical Thinking

1. The word *volunteer* usually suggests someone of good will who is serving others. The volunteers Fox discusses are serving themselves out of a desire to have more freedom and convenience.
2. Fox seems genuinely irritated by the demands of the Great Labor Transfer, but she also seems to exaggerate the trend. Whether students believe that Fox is exaggerating or not, be sure that they support their view with specific examples from the text.
3. There is some sarcasm in paragraph 10. For example, it does not require medical skill to "starve" oneself before surgery, as Fox suggests. However, Fox does appear to believe that the Great Labor Transfer was successful in the medical realm—that consumers proved able to do at least some of what nurses had once done—and thus she is not saying the opposite of what she means.
4. Encourage students both to (a) predict the future effects of the Great Labor Transfer in the areas that Fox has mentioned and (b) brainstorm and then consider other contexts that Fox does not mention.

Writing Practice

1. Remind students to refer to Chapter 1, Understanding the Writing Process, especially as they brainstorm and organize examples of the "volunteer" work they do.
2. Remind students to choose the examples that are most supportive of their argument. For

example, they may wish to focus on the benefits of pumping one's own gas and doing one's own grocery shopping but leave out a discussion of medical outsourcing.

NARRATION

"Orange Crush" (p. 643)

Yiyun Li reminisces about her childhood "crush" on the orange-flavored drink Tang. In doing so, she describes the China of her childhood, reflects on the value of thriftiness, explores the seductiveness of advertising and the pull of trends, and suggests that growing up means overcoming one's illusions.

Focus on Meaning

1. For Li and her family and friends, Tang represents wealth and luxury; to them, a bottle of Tang, even an empty one, is a status symbol. The advertisement, with its spacious, bright kitchen and beautiful models, brings to life the luxury that Tang represents (3).
2. Li's father was thrifty and avoided drinks made with "chemicals" in favor of homemade drinks like dried citrus peels boiled in water.
3. Li learns to see her crush on Tang as an unattainable fantasy. She realizes that she will never have a "Tangy life"; no one will. Listening to her mother and a neighbor talk about how young men may throw away money during courtship but will settle into thriftiness as married men, she concludes, "Every dream ended with this bland, ordinary existence" (13).
4. A "Tangy life," according to Li, is a life of luxury, a life in which thriftiness does not get in the way of pleasure.

Focus on Strategy

1. Li appears to be writing for an American audience. She describes how seductive the promise of an American lifestyle was to her and to everyone around her, something that she would presumably not need to explain to a Chinese audience who shared her perspective.
2. The unstated thesis of "Orange Crush" is that, to Li and her family and friends, Tang was a symbol of luxury; however, like any status symbol, its promise would eventually turn out to be empty. In paragraph 7, Li describes how

Tang was regarded with reverence, setting the stage for Li's disillusionment in the final paragraph.

3. By opening the essay with a description of her father's cold remedy, Li shows the thriftiness she was reacting against, helping readers understand her attraction to the luxury that Tang represented.

4. Through the exchange of dialog in paragraphs 10–12, the reader sees the shift in Li's perspective. With help from the older women's frank words, Li moves from fantasizing about the luxury that Tang represents to seeing that Tang is a "waste of money," a luxury that cannot be sustained.

5. By using first-person pronouns, Li makes this a story about her own transformation—she goes from being charmed by luxuries out of her reach to feeling jaded and cautious about life and what it has to offer. This is a personal narrative told not so much *about* Tang as *through* Tang.

Focus on the Pattern

1. Transitions include "the year I turned 16" (3); "near the end of the ad" (5); "Until this point" (6); "When it was my turn" (9); and "Two months later" (10).

2. *Exemplification:* "Even the sturdy glass containers that the powder came in were coveted. People used them as tea mugs. . . . Even my mother had an empty Tang bottle" (7). *Description:* "The kitchen was spacious and brightly lighted" (3); "The drink itself, steaming hot in an expensive-looking mug that was held between the child's mittened hands, was a vivid orange" (4). *Comparison and contrast:* the contrast between the kitchen and the people in the Fruit Treasure ad and the kitchen and the people in Li's life in China (3).

Focus on Critical Thinking

1. Ask students to think about what their younger siblings, their nieces and nephews, or their own children repeatedly ask for. Remind them that this fascinating product need not be food or drink but could be anything—perhaps a coveted toy or game or electronic device.

2. Remind students that Li, as an adult living in America, loses interest in Tang long before she sees bottles of it in a supermarket and

notices that they are "neither expensive nor trendy" (13).

3. If students are having trouble with this question, you might point them to the following excerpts: "My father . . . purple-colored medicines" (1–2); "The Tang ad . . . the West and its capitalism" (6); "Even my mother . . . Tang-filled life" (7–8).

Writing Practice

1. Show students how Li's essay is really a narrative about a personal transformation (she goes from starry-eyed to skeptical). Challenge students not just to tell about the food but also to use the food to tell about themselves.

2. Ask students who have little experience of foreign countries to think about ethnic restaurants they have visited or people they know from other countries who might have introduced them to an "exotic" food.

"Pick One" (p. 646)

A few weeks into his fourth-grade year, David Matthews moved from a school in the Maryland suburbs of Washington to one in inner-city Baltimore. There, he was confronted with the question of his race: was he black or white, the other kids wanted to know. At lunch, he was forced to "pick one," and his choice to sit with the white kids would define him for years to come.

Focus on Meaning

1. More blacks lived in Matthews's new home, inner-city Baltimore, than in his old home, the Maryland suburbs of Washington. His new home also featured "many houses connected to one another, block after block" and "many people on streets, marble stoops and corners" (1).

2. Matthews's new school was a shock to him because 80 percent of the kids were black. Matthews, a mixed race child whose skin was neither "milky enough to classify me as white or swarthy enough to render me black (27)," was painfully aware that he didn't belong with the black children, but he was not sure he belonged with the white children, either. He felt "utterly on [his] own." (2)

3. Matthews's skin tone was different than any of the other kids'. While the black kids "ranged in shades from butterscotch to Belgian

chocolate" and the white kids had "red and alabaster faces" (3), Matthews's was yellowish. While this "sallow complexion" and his "fine, limp hair" (3) made Matthews look not black, his thick lips and flared nose made him look not white.

4. In the cafeteria, where the kids segregated themselves by race, Matthews chose to sit with the white kids. He was intimidated by the black kids, whose actions, words, and attitude he couldn't mimic, and, at the same time, he was comforted by the white kids' hairstyles and clothing, which matched his own.

5. Matthews feared urban blacks because he didn't know how to negotiate their world: a faux pas on his part could have led to a "table-clearing brawl" (8). On the other hand, he envied how they carried themselves with a "loose, effortless charge" that made them seem "alive and cool" (8).

6. The "code of the cafeteria table" (10) is the unspoken rule that you are racially defined by the company you keep. If you sit with the white kids, as Matthews did on his first day in Baltimore, you are considered white.

Focus on Strategy

1. The statements "I had never seen so many black people in all my life" (1) and "I had never felt so utterly on my own" (2) are both short and punchy, perhaps meant to surprise the reader with their finality; they are strong statements, and there is nothing circuitous or qualified about them. The first statement predicts that Matthews will choose to sit with the white kids. The second statement predicts that Matthews will nevertheless have a hard time making this choice, since he feels like an outsider to both the white kids and the black kids.

2. When Matthews says, "I was no explorer" (7), he means that he did not feel adventurous or bold in the unfamiliar environment; he was ready to play things safe.

3. Students may have trouble imagining how readers of another race might react to this essay. To help them step back from their personal perspective, assign them to edit the essay, replacing "black" with "white" and vice versa (or provide them with a ready-made edited version). How do students' reactions

change when they read this mirror version of the essay?

4. For Matthews, as a mixed race child, identifying himself as either black or white (mixed was not an option) was a choice that was both "necessary and impossible" (6). This is the central idea in Matthews's essay, and it is most clearly articulated in paragraph 6.

5. "By the code of the cafeteria table, which was just as binding in that time and place as the laws of Jim Crow or Soweto, I was white" (10): this summary statement echoes Matthews's main idea that it was mandatory for him to identify himself according to the racial binary of his time and place (the 1970s in inner-city Baltimore), even if neither identification — black or white — was wholly true. In other words, identifying himself as either black or white was both "necessary and impossible" (6).

6. Answers will vary. As a challenge, ask students to imagine situations that may have complicated Matthews's racial identification as a teenager.

Focus on the Pattern

1. The narrative covers a single morning.
2. The events take place in the classroom, in the hallway, and in the cafeteria.
3. Transitions that move readers from one time and place to another: "Nothing prepared me for walking into that public school classroom, already three weeks into fourth grade" (2); "In the hallway, on the way to class" (4); "At lunchtime that first day, teetering on the edge of the cafeteria" (7); and "Lunch tray in hand . . . I headed toward the kids who looked most like me" (9).
4. Matthews uses dialogue in paragraph 5, when the kids surround him and pepper him with questions. Other voices students might like to hear include those of Matthews, Matthews' father and his "bebop-era revolutionary friends"(7), and the "ruddy boy" (9) that Matthews sits next to at lunch.

Focus on Critical Thinking

1. Opinions may vary, but Matthews identifies himself in this essay as "mixed" (6).
2. You may wish to ask students (especially those who cannot answer this question from personal experience) to consider President

Obama. Like Matthews, President Obama's mother was white and his father was black. To what extent is President Obama forced to "pick one"? Does he identify himself differently to different audiences or in different contexts?

3. Answers may vary, but students may feel that this choice is not quite as stark as it used to be.

Writing Practice

1. Students may consider any group of people joined by common interests, histories, passions, or prejudices — from childhood or workplaces cliques to affiliations based on ideology, religion, or culture.

2. In particular, encourage students to identify and explore Matthews's feelings as a nine-year-old or a teenager. Ask them to bring to life the isolation, confusion, and uncertainty that Matthews recounts.

DESCRIPTION

"An American in Mexico" (p. 650)

In this essay, Alex Espinoza travels with his mother to his family's property in El Ojo de Agua, Mexico. More than thirty years before this trip, Espinoza's mother had built a house there, where she had lived with Espinoza's siblings. By the time Espinoza was born, however, his mother had moved their family north — first to Tijuana, and then to Los Angeles — to be closer to Espinoza's father, a day laborer. Espinoza "really wanted to connect to that land" (11), but even after making the trip, he felt removed from the place and was unable to grasp the "complicated feelings" (3) it evoked in his siblings.

Focus on Meaning

1. Espinoza was born in Tijuana and grew up outside of Los Angeles. Most of his older siblings, by contrast, were born in El Ojo de Agua, a village in Michoacán, on a parcel of land that was in their mother's family. Whereas Espinoza's childhood entertainment included a BMX bike, "Star Wars" action figures, and cable TV, his siblings' pleasures were simpler: handmade dolls, mesquite trees for climbing, and eggs stolen to sell for candy. Espinoza's childhood differed from

his siblings' because he was born during his family's gradual move north, to reunite with Espinoza's father in Los Angeles.

2. Espinoza finally decided to visit El Ojo de Agua because he wanted to understand his siblings' complicated feelings toward their former home and because he wanted to connect to the land as his siblings had as children.

3. Espinoza means that the house existed for him only in his imagination, and that it had taken on the magnified dimensions of imagination rather than being grounded in reality.

4. Espinoza's photos reveal only "sections of walls, windows and dark doorways" (11). Missing from the pictures are the feelings that the place evoked in Espinoza's siblings; these feelings continue to be out of reach to Espinoza.

5. Espinoza thinks his trip did not fulfill its purpose. He went to El Ojo de Agua to connect with the land and with the past, and to grasp some of the things his siblings understand firsthand, such as sacrifice. However, he comes away without a connection to the land or the past, and with no better understanding of his siblings' "close, deep and also painful" relationship to Mexico (37).

Focus on Strategy

1. To clarify to readers the purpose for his trip to El Ojo de Agua, Espinoza uses the first three paragraphs to describe his family background. He explains that most of his siblings grew up in El Ojo de Agua, while he did not; that, because of this difference, his siblings had always felt a deep and painful connection to Mexico, whereas Espinoza had always felt disconnected from and uninterested in the country; and that, as an adult, he was drawn to make the trip so he could attempt to understand his siblings' feelings and forge his own connection with the place.

2. *Possible thesis statement:* "I traveled to Mexico to grasp my siblings' deep connection to the place, but I came away feeling as disconnected from it as I had always felt; simply traveling to the place where my family had experienced hardship and sacrifice was not enough to make me really understand such challenges."

3. Remind students that they should articulate the essay's subject matter and "message" before

answering this question. Possible subject matter: one man's failed attempt to connect with a place that holds power for his family members but with which he has no personal history. Possible "message": a deep connection with a place is not easily forged; a visit is not enough to create such a connection.

Focus on the Pattern

1. Paragraphs 6–10 convey a dominant impression of the house as abandoned and bare.
2. Espinoza organizes his description from far to near, and from outside to inside.
3. Espinoza might have used transitional words or phrases to move readers from the entrance to the property to the road, and from the reservoir to the house. The relationship between these elements is not totally clear.
4. Espinoza combines subjective and objective description. For example, he uses subjective description when he says it was "threatening to rain" (6) or that the house was "nothing more than four walls" (8), conveying an impression of the place, and the house, as dim and small.

Focus on Critical Thinking

1. Answers will vary. It is unclear whether Espinoza sees his family as American; he certainly notices their "close, deep" connection to Mexico (3).
2. Espinoza says that his siblings' connection to Mexico was "close, deep, and also painful" (3). He describes the fun they used to have as well as the "hardships and misfortunes" (2) they endured in El Ojo de Agua. This textual evidence suggests that Espinoza's siblings' "complicated feelings" (3) may have involved both affection for their home and relief to be free of the pain it caused them.
3. Answers will vary. Paragraph 9 suggests that Espinoza's mother has separated herself from her past; she seems surprised—almost pushed off-balance—by the physical reminder of the house she used to live in, as if she had forgotten that part of her life.
4. Answers will vary. Espinoza may feel less connected to his family after the trip, since his visit erased the mythic image he had of the land and the house, and he did not establish a connection to the place.

Writing Practice

1. Remind students to be aware of the elements of description they explored in this reading's Focus on the Pattern questions. For example, as they write, they might ask themselves questions such as these: What dominant impression am I creating? How is my description organized (side to side, far to near, outside to inside)? Have I included enough transitional words and phrases to move readers from one part of the subject to the next? Is this a subjective or an objective description?
2. You may wish to use this writing activity as an opportunity to engage students in a conversation about audience and purpose.

"A Fable for Tomorrow" (p. 653)

Rachel Carson describes a blight on a beautiful American town. Her imagined description—a "fable for tomorrow"—is designed to wake readers up to the dangers of pesticides. Carson's 1962 book *Silent Spring*, from which this excerpt is taken, led to the ban on DDT.

Focus on Meaning

1. A fable is a fictitious narrative designed to illuminate a useful truth. Here, Carson tells the story of a rural town, full of natural beauty, that sickens under the assault of chemical pesticides. Carson constructs the blight on her fabled town by combining and magnifying the ills that have befallen real towns. Carson's fictitious narrative is a "fable for tomorrow" because it is intended to illuminate the frightening effects of pesticides on living things and shock readers into choosing a better future.
2. Carson describes the cause of the "strange blight" in paragraph 7—the spraying of pesticides: "In the gutters . . . a white granular powder still showed a few patches; some weeks before it had fallen like snow."
3. Signs that the town has changed include that farm animals, birds, and people sicken and die (3); the chickens and pigs cannot reproduce (5); the bees have died, so the apple trees are not pollinated (5); the roadside vegetation has died (6); the fish have died (6).
4. The townspeople are confused and dismayed: they find the blight "strange" (3, 4); deaths

among them are "sudden and unexplained" (3); the doctors are "more and more puzzled" (3); the farmers complain that their piglets are dying (5).

5. When she says "the people had done it them-selves" (8), she means that the farmers had chosen to spray the pesticides that created the blight.

6. The "stark reality" (9) that Carson warns against is a pesticide blight that affects all liv-ing things.

Focus on Strategy

1. Carson likely opened her book with this story in order to shock people into paying atten-tion to her message. She probably expected readers to react with fear and disgust. Today's readers may not be as frightened as readers in the past, since Carson's book led to a ban on DDT use.

2. Carson probably expected to frighten and enlighten readers. Her "fable" of environmen-tal collapse is frightening because, although it is fictitious, it is created by combining real events. It is enlightening because it reveals the damage that pesticides can cause.

3. By telling the story in the past tense, Carson makes the story seem more real—and more frightening. In her fable, the tragedy is not merely a possibility but a "stark reality."

4. Answers will vary, but students may find that Carson's admission that the town does not exist *does* weaken her essay—at least initially —either because it undermines readers' trust in Carson or because it suggests that Carson is blowing things out of proportion.

5. Examples of strong language include "shadow of death" (3) and "stricken suddenly" (3).

Focus on the Pattern

1. In paragraphs 1–2, Carson identifies the fol-lowing positive features of the town: its pro-ductivity ("a checkerboard of prosperous farms, with fields of grain and hillsides of orchards"); its beautiful vegetation ("In autumn, oak and maple and birch set up a blaze of color that flamed and flickered across a backdrop of pines"); its healthy wildlife ("foxes barked in the hills and deer silently crossed the fields"); and its attrac-tiveness to outsiders, who engaged in a kind

of eco-tourism ("The countryside was, in fact, famous for the abundance and variety of its bird life, and when the flood of migrants was pouring through in spring and fall people traveled from great distances to observe them. Others came to fish the streams . . .).

2. In paragraphs 3–7, Carson identifies the fol-lowing negative features, among others, of the town: its puzzling sicknesses among ani-mals and humans (3); its stillness without birds and silence without bees droning in the trees (4, 5); its browned and withered road-side vegetation (6).

3. Carson transitions from positive to negative description with this sentence: "Then a strange blight crept over the area and every-thing began to change" (3).

4. This is a subjective description. In her description of the town, Carson uses words that evoke strong positive or negative reac-tions in readers. For example, Carson first describes the town as a place where "all life seemed to live in harmony with its surround-ings" (1) and where even the roadsides were "places of beauty" (2); then she describes the change that brought a "shadow of death" and a "strange stillness" (3, 4).

Focus on Critical Thinking

1. Carson chooses to make the town into Any-where, U.S.A., so that the fable will feel rele-vant to every American.

2. *Possible answer:* Carson's predictions have not come true, in large part because this essay motivated a ban on DDT. However, there are still many threats to human, ani-mal, and environmental health, including threats from pesticides.

3. Answers will vary. Climate change is one pos-sible answer.

Writing Practice

1. You may wish to use this writing practice as an opportunity to talk about use of highly charged language by those arguing on behalf of the environment. What is the benefit of using strong language? What are the possible risks?

2. Remind students that increasing tempera-tures are not the only predicted effects of global warming. Other predicted or present

effects include extreme weather, such as droughts, cyclones, and tsunamis; ocean acidification; and rising sea levels.

PROCESS

"Mummy Arts" (p. 656)

In the style of a cheerful instructional article in a cooking magazine, Adam Goodheart describes how to make a mummy. Although his tone is silly, Goodheart manages to convey quite a bit of information about ancient Egyptian mummification in this essay.

Focus on Meaning

1. The Ancient Egyptians practiced mummification so that the spirits, or *ka*, of their dead could identify their own corpses.
2. Equipment and supplies needed for mummification include an iron hook (2); a flint knife (3); palm wine (3); alabaster jars (3); natron, a natural salt (4); frankincense, sacred oil, myrrh, and other spices (4); a sheet of gold (4); sawdust, butter, and mud (5); bedsheets (6); pine resin (6); and amulets (6).
3. The following steps are included in the "evisceration" stage of the process (2 and 3): relocate to a well-ventilated tent; cleanse the body; break the nose by pushing a long iron hook up the nostrils; use the hook to remove the contents of the skull; discard the brain; make an incision on the left side of the abdomen; remove the internal organs through the incision; wash the organs in palm wine and set them aside.
4. The following steps are included in the "salting and stuffing" stage of the process (4 and 5): fill the abdominal cavity with natron; cover the body with natron; leave the body for forty-two days; remove the natron; anoint the head with frankincense; anoint the body with sacred oil; pack the skull and abdomen with myrrh and other spices; cover the incision with a sheet of gold; and stuff the corpse's skin with a compound of sawdust, butter, and mud.
5. The following steps are included in the "wrapping up" stage of the process (6): pour molten pine resin over the body; bandage each of the extremities separately, including fingers and toes; repeat the resin and band-

aging process; place at least one amulet between the layers of bandages; and make sure the last layers secure the arms and legs to the body.

Focus on Strategy

1. Goodheart uses commands and "you" for comic effect, and to bring the process of mummification to life.
2. Answers will vary. Goodheart does seem to want to inform and educate readers; his attention-grabbing strategy of using commands and "you" helps him do this. However, in bringing out the absurdity of the Egyptian mummification process, he may have another purpose: to make present-day readers examine and question the rituals in their own lives.
3. Goodheart's tone is casual, even silly. It is evident right away that his essay is not a serious treatment of the topic. For example, Goodheart says that the *ka* returns "now and then . . . to snack on the food" (1) in the tomb, as if the spirit were popping into his kitchen throughout the day. Students' responses to Goodheart's lighthearted approach may vary.
4. *Possible thesis statement:* The art of mummification is not for the faint of heart, but with the right equipment and supplies, anyone can practice the ancient art of preserving their loved ones. Possible placement: the end of the first paragraph.
5. Answers will vary. The last paragraph is not part of Goodheart's instructions, but it adds an additional amusing detail.
6. Answers will vary. The title "Mummy Arts" suggests that the essay's purpose is to instruct readers about an art form or describe the steps in a craft. It is an inviting title that makes mummification seem accessible.

Focus on the Pattern

1. Goodheart's use of such transitional words as *after*, *then*, *next*, and *while*, and his use of commands and "you" indicate that this essay is a set of instructions.
2. Cautions and reminders include "please make sure that the loved one in question is fully deceased" (1); "it's best to have a friend do this, since the person who cuts open the body must be pelted with stones" (3); "Don't

overdo it, though" (5); "Go easy on the resin" (6); and "Careful labeling will prevent embarrassing mix-ups later on" (7). These warnings allow Goodheart to add funny factoids about mummification, such as that a queen's overstuffed face "split open like an old sofa" (5) or that a mummy thought to be a princess turned out to be a pet baboon (7).

3. Answers will vary. Goodheart's categories wouldn't be out of place in a cooking magazine with a cutesy, cheerful tone. The incongruity of that tone with the usual seriousness that surround mummies makes for comic effect. Students may come up with other, funny categories.

4. The steps in the process, which are presented chronologically, are as follows: clean the body; remove and discard the brain; remove the internal organs, which will be preserved separately; salt the body to dry it out; anoint and fill the body with oils and spices; cover the abdominal incision with a sheet of gold; stuff the corpse's skin; pour molten pine resin over the body; and apply two layers of bandages to the body.

5. Transitional words include *after, then, next, once,* and *while.* Transitional phrases include "After cleansing the body" (2); "Then use the hook" (2); "Next, take a flint knife" (3); "After you've stoned your friend" (3); "Once the abdominal cavity is empty" (4); "Having removed the natron" (4), "While the resin's still tacky" (6); and "Then brush on another coat" (6).

Focus on Critical Thinking

1. Answers will vary. The graphic details assure readers that nothing about the process is being held back out of a sense of delicacy. This lack of evasiveness may be appealing in itself, especially when applied to a fascinating ancient subject that readers will know little about.

2. Answers will vary. Even though the essay is presented in a lighthearted way, Goodheart manages to convey a lot of factual information about Egyptian beliefs and customs.

3. Answers will vary. Other steps that are clearly not part of the process include relocating to a well-ventilated "tent" (2) and wearing a jackal-head mask (2).

Writing Practice

1. After students complete this writing practice (or during the planning stage), you may wish to have them compare and contrast their essay with Goodheart's. What did they add or subtracted from the basic set of instructions in the process of rewriting them for their particular audience and purpose?

2. Challenge students to create as vivid a mental picture in their essay as Goodheart does in "Mummy Arts." You may wish to highlight for students the vivid details in Goodheart's essay (or have them do this as a class or individually). This will help them see the number and type of details that are necessary to bring a process to life.

"My Grandmother's Dumpling" (p. 659)

Amy Ma explains the process of dumpling-making for Lunar New Year and conveys the event's importance to her family and in her culture. The engine behind the "great dumpling cook-off" is Ma's grandmother, whose forceful voice echoes throughout the piece.

Focus on Meaning

1. Cousin Mao Mao folds her dumplings in the style of the rat. Aunt Yee makes "[t]wo distinct pleats in a fan-shaped dumping" (3). Grandmother's dumplings are flat and crescent shaped with a smooth edge. The author's dumplings are like her grandmother's but with a "flower edge" (3). Each woman in the family has a distinct folding pattern that marks her "as surely as her fingerprints" (1).

2. Dumplings symbolize prosperity because they are shaped like the gold and silver coins of the Yuan and Ming dynasties. They also symbolize a letting go of the past because part of their name means "the end of something." Thus, they are eaten on Chinese New Year to celebrate prosperity and the letting go of the past. For Ma, dumplings remind her of the Taipei kitchen where she and the other women in her family learned to make them under the watchful eye of her grandmother.

3. In addition to teaching the women how to make dumplings, Ma's grandmother presides over a kind of cultural training. For example, she teaches superstitions—"Women who

fold dumplings with one hand won't have children" (23)— and establishes standards of acceptable behavior—"What good is a wife who makes lovely dumplings if there's not enough to feed everyone?" (24).

4. Ma seems to see two levels of magic in the dumplings. First, she understands their symbolism—"filling your stomach with edible replicas of ingots was thought to ensure a year of prosperity ahead" (9). Second, she sees the dumpling-making process as a special night of training under the family matriarch, and as a kind of "culinary theater" requiring careful orchestration and Zen-like rhythms (11).

Focus on Strategy

1. To help readers understand the significance of making dumplings, Ma uses paragraphs 1–11 to describe how the process fits in to the tradition of Lunar New Year.
2. *Possible answer:* Ma wanted to tell readers about an important part of her childhood and her culture.
3. These quotations help Ma convey her grandmother's role in the dumpling-making process. The quotations show Grandmother as a forceful matriarch, full of cautions, criticisms, and advice. They also reveal Ma's attentiveness to what her grandmother said.
4. Ma's target audience is probably American women of Ma's age, who would be charmed and enlightened by this portrait of women in a family in China.
5. In paragraphs 5–10, Ma details the traditions of Lunar New Year, indicating that her essay is intended to inform and is aimed at an audience unfamiliar with Chinese traditions.

Focus on the Pattern

1. Ma does not address readers directly or instruct them how to perform the steps in the dumpling-making process. Instead, she describes how she and her female relatives made dumplings.
2. The dumpling-making process is described in paragraphs 15–31. The whole process of cooking, presenting, and then eating the dumplings—from Grandmother unloading the dough from the refrigerator to Grandfather taking the first bite—spans paragraphs 15–39.

3. Ma's purpose is not to teach others how to make dumplings but to bring to life a special tradition in her family and culture. If this essay were written as a set of instructions, Ma would have included her Grandmother's cautions, such as not to overmix the dough.
4. The main steps in the dumpling-making process are to roll the dough into logs; prepare the filling; cut off equal-size segments of the dough; flatten the dough segments into circles; fill and fold the dumplings; and, just before serving, boil the dumplings.
5. Transitional words and phrases include "To start" (15); "Meanwhile" (16); "Then" (19); "First" (19); "When" (27); "By the time" (31); "With only the boiling of the dumplings left to do" (32); "Around 5 a.m." (33); "Before long" (34); "At 9 a.m. or when the guest count reached 10" (35); "By the fourth time" (35); "Before the first bite" (39); and "Then" (39).

Focus on Critical Thinking

1. *Possible answer:* Ma's grandmother is the essay's central focus. Her voice is almost the only voice we hear, and Ma makes clear that it is her grandmother's energy and direction that propel the dumpling-making process. This is especially clear at the end, when Ma tells readers, "The dumpling ritual slowly faded after Grandmother's passing in 1999" (41).
2. Answers will vary. You may wish to remind students that a memoir is a narrative composed from personal experience. The dumplings may be narratives in the sense that they "contain" the story of a matriarch training the generations of women below her—the story of the dumpling-making process. But, if the dumplings are made in set patterns given to each woman by Grandmother, do they reflect personal experience? Does Ma use "memoirs" to mean something other than a narrative composed from personal experience? For example, perhaps she is using the word merely to mean something that identifies its maker, in the same way she uses "fingerprint" in paragraph 1.

Writing Practice

1. To help students develop their introductory paragraphs, you may wish to have them look

back at paragraphs 1–10 of Ma's essay. How much space does Ma devote to her family's dumpling-making tradition? to the cultural and historical roots of the dumpling tradition? How does she weave the personal and cultural/historical threads together? Encourage students to think about whether they would like to include personal background, cultural/historical background, or both; how much of each they will include; and how they will connect the two elements.

2. Draw students' attention to the fact that the audience for this writing practice is very different from Ma's audience in "My Grandmother's Dumpling." Rather than addressing an American audience unfamiliar with Chinese traditions, students doing this writing practice will be addressing young Chinese-American girls, the daughters of the author. The tone may be more personal and different information will be presented.

Cause and Effect

"The Poncho Bearer" (p. 667)

John Schwartz, a technology writer for the *New York Times,* explains both the causes and effects of his middle child Sam wearing a poncho to high school every Friday. He explains that no one, not even Sam, was aware of the effects his actions would have.

Focus on Meaning

1. Later in the essay, Schwartz tells readers that Sam explained at least part of the "why" of it in an English essay: "He wrote that he started wearing it because, when he tried it on at home, it made him laugh" (14). Schwartz also makes clear that Sam's personality—"he's always made his own path" (6)—and the silent support he receives at home—"I never gave Sam any trouble about the poncho" (12)—combine to make Sam unself-conscious about wearing the poncho to school.

2. Sam's own words show that he has a light-hearted sensibility—he likes to have fun and to create fun for others. Sam's essay, in particular, reveals his humor; it also shows him to be thoughtful and unpretentious. He gives real thought to the "whys" of his behavior and makes light of them through exaggeration.

3. Dick's experience inspired Schwartz to treat his children with the same respect and support that his father showed to Dick.

4. Answers will vary. Schwartz means that Sam has begun to thoughtfully shape his identity.

Focus on Strategy

1. The event in Dick's life taught Schwartz to "stand up for his children no matter what" (11). As a result, Schwartz silently supports Sam, allowing him the freedom to explore his identity without feeling disapproved of by his family.

2. *Possible answer:* This essay appears to be directed at parents. When Schwartz says, "As we all know, high school for most teenagers is a time of intense pressure to conform" (4), we know immediately that he is addressing adults, not teenagers. He also refers to Sam as "our middle child"—a formulation that would be especially at home in a conversation between parents—and ends with a statement that would best be appreciated by fellow parents: "That good feeling lasted about a week, until I got an instant message from my daughter at college: *I got a tattoo today*" (20–21).

3. Answers will vary. The point Schwartz is trying to get across is that the main duty of adolescence is to carve out one's identity, and that parents can support this process by standing up for their children's choices.

4. *Bearer* means "one who wears." In this essay, it also suggests a sense of duty. As Sam writes in his essay, the next "poncho bearer" will take on not just the billowy cloak but also its attendant obligations. To Schwartz, *bearer* may also echo the essay's theme: every teenager bears the duty of defining him- or herself.

5. Answers will vary. In the last line, Schwartz makes light of himself by showing that the "light touch" he has just boasted about does not always come easily: he finds his daughter's tattoo hard to swallow. This last line lightens the tone of the piece, after Schwartz soberly declares that "Defining yourself is the central question of adolescence" (19) and congratulates his son (on beginning to answer the question well) and himself (for not getting in the way of that answer).

Focus on the Pattern

1. The essay's emphasis is on both causes and effects. Sam's father ponders the causes of Sam wearing the poncho, but in the second half of the essay, he devotes just as much thought to the effects of wearing the poncho on Sam, on Sam's family, and on Sam's coaches, classmates, and teammates.

2. Sam's reasons include that when he tried it at home, it made him laugh (14); wearing the poncho has become something of an obligation (14); if he stops wearing it, more than half the school will forget that the weekend is about to come up (15); it is his duty in this strange society to remind his classmates of good times ahead (15). Schwartz's reasons include that Sam has often found ways to stand out in situations where others try to fit in (5); and Sam was using the poncho to "define" himself (19).

3. Sam's decision to wear the poncho forces those around him to take his unusual choice in stride. His coaches come to see that Sam's Friday attire does not compromise his seriousness during sporting events. His father, the author of the essay, approaches the poncho as a kind of test—which he passes by not objecting to Sam's choice.

Focus on Critical Thinking

1. Several details are useful: Schwartz explains that his son "has often found ways to stand out in situations where others try to fit in" (5); Sam "has always found his own path" (6); and Schwartz's own brother and father had stood up for their rights to look or act differently.

2. The haiku shows the power Sam derives from wearing the poncho. He "strides"—the word suggests purpose and forcefulness—and he does so quickly: he is a blur of color. The strong and gusty wind showcases Sam's own strength and flair; in particular, it billows the poncho dramatically behind him.

3. Answers will vary. Schwartz describes the poncho very briefly: "It is brightly colored, or more accurately, blinding" (3).

4. Answers will vary. The essay is arguably about Sam and his effort to define himself, and arguably about Schwartz and his triumph of hands-off parenting.

Writing Practice

1. Remind students that *motives* in this context is synonymous with *causes*.

2. You might wish to use this writing activity as an opportunity to review the difference between *affects* and *effects*.

3. For this writing practice, you might divide the class into groups and ask them to create lists of the causes and effects of feeling out of place in high school.

"At the Heart of a Historic Movement" (p. 670)

John Hartmire, whose father was César Chávez's executive director of the National Farmworker Ministry, describes his ambivalent feelings about the experience of growing up at the center of a social movement. Students may not be familiar with Chávez (1927–1993), who fought for the rights of migrant farm workers, leading a highly publicized five-year strike in the 1960s during which he encouraged Americans to boycott table grapes as a show of support. After winning a long battle with the Teamsters for control of the field workers in 1977, Chávez and his United Farm Workers organized a number of generally successful strikes and boycotts to get higher wages and better working conditions for grape and lettuce growers. While acknowledging the social benefits of the movement, Hartmire describes the personal losses experienced by a child who grew up feeling that his father cared more about the movement than about his family.

Focus on Meaning

1. In paragraph 1, Hartmire describes sweating through protest marches while his friends were at the beach. He gives further examples of the kinds of family and social experiences he missed in paragraph 5. He blamed Chávez for ruining his childhood.

2. Have students name a few contemporary political or cultural icons and ask them to imagine what it might be like if one of their own parents worked for or with that person. What would be some of the advantages and disadvantages?

3. Hartmire is referring to Chávez's long and well-publicized struggle to unionize farm workers and protect their rights, an effort best

remembered for the strikes and grape boy-cotts of the 1960s and '70s.

4. Ask students to read through the essay and make a list of the positive and negative effects Hartmire associates with Chávez. Which list is longer? Which list is more important?

5. Hartmire begins with a description of Chávez as "larger than life" and ends by talking about him as a person, a quiet individual, and a father. Throughout the essay he moves back and forth between the man and the myth, the cause of individual losses and the impetus for social gains. His feelings about his father also vacillate between pride and loneliness; the next-to-last paragraph shows that he is still wrestling with these conflicting emotions.

6. Students may point to the language in the next-to-last paragraph ("I just wonder if the price has to be so damn high") as an example of the bitterness he still feels—a bitterness that seems to be directed at Chávez but more at Hartmire's father, who was absent during much of his childhood and who seemed more concerned about union issues than about family matters.

Focus on Strategy

1. By using versions of the same question to introduce and conclude his thoughts, Hart-mire effectively frames his essay and gives it relevance for contemporary readers. The girl's question reveals that most people of her generation don't know much (or anything) about Chávez, despite his historic influence and even though his name continues to dom-inate the physical and cultural landscape of America. You might point out that Hartmire reframes the question in his last paragraph, focusing on how well he knew the individual man, rather than the public icon—and con-cluding that he is largely ignorant as well.

2. *Newsweek* is a news-oriented, general-interest publication with an audience of relatively edu-cated readers who wish to stay current with politics and culture. Students should notice that Hartmire assumes the kind of historic knowledge readers might gain in college or through reading, but also provides plenty of detail and appeals to their shared experiences and emotions as children and/or parents.

3. Some students will be frustrated by Hart-mire's obvious assumption that readers know

the history, but even for those wholly unfa-miliar with Chávez and his fight, the article gives just enough information to ground Hartmire's thoughts on the sacrifices individ-uals often must make for social progress. (Ask students if they have seen any of their peers sporting the iconic Chávez T-shirt popular on many college campuses. Did they know, or maybe wonder, what the image was about?)

4. Students should support their answers with references to the text.

5. The quotation marks indicate irony and ambivalence: although Hartmire knew that his father's absences were for the greater good, he wasn't happy about the situation and didn't really accept it. He still feels ambivalent, although his outlook seems to have matured.

6. The personal elements *are* Hartmire's point. Although the essay is purportedly about Chá-vez and his legacy, Hartmire is really writing to explore the personal sacrifices that social progress sometimes demands of individuals.

Focus on the Pattern

1. Hartmire cites his father's acceptance of a job as the director of the National Farmworker Ministry as the reason for his family's involvement with Chávez's cause. He also suggests that his father took the job because he shared Chávez's vision and had a passion for social justice.

2. Of the many effects he cites, Hartmire emphasizes his own feelings of abandonment and frustration as a child. He does, however, acknowledge that his father's work was valu-able and that Chávez "left the world a better place than he found it" (7).

3. Answers will vary, of course, but encourage students to think beyond those causes and effects specific to Hartmire and his immedi-ate family. They should consider, instead, the larger events that inspired Chávez as well as the lasting influences of his movement.

4. The emphasis is almost wholly on effects.

Focus on Critical Thinking

1. Although Chávez sparked significant im-provements in the 1960s and '70s, students will likely be aware that migrant farm work-ers continue to struggle with exploitation and discrimination (at least two other articles in the same issue of *Newsweek* touched on issues

of immigration and labor in the United States). At the same time, Hartmire's theme—the personal costs of social progress—would likely apply to the participants of any political movement taking place today.

2. Probably not. Even the younger Hartmire acknowledges that his father tried to stay connected with his family. The elder might counter that he did the best he could or that all parents make sacrifices to support their families. He might also argue that the political involvement gave his children more than it took from them—in the form, for example, of heightened awareness or a better world.

3. Ask students to imagine themselves to be members of Hartmire's family. What advantages would they have had with a "normal" bus-driver/plumber father? What would they have missed?

4. Answers will vary, as this is a personal opinion question, but students should understand that the tensions between competing responsibilities are not easily resolved.

Writing Practice

1. Assure students that you are not looking for essays showing the kind of involvement in history that Hartmire's article contains, just a description of a famous person whose life, philosophy, or achievements had an impact on the way their family lived or on their family values.

2. Decide whether you are going to restrict this essay to those famous people who have changed society in broad and tangible ways, or whether students should instead write about personal heroes—family members, community members, church members—who have had a distinct effect on their lives, or whether either approach is acceptable.

3. Students whose schools were not named after an individual can instead write a letter to their school newspaper arguing for a change of name and describing the individual whom they feel the school should honor.

COMPARISON AND CONTRAST

"My Two Lives" (p. 674)

Jhumpa Lahiri, an Indian-American, contrasts her childhood and adult views of her dual identity. As a child, Lahiri felt that her Indian and Ameri-

can identities canceled each other out, making her nothing. As an adult, Lahiri understands the richness of her dual identity and is able to claim both sides of herself. She explains that her writing helped her achieve this transformation.

Focus on Meaning

1. As a child, Lahiri's world of American school, books, music, and television (3) stood in contrast to the world of songs, clothes, and memories from India that her parents inhabited (2). Lahiri's family had immigrated to America more recently than the families of her school friends "so that the ethnic roots they claimed had descended underground whereas mine were still tangled and green" (3).

2. Lahiri went from being unable to fully claim either of her identities to being able to embrace both. She achieved this through writing about the Indian-American experience.

3. Lahiri went from feeling that her life was impoverished by her dual identity to feeling that it was enriched.

4. As a child, Lahiri felt that she was neither entirely Indian nor entirely American. Her American and Indian selves were always "canceling each other out" (3)—because one existed, the other could not. As an adult, she still acknowledges the imperfection of a bicultural identity—she is indeed neither entirely Indian, nor entirely American. But realizing that her Indian and American selves can both exist, she also sees her bicultural identity as a source of richness. Rather than being nothing, she is two things.

5. Lahiri feels American in her grasp of the English language and in her familiarity with American culture, through school, books, music, and television. She feels Indian in her name, in her looks, in her ability to speak Bengali, and most of all through her connection to her parents, who seem to her like anchors to another world.

6. Lahiri feels that she is not entirely Indian. Her strong connection to her parents anchors her to her Indian identity, legitimizing it. She predicts that when they are gone, her feeling of connection to that identity will be weakened.

Focus on Strategy

1. As a young girl, Lahiri felt torn between two cultures, but today she is secure in her cultural identity. Although her identity is still

shifting, she predicts that her American side will soon begin to gain "ascendancy and weight" (7).

2. Immigrants must separate themselves from their homes—a painful process that involves deprivation from the people, places, and culture that they know and love. However, their children are in a position to explore and thrive. While her parents are alive, Lahiri will feel connected to their foreignness; their Indian identity has contributed to her struggle to define herself. When they are gone, she predicts that her American side will "gain ascendancy and weight" (7), and she will be able to experience the "sense of arrival and advantage" that is promised to the children of immigrants (7).

3. Lahiri is writing as a writer. Her struggle to define herself was resolved through writing, and she will continue to explore this struggle in fiction (7).

4. Lahiri's purpose seems to be to explain her two roles to those who identify with only one culture or nationality. She steps back to describe in paragraph 7 "the immigrant's journey" and "the sense of arrival and advantage" that the "subsequent generation" enjoys, making these experiences easy for an outsider to grasp.

Focus on the Pattern

1. Lahiri is comparing her childhood self with her adult self.

2. This is a subject-by-subject comparison.

Sample scratch outline:

Subject A: My childhood self

Point 1: I took pains to hide my Indian side from my American friends.

Point 2: My parents' Indian music, memories, and clothes seemed precious and outdated.

Point 3: I spoke English fluently and entered American culture.

Point 4: My parents told me I would never be American.

Subject B: My adult self

Point 1: Now, I only need to say I am "Indian-American" and people understand.

Point 2: When my husband and I were married in Calcutta, friends were full of enthusiasm for the place.

Point 3: I no longer feel compelled to hide the fact that I speak Bengali.

Point 4: In my fiction, I will continue to explore what it means to be Indian-American.

Focus on Critical Thinking

1. Answers will vary. You might ask students to imagine what loyalty to the old and fluency in the new *looks* like. For instance, have them think of someone they know or someone famous who embodies loyalty to one culture and fluency in another.

2. Answers will vary. Challenge students to examine the evidence in the text to help them consider what Lahiri's parents might value.

3. Answers will vary. Ask students to brainstorm reasons it might be easier to maintain a dual identity as a writer. Then ask them to brainstorm reasons it might be easier to maintain a dual identity in one's personal life.

Writing Practice

1. Students might also consider roles that are dependant not on other people but on activities—for example, artist, basketball player, or cook.

2. Here are some questions that students might consider: How are the experiences of Lahiri, Cofer, and Matthews colored by stereotypes or outside opinions about what they should be, what they should look like, or how they should act? Do Lahiri, Cofer, and Matthews describe turning points in their understanding of their dual identities? How do these turning points differ? What resources do Lahiri, Cofer, and Matthews turn to as they negotiate their complicated identities? How do parents play a role in each of these essays?

"The Transaction" (p. 678)

William Zinsser sets up a point-by-point comparison of two extremes: (1) the person who writes as a hobby, finding composing easy, getting everything right the first time around, waiting for the right inspiration and mood, socializing with others, and enjoying the whole process; and (2) the person who writes for a living, finding writing difficult, working systematically through writer's block, rewriting and rewriting, avoiding symbols and valuing direct communication, working alone, and struggling daily to find the right words. Zinsser's thesis appears in paragraph 13: "For there isn't any 'right' way to do such personal work. There are all kinds of writers and all kinds of methods, and any method that helps you to say what you want to say is the right method for you."

Focus on Meaning

1. Dr. Brock's approach to writing is enthusiastic, unrestrained, and celebratory. Zinsser's approach to writing is sober, regimented, and painstaking.
2. Zinsser believes "the product that any writer has to sell is not the subject being written about, but who he or she is" (15). A successful writer, in Zinsser's view, conveys something about him- or herself, thus creating a relationship with the reader.
3. Zinsser values "aliveness," honesty or transparency, and concision (16).
4. Zinsser portrays Dr. Brock as a free spirit through this detail.

Focus on Strategy

1. Answers will vary. The interview format allows Dr. Brock and Zinsser to speak in their own words. It is an economical way to compare and contrast the two authors. It also places the reader firmly in the context of the event described.
2. Answers will vary. Zinsser seems to want to startle the reader by showing the stark differences between Dr. Brock and himself. This helps the reader see just how different two authors can be, preparing the reader for Zinsser's main point that "any method that helps you to say what you want to say is the right method for you" (13).
3. Answers will vary. The two writers' approaches are *very* different, perhaps even exaggeratedly so. (Surely they must have agreed on *something*.)
4. When Zinsser talks about "the real man or woman behind all the tension" (14), he is referring to what is essential and authentic, not stiff or false, about the writer. According to Zinsser, the "transaction" is the transfer of this authentic self from writer to reader.

Focus on the Pattern

1. By organizing his essay around questions, Zinsser designs his essay as a point-by-point

comparison. Each question—What was it like to be a writer? Was it important to rewrite?—is a "point" addressed by Zinsser and Dr. Brock.
2. The point-by-point comparison in paragraph 13 begins with "Some people write by day . . ." and ends with "they have fiddled endlessly with the first." Here, Zinsser compares imaginary writers on each of several points (time, noise, method, revision style), just as he has compared himself and Dr. Brock on each of several points.

Focus on Critical Thinking

1. Answers will vary. Remind students that rewriting may not mean creating an entirely new draft; it might mean tweaking as one writes.
2. Answers will vary. Challenge students to rephrase this statement before addressing it. Possible rephrasing: "When we write, we create personas that reflect fewer dimensions of ourselves than actually exist."
3. Zinsser's comment in paragraph 12 ("At the end Dr. Brock told me he was enormously interested in my answers—it had never occurred to him that writing could be hard") indicates that Dr. Brock would likely welcome Zinsser's conclusion that "[t]here are all kinds of writers and all kinds of methods" (13).

Writing Practice

1. Other questions students might respond to include the following: How much and what kind of interaction do you have with other students in classes, study groups, and other academic contexts? How do these interactions affect your learning? What resources do you turn to when you need to make sense of difficult concepts?
2. Answers will vary. Alternatively, you might ask students to address this question in the context of some other activities they engage in regularly, such as painting, cooking, welding, gardening, or taking photographs.
3. Answers will vary. You may wish to ask students to reread paragraphs 15–16. Encourage them to consider their deep enthusiasms and the experiences that have changed them.

CLASSIFICATION

"But What Do You Mean?" (p. 681)

In this essay, Deborah Tannen focuses on miscommunication between men and women in the workplace. She divides her subject into seven categories of "conversational rituals." These include apologies (a female conversational ritual) and fighting (a male conversational ritual). (Other conversational rituals, such as criticism and praise, have gender-specific versions.) Tannen writes for an audience of women, cautioning them to learn how to negotiate male conversational styles—or risk being disadvantaged in the workplace.

Focus on Meaning

1. When she says "conversational rituals" (2), Tannen means exchanges in which literal meaning fades into the background, and that carry implied purposes—such as showing that you are taking the other person's feelings into account.
2. Tannen identifies the following categories of conversational rituals: apologies, criticism, thank-yous, fighting, praise, complaints, and jokes.
3. According to Tannen, learning the conversational rituals of the other sex can help us avoid misunderstanding. In particular, women who learn how men interact can avoid putting themselves at a disadvantage in the workplace and can also sidestep frustration and hurt feelings caused by clashing conversational styles.
4. To a man, a woman who apologizes can seem to be putting herself down. Since she appears to be taking the blame for problems, she may be seen as responsible for them. However, if she does *not* apologize, she may be seen by other women as "hard-edged" (9).
5. Tannen identifies two styles of criticism: softened or straight. Softened criticism has the advantage of showing others that you are taking their feelings into account; however, it is more time- and labor-intensive for the speaker. Straight criticism is itself a kind of compliment, since it implies that the criticized person is good enough—and confident enough—not to need reassurance; however, it can be hard to swallow, especially for those not used to it.

6. In many rituals typical of women's conversation, the speaker puts herself in a position of blame or indebtedness because she expects the other person to meet her halfway. For example, if she apologizes, she expects a reciprocal apology so that blame is shared. If she says thank you, she expects a reciprocal thank you so that indebtedness is shared. Thus, the first speaker takes all the blame or indebtedness initially, and then relies on the goodwill of her conversational partner to give half of it back.
7. Most men enjoy verbal sparring, in which they present their strongest case, wait for their conversational partner to call out their weaknesses, and respond to those objections. Many women, by contrast, view verbal sparring as a personal attack and find contentiousness in the workplace distracting or upsetting.
8. Many men do not understand that when women give or expect praise or when they complain, they are merely engaging in a conversational ritual, not asking for a critique or asking for help solving a problem.
9. When it comes to humor, men tend to enjoy teasing one other, while women tend to mock themselves.

Focus on Strategy

1. Tannen's title "But What Do You Mean?" reminds readers of the frustration of conversational confusion. A possible alternate title is "The Communication Gap in the Workplace."
2. *Thesis:* "when men and women interact—especially at work—it's often women who are at the disadvantage" (2).
3. Answers will vary.
4. This essay is aimed at women in the workplace, especially employees. It might appear in a women's magazine.
5. Tannen does support her statement that "There is no 'right' way to talk" (30). For example, in comparing softened or straight criticism, she says, "Those who are used to ways of talking that soften the impact of criticism may find it hard to deal with the right-between-the-eyes style. It has its own logic, however, and neither style is intrinsically better" (12). Throughout, her purpose is to illuminate conversational differences and show

how they disadvantage women; however, she doesn't judge one style as "intrinsically better" than the other.

Focus on the Pattern

1. Tannen's essay is a classification, with subheadings dividing her subject into categories. This organizational structure works well because it allows Tannen to elaborate on each conversational ritual with anecdotes and excerpted conversations. Had she chosen to structure her essay as a comparison and contrast, she probably would have needed to condense these points to provide a more focused comparison. However, her decision to structure her essay as a classification rather than a comparison and contrast also has drawbacks. Tannen risks repeating herself when points recur, and she has fewer opportunities to make overarching conclusions because the focus is on developing each part that makes up the whole rather than directly addressing the whole. (The whole: the differences between men's and women's conversational styles; the parts: the particular areas of miscommunication that Tannen addresses.)

2. Answers will vary. Instead of straightforward, descriptive headings, Tannen might have used interesting but recognizable phrases from each of the ritual conversations she addresses.

3. Answers will vary. You might challenge students to add one or two transitions to evaluate what difference transitions would make.

Focus on Critical Thinking

1. Answers will vary. Male students might have trouble answering this question. Consider inviting them to provide their perspective—for example, by asking "What conversational rituals do I find baffling, frustrating, or counterproductive when I interact with women in the workplace?"

2. Answers will vary. Students may find it helpful to recall examples from their own experience of positive workplace interactions between men and women.

3. Answers will vary. This question lends itself well to group work. Divide students into groups representing the seven categories of miscommunication that Tannen identifies

(apologies, criticism, thank-yous, fighting, praise, complaints, and jokes). Then ask each group to brainstorm examples of miscommunication in the classroom, focusing on the conversational ritual their group represents.

Writing Practice

1. This writing practice would follow well from the group exercise described above (in Focus on Critical Thinking #3).

2. You may wish to discuss with students how Tannen integrates aspects of comparison and contrast into her classification essay, and how they can do the same. (Also see Focus on the Pattern #1).

"The Dog Ate My Disk, and Other Tales of Woe" (p. 689)

Using exaggeration, sarcasm, and other forms of humor, Professor Carolyn Foster Segal presents five categories of student excuses: the family, the best friend, the evils of dorm life, the evils of technology, and the totally bizarre. Her tone is amused, annoyed, and unapologetic.

Focus on Meaning

1. Segal views the claim of a grandparent's death as "the grandmother of all excuses" (2) because she hears it so often.

2. Students' friends always seem to have boyfriend/girlfriend troubles, to be throwing up blood, or to have deaths in their families.

3. According to Segal's excuse-making students, dorm life involves distractions such as partying and loud crying.

4. Technology causes many problems for students. For example, students may be unable to save or print their work, or they may encounter mysterious obstacles when they try to attach files or write to the class newsgroup.

5. One of Segal's students claimed to have been in the hospital with a severed tendon, the result of a freak accident involving her neighbor's chainsaw. On another occasion, the student claimed that she would be in Rome, keeping a date she had made with a man she had met online.

Focus on Strategy

1. With subtle word choices, Segal indicates her audience comprises readers of the *Chronicle*

of Higher Education. For example, Segal writes that she worked as an "adjunct" (5). She does not define the unusual word because her audience of college faculty and administrators will know just what she means. She also writes, "The death of the grandfather/grandmother is, of course, the grandmother of all excuses" (2). The "of course" is intended as a kind of wink to readers familiar with student excuses.

2. Segal's mention of the cartoon on her door tells readers that she has a sense of humor about her subject (she does not take the problem of students' excuses *too* seriously), and that she has made an effort to communicate her position in creative and varied ways, including the cartoon on her door and a "lengthy warning" in her syllabus. Knowing that Segal has given her students fair warning and that she is reacting to their excuses with lightness and humor makes readers more likely to trust Segal and to read on.

3. Answers will vary. The sentence listing Segal's categories may make readers more eager to read on; however, the essay would not be harmed much if the sentence were cut.

4. Answers will vary. Examples of sarcasm include "What heartless teacher would dare to question a student's grief or veracity?" (2) — Segal does question her excuse-making students' grief and veracity, and she does not really consider herself to be heartless — and "This heartwarming concern for others extends beyond the family to friends . . . " (4)— Segal does not believe students are really demonstrating "heartwarming concern for others" but instead are lying to avoid a deadline.

5. Answers will vary. The last detail ("she trusted that I—just this once—would accept late work if the pope wrote a note") is so incredible that it serves as a kind of punchline for Segal's essay.

Focus on the Pattern

1. Segal identifies the following categories of excuses: the family, the best friend, the evils of dorm life, the evils of technology, and the totally bizarre.

2. Segal seems to present her categories of excuses from most to least common. Or at least she *begins* with the most common

excuses — deaths in the family — and *ends* with least common—unique, bizarre excuses. However, it's unclear whether the three middle categories follow this pattern.

3. Answers may vary. Possible smaller categories: medical emergencies and travel emergencies.

Focus on Critical Thinking

1. Answers may vary. Possible additional categories include conflicts with work, conflicts with sports, and accidents and medical emergencies.

2. Answers will vary. Students should assess the validity of the excuses *assuming they were true.*

3. Answers will vary. Remind students to provide *textual evidence* by returning to particular sentences or passages that they reacted to with hunger or offense.

4. Segal sees the humor in her situation, but she is laughing *at,* not *with,* her students. She finds their excuses laughably transparent. Her derisive attitude might be explained by the sheer number of excuses that Segal has heard — "week after week, semester after semester, year after year" (1) — making her increasingly tired and skeptical of her students' stories.

5. Addressing an audience of students, Segal could still use sarcasm to show how little she thinks of students' excuses. However, she might want to lighten her sarcasm by mentioning some laudable student behaviors. She might at least acknowledge that not all excuses are invented and that many students do turn their work in on time.

Writing Practice

1. You may wish to use this writing practice as an opportunity to address the use of humor. How does sarcasm differ from irony or satire? Can students find examples in Segal's writing of understatement or exaggeration? Consider providing examples of each of these types of humor to help students identify them in their reading and use them in their writing.

2. Here are several possible types of unacceptable behavior by a teacher: favoritism that affects grading, a tendency to lose student work or return it very late, comments that discourage students, and sexism or racism.

3. You may use this writing practice as an opportunity to present formatting guidelines for different types of letters.

DEFINITION

"The Wife-Beater" (p. 693)

In this essay, Gayle Rosenwald Smith defines *wife-beater*—the popular ribbed undershirt—using a formal definition as well as exemplification, description, and other patterns of development. In doing so, she argues that the name *wife-beater* is disturbing and even dangerous because it teaches that spousal abuse is acceptable.

Focus on Meaning

1. According to Smith, everyone wears wife-beaters.
2. Smith most objects to the name of the shirts.
3. Smith is concerned that our fashion choices signal a return to male dominance, especially male physical control over women.
4. Smith believes the "worst difficulty" (15) with the shirt's name is that it teaches young people a dangerous lesson: that violent men are sexy.
5. Smith suggests that the shirt's name be changed, perhaps to something "connoting flattery—not violence" (12). She does not suggest that people should stop wearing wife-beaters.

Focus on Strategy

1. Answers will vary. The opening sentence is short and startling—it piques the reader's attention. If everyone wears wife-beaters, readers want to know why. What about these shirts makes them so universally attractive? This opening strategy also establishes the importance of Smith's topic: the shirts and their name affect not just a segment of the population but "everyone."
2. Answers will vary. Smith's use of informal language may make her message more palatable, especially to young readers. If her language were more formal, readers might consider her old-fashioned or out of touch—and therefore not worth listening to.
3. Smith's purpose is to argue that the name *wife-beater* is disturbing—even dangerous, if

the name teaches people to associate manliness with violence. She does not express this purpose as a thesis statement.
4. Answers will vary. Women may respond with more sensitivity to the name *wife-beater*. As Smith argues, the name implies an acceptance of violence toward women. Women more than men are in a position to worry about such acceptance translating to real violence.
5. Answers will vary. Smith seems especially concerned about the views of people under twenty-five, who "do not seem to be disturbed by the name" (5) and whose continued use of it could teach "the wrong thing about men" (15). She seems to worry that readers under twenty-five may not be receptive to her points: "Wearers under 25 may not want to hear this, but here it is" (13).
6. Possible conclusion rewrite: If the name *wife-beater* gives young people the idea that violent men are sexy—if the name places a stamp of approval on male physical control over women—it ought not to be used, especially for a piece of clothing so universally worn.

Focus on the Pattern

1. Smith presents a formal definition of *wife-beater* in paragraph 7.
2. In paragraphs 8–10, Smith supplies information about the origin of *wife-beater* to show that the name is not an empty label but in fact references spousal abuse.
3. Patterns of development used in this essay include *exemplification* in paragraphs 1 (exemplifying the popularity of *wife-beaters*) and 13 (exemplifying the seriousness of spousal abuse); *description* in paragraph 4 (describing *wife-beaters*); *comparison and contrast* in paragraph 11 (comparing fashion trends); and *cause and effect* in paragraph 8 (showing the origin of the term *wife-beater*).

Focus on Critical Thinking

1. Answers will vary. Smith seems to think that readers under twenty-five will consider her concern about the term *wife-beaters* out of proportion to the threat the name actually poses. Challenge students to put themselves in Smith's shoes. She knows that readers under twenty-five will think that her distress is over-

the-top, and yet she has written an impassioned essay anyway. Can students see where Smith's passion comes from? Does paragraph 13 help them understand her perspective?

2. Answers will vary. Real alternative terms: A-shirt, ribbed tank, singlet.
3. Answers will vary. Some items of clothing are viewed negatively because of what they represent—for example, baggy pants may represent gang culture. Other items of clothing are viewed negatively because of features of the clothing itself—tight or skimpy clothing, for instance, may reveal a woman's curves or skin.
4. Answers will vary. A possible characterization: The name *wife-beater* teaches people to accept male dominance through physical control, which makes spousal abuse more likely.

Writing Practice

1. Students can get a good start on this writing practice by brainstorming answers to the following questions: What does the article of clothing look like? Who wears the article of clothing? What associations does the article of clothing have for its wearers? What impression does the article of clothing make on others?
2. Make sure students understand that they should define a *type* of person, not a particular person.

"Triskaidekaphobia" (p. 696)

In this entertaining essay, Paul Hoffman defines *triskaidekaphobia,* fear of the number 13. He focuses on the origins of triskaidekaphobia and on historical examples of the superstition.

Focus on Meaning

1. Triskaidekaphobia is fear of the number 13.
2. Hoffman cites the following evidence of triskaidekaphobia: high-rises that skip the number 13 when labeling their floors; hospitals that skip the number 13 when labeling their rooms; the popularity of the movie *Friday the 13th*; and newspaper tabloid stories about the number 13, such as those about the thirteenth *Apollo* mission.
3. Napoleon, J. Paul Getty, Herbert Hoover, and Franklin Delano Roosevelt suffered from triskaidekaphobia.

4. Hoffman thinks that triskaidekaphobia originated with ancient Pythagorean numerology, in which the number 12 "has always represented completeness," whereas the number 13 "lies just beyond completeness and, hence, is restless to the point of being evil" (5).
5. The purpose of the Thirteen Club was to dispel fear of the number 13. The club began with a group of 13 New Yorkers and soon grew to 1,300 members around the world. The club has tried to counter triskaidekaphobia by holding gatherings that snub superstition and by collecting and promoting lucky stories about the number 13. They have had successes, such as convincing Maria Cristina, queen regent of Spain, to name her son Alfonso XIII. But people still fear the number 13.

Focus on Strategy

1. *Possible thesis:* Triskaidekaphobia, or fear of the number 13, is an ancient affliction that persists today; efforts to vindicate the number 13 have not been entirely successful.
2. Hoffman seems to be both critical of and sympathetic to triskaidekaphobes. He claims to be both "hardly impressed by the historical evidence" and "distressed by the mathematical evidence" in favor of 13's wickedness (15).
3. Answers will vary. Hoffman's historical examples of triskaidekaphobia include newspaper tabloids blaming the number 13 for the aborted *Apollo* mission of April 1970 (2); FDR avoiding dinner parties of 13 and train travel on the 13th (4); members of the Thirteen Club failing to show up, out of fear, for a London branch dinner defying superstition of the number 13 (11); a letter written to the Thirteen Club, in which the author told of his "luck" in escaping the curse of the number 13 by not believing in it (12); the registration of Princess Margaret, in 1930, as birth number 14, although she was really number 13 (13); the renaming of a train platform from 13 to 12a for Queen Elizabeth (13); and a Columbia University study in which 10 percent of subjects thought it was unlucky to have anything to do with the number 13 (14). These historical examples seem merely to document fear of the number 13, not to justify it, although several of the examples, such

as the *Apollo* mission and the letter about escaping the curse of 13, are compelling anecdotes that make triskaidekaphobia at least understandable.

4. Answers will vary. Hoffman's mention of the cost of triskaidekaphobia to American businesses provides evidence of the phenomenon's reach. This information suggests that triskaidekaphobia is not just real but also widespread and consequential. In this essay, Hoffman is merely establishing the existence, extent, and fixedness of triskaidekaphobia, making an argument that it is bad and should be extinguished. For this purpose, just a mention of the cost of triskaidekaphobia is enough.

5. Hoffman seems to expect most readers to be at least sympathetic to triskaidekaphobes, if they are not triskaidekaphobes themselves. In discussing historical triskaidekaphobes, Hoffman's tone is amused, especially at the intensity of their fear and the lengths to which they will go to avoid the number 13, but he is not scornful. He calls triskaidekaphobia "an affliction" (3) — indicating that he does not consider it justified — and he says he is "hardly impressed by the historical evidence in favor of 13's wickedness" (15). On the other hand, he understands that many people suffer from triskaidekaphobia, and even he is "distressed by the mathematical evidence" implicating the number 13 (15).

Focus on the Pattern

1. In addition to exemplification, Hoffman uses the following patterns of development: *narration* in paragraphs 7–8 (narrating the story of the original Thirteen Club) and paragraphs 10–11 (narrating the story of the London branch of the Thirteen Club); *description* in paragraph 10 (describing the London branch dinner); and *cause and effect* in paragraph 5 (indicating one possible cause of triskaidekaphobia, ancient numerology).

2. *Sample one-sentence definition:* Triskaidekaphobia is fear of the number 13. *Sample one-paragraph definition:* Triskaidekaphobia, fear of the number 13, is an old superstition that persists today. It has roots in ancient numerology, in which 13 was thought to be unstable because it is one more than 12, a number that represents completeness (think

of the 12 months or the 12 zodiac signs). Even ancient mythology and biblical stories reflect triskaidekaphobia: Jesus was crucified after he and his twelve disciples — thirteen altogether — dined together; and in Nordic mythology, a demon caused the death of the god of light by adding one to their dinner party of 12. Although efforts have been made to dispel triskaidekaphobia, the fear of 13 remains. Many hospitals and hotels avoid rooms and floors labeled 13, and some people still refuse to entangle themselves with the dangerous number.

3. Answer will vary. Paragraphs 7–13 tell about the Thirteen Club, which has tried to vindicate the number 13. These paragraphs give Hoffman more opportunities to provide examples of triskaidekaphobia. They also show how entrenched triskaidekaphobia is: even organized efforts to dispel fear of the number 13 have yielded only lukewarm success.

Focus on Critical Thinking

1. Answers will vary. *Possible answer:* Perhaps people in modern society are superstitious about the number 13 because people have historically been superstitious about the number 13. And since our modern-day superstition is rooted in past superstition, it makes sense to focus on historical background here.

2. Answers will vary. You may wish to point out to students that, even though Hoffman's discussion of the Thirteen Club is lengthy, he uses it as a starting point for additional, related examples of triskaidekaphobia. Challenge students to identify where Hoffman integrates examples throughout paragraphs 7–13.

3. Answers will vary. Other kinds of information Hoffman might have offered include fear of other numbers in other cultures (e.g., fear of the number 4 in China, Korea, and Japan) and additional modern examples of triskaidekaphobia (e.g., software companies avoiding labeling their new software versions with the number 13).

Writing Practice

1. Phobias that students might define include *acrophobia*, fear of heights; *glossophobia*, fear of public speaking; *nomophobia*, fear of being out of cell phone contact; and *musophobia*,

fear of mice and rats. These and many other phobias are listed at **http://en.wikipedia.org/wiki/List_of_phobias**.

2. Other examples include suffering bad luck if a black cat crosses your path, if you walk under a ladder, or if you kill a spider in the house, and avoiding bad luck if you cross your fingers.

ARGUMENT

"Don't Hang Up, That's My Mom Calling" (p. 702)

Bobbi Buchanan humanizes the "anonymous voice on the other end of the line" (1) by introducing readers to her mother, who, at seventy-one, finds herself working as a telemarketer. In paragraph 3 the writer gives some demographic information about the "more than six million . . . Americans who work in the industry." She disagrees with the exemption to the do-not-call list given to politicians and others, arguing that the list will eventually lead to increased costs for consumers. She asks that readers respond to telemarketers politely and concludes by describing her mother.

Focus on Meaning

1. According to Buchanan, the telemarketing workforce is mostly women, mostly minorities, and almost entirely non-college graduates. In addition, a quarter are single mothers and almost a third are previous recipients of welfare. Thus, the telemarketing workforce is comprised of groups who are more likely to face obstacles such as discrimination (women and minorities); lack of support (single mothers); poverty (welfare recipients); and low job flexibility, security, and pay (non-college grads). Thus, as a group, telemarketers are "used to hardship" (3).

2. It is easier for big businesses than for small businesses to resort to more expensive kinds of advertising than sales calls.

3. As an unskilled, elderly, and physically limited worker, telemarketing was a way for Buchanan's mother to supplement her Social Security income after her husband's death ended his pension benefits. Buchanan's mother worries that she will lose her job and will be unable to find another.

4. Buchanan wants readers to imagine "a hard-working, first-generation American; the daughter of a Pittsburgh steelworker; a survivor of the Great Depression; the widow of a World War II veteran; a mother of seven, grandmother of eight, great-grandmother of three" (7).

Focus on Strategy

1. In paragraph 1, Buchanan divides Americans into two main camps: some consider telemarketers pests, nuisances, and invaders of privacy; others view them as anonymous voices. In paragraph 6, she addresses readers directly, advising them to "breathe deeply and take a silent oath to be polite" before picking up the phone. Thus, Buchanan implies that she believes readers will fall into the categories she established in the first paragraph: they will view telemarketers either as pests or as anonymous voices who do not deserve politeness, and they will thus need to make a conscious effort to temper their annoyance and restrain their rudeness.

2. Paragraph 1 prepares readers for the thesis by introducing Buchanan's mother— LaVerne—and by showing what LaVerne is up against: people who view her either as a pest or as an anonymous voice.

3. To increase readers' sympathy for telemarketers, Buchanan presents statistics about the demographics of the telemarketing workforce. These statistics reveal that telemarketers come from some of the most disadvantaged groups in America but are nevertheless choosing to work. As struggling workers, they personify the "great American way" that Buchanan refers to in her thesis (1).

4. Buchanan includes this information to increase readers' sympathy for her mother, who is apparently not just hard-working but also long-suffering, patiently enduring wrongs and difficulties.

5. Answers will vary. Buchanan hopes to get readers to respond humanely to telemarketers.

Focus on the Pattern

1. Buchanan makes the following arguments: *First,* LaVerne is a generous, patient, and hardworking person—a woman who is a "pillar of strength" (2) to the seven children she stayed home to raise, and who is patient and

hard to discourage at her part-time telemarketing job. *For these qualities, she deserves at least politeness. Second,* small businesses and struggling workers like LaVerne suffer when Americans put themselves on the do-not-call list. *Americans should continue to be open to telemarketing.*

2. In paragraph 4, Buchanan addresses the counterargument that telemarketers are annoying and intrusive. In response, she points out that when American consumers block telemarketing, they force companies to spend more money on alternative advertising, the cost of which is passed on to consumers. In other words, telemarketing may mean intrusive calls at dinner, but blocking telemarketing means something worse—the increased cost of consumer goods.

3. Patterns of development used in this essay include *exemplification* in paragraphs 2 (exemplifying why LaVerne is a "pillar of strength") and 5 (exemplifying LaVerne's patience); *classification* in paragraph 1 (classifying people into those who view LaVerne as a pest, those who view her as an anonymous voice, and those who think she personifies the American way); *comparison and contrast* and *cause and effect* in paragraph 4 (comparing the effects of the do-not-call list on big versus small businesses); *process* in paragraph 6 (describing how to politely handle a telemarketing call); and *description* in paragraph 7 (describing LaVerne).

Focus on Critical Thinking

1. Answers will vary. *Possible answer:* Through glimpses of her mother's personality and background and through statistics about the demographics of the telemarketing workforce, Buchanan successfully humanizes telemarketers. However, she does not adequately address possible counterarguments. For example, she argues that when Americans say no to telemarketing, they say yes to more costly forms of advertising—for which they will bear the costs—and they also harm small businesses that can't afford these more expensive options. However, she does not adequately support this assertion. Why can't small businesses replace telemarketing with low-cost Google AdWords, for example? Similarly, Buchanan writes that her mother wor-

ries that she will not be able to find another job, but she does not substantiate this worry. Is telemarketing really one of the only jobs available to unskilled, physically limited workers?

2. Answers will vary. You might wish to encourage students to think about people who act as pillars of strength for their own families or communities. Ask students to identify the characteristics of these people. Does LaVerne share these characteristics?

3. Answers will vary. Point students to paragraphs 1, 2, 5, and 7.

Writing Practice

1. To begin this assignment, have students ask themselves questions like these: "What criticisms did my friends and family make?" "What reasons did they give for their criticisms?" "Why did I accept the job?" "How did the job meet or fail my expectations?"

2. Remind students that they can support their topic sentence with either one main reason and several sentences of detailed explanation, or several supporting reasons presented in order of increasing importance.

"For Most People, College Is a Waste of Time" (p. 704)

Charles Murray argues for a system of certification tests to replace today's all-purpose bachelor degree. He believes that such a system would make educational goals more focused and the means of attaining them more flexible, thus widening opportunity and removing unfair advantage.

Focus on Meaning

1. To an employer, a bachelor's degree at least guarantees "a certain amount of intellectual ability and perseverance" (5) in a job applicant—the amount needed to pass four years of college courses. But the catchall BA does not reflect the applicant's depth or area of knowledge. An applicant's college experience might have given him or her a deep grasp of knowledge relevant to the job or, equally, a vague familiarity with knowledge irrelevant to the job.

2. The CPA exam is a good model for the certification tests that Murray advocates because

it tests the depth of a job applicant's relevant knowledge.

3. Murray identifies two major advantages of certification tests. First, they would increase educational opportunity by removing the stigma of nontraditional (e.g., online) colleges and the "halo effect" of highly regarded (e.g., Ivy League) colleges; they would do this by focusing attention away from the BA's amorphous symbol of achievement and toward real measures of competency. Second, they would put intellectual ability on a more equal footing with other sorts of abilities, such as those of cooking and welding. Murray does not identify any disadvantages of certification tests that are not shared by the BA, although he does say that certification tests would not remove "the problems associated with differences in intellectual ability" that exist with the BA (10). Note that Murray actually regards the "disadvantage" in paragraph 13 as an advantage.

4. Murray means that a competency gained in college would not be privileged over a competency gained outside of college. He believes this would be good because it would "create a society in which it's what you know that makes the difference," and such a society would be fairer.

5. Murray means that, because of our reverence for the BA, young people who choose not to go to college in favor of learning a skill such as cooking or welding are seen as being in a second tier, inferior to the academic one.

Focus on Strategy

1. Murray seems to think that readers will be receptive to his argument. In paragraphs 1–3, he asks the reader to imagine a scenario in which he or she, starting from scratch, was reviewing a proposal for a system of postsecondary education like the one we have today. Murray expresses his confidence that the reader would consider such a proposal—a mirror of our current system—to be cruel. Murray seems to think that once he helps readers get some objective distance from the current system, they will share his view that it is insane.

2. In his thesis in paragraph 6, Murray proposes a solution. The previous paragraphs are devoted to establishing the problem and to artfully (especially through the imagined sce-

nario in paragraphs 1–3) bringing the reader around to Murray's perspective on it.

3. The main points that Murray makes to support his thesis that young people entering the job market should have a certification, not a degree, are as follows: certification tests can reveal authentic competence (7); would be appropriate replacements for most college majors (8); would strengthen, not undermine, traditional liberal-arts education (9); would remove obstacles to educational opportunity such as residence and expensive tuition (11); could be established easily, such as through coordination between a test creator and a major employer (15); and would put academic mastery on an equal footing with skills mastery (17).

4. Answers will vary. *Evidence that certification tests can reveal authentic competence:* the CPA exam. *Evidence that certification tests would be appropriate replacements for most college majors:* the applicability of CPA-like exams to two-thirds or more of college majors. *Evidence that certification tests would strengthen traditional liberal-arts education:* speculation, but no specific evidence. *Evidence that certification tests would remove obstacles to educational opportunity:* the elimination of requirements like residence, tuition, and four years of schooling. *Evidence that certification tests could be established easily:* the existence of a tipping-point effect and of powerful companies that could create that effect. *Evidence that certification tests would put academic mastery on a equal footing with skills mastery:* no specific evidence.

5. Murray mentions the following objections: certification tests might undermine the incentives to get a traditional liberal-arts education (9); certification tests will not get rid of the problems associated with differences in intellectual ability (10); and technical barriers might stand in the way of establishing a system of certification tests (14). Other possible objections that Murray does not mention include the following: in a system of certification tests, people would not be exposed to subjects like poetry, which are enriching but without practical relevance; people would need to decide on their career path before they had a chance to explore a range of possibilities.

6. In his last paragraphs, Murray emphasizes the idea that certification tests would put academic mastery on an equal footing with skills mastery. Students may notice that this is a different (although related) idea than the one Murray has developed throughout his essay: that certification tests would remove obstacles to educational opportunity.

Focus on the Pattern

1. Murray's essay is characterized by strong topic sentences that unify the paragraphs and help readers follow the discussion as they move from one paragraph to another.
2. Murray uses few transitions. Instead, he relies on the strength of his topic sentences and the intuitiveness of his logic to move readers through his argument.

Focus on Critical Thinking

1. Answers will vary. In paragraphs 14–15, Murray addresses the objection that his plan is impractical. Do students find Murray's response to this objection convincing? If not, what issues do they think Murray has failed to address?
2. Answers will vary. Other groups of students that might be hurt include those who enter college without firm career goals, who would benefit from the opportunity to discover new subject matters and who are poor test-takers, whose competency would be more accurately measured in traditional college courses (e.g., through essays, in-class discussion, or group work).
3. Answers will vary. Ask students to imagine their educational career under a system of certification tests. Would they still be motivated to pursue a liberal-arts education? Why or why not?

Writing Practice

1. Remind students that even email messages should contain correct grammar, punctuation, and capitalization.
2. Students may instead view college from the perspective of the culture. For example, perhaps the purpose of a liberal-arts education system is to create a certain kind of society.

"Impounded Fathers" (p. 708)

This editorial by Edwidge Danticat appeared in the *New York Times* on Father's Day 2007. It uses anecdotes to argue that the United States should reconsider how it handles issues of immigration.

Focus on Meaning

1. Danticat takes the opportunity to commemorate fathers who are absent due to America's immigration policies.
2. The predicament of other fathers is "poignant" for Danticat because her own father died in May 2005.
3. The fathers in these paragraphs are all stressed or harmed by the actions of the Department of Homeland Security.
4. The Department of Homeland Security deports hard-working men, breaking up their families. In some cases, these men die.
5. Answers will vary. Danticat is referring to the value that Americans place on family cohesiveness.

Focus on Strategy

1. Danticat relies almost entirely on anecdotes to carry her argument. She seems to believe that these stories, almost by themselves, will be powerful enough to sway readers to share her perspective. She thus appears to think that readers will be receptive to her ideas.
2. Answers will vary. Danticat gets readers to sympathize with noncriminal immigrants by telling of several fathers who are hardworking, blameless, and important to their families.
3. Answers will vary. Danticat introduces arguments against her position in paragraph 7 when she describes "the goals of the operation."
4. So that readers can understand the powerful impact the problem has on individuals, Danticat places her thesis *after* the many examples of children losing their parents. The thesis appears in paragraph 8: "So while politicians debate the finer points of immigration reform, the Department of Homeland Security is already carrying out its own. Unfortunately, these actions can not only plunge families into financial decline, but sever them forever."
5. Answers will vary. Danticat appeals to emotion in paragraphs 1–6, 8–9, and 11. She appeals to logic in paragraphs 7 and 10.

Focus on the Pattern

1. Danticat's argument is an inductive one because it moves from the specific to the general.
2. Answers will vary. Danticat presents her points in the following order: Many families are damaged by the immigration project titled Operation Return to Sender. Although one of the goals of the project is to catch and deport criminals, many immigrants without criminal records are deported. The fates of the American-born children of these men should be taken into account. Instead, these children may feel abandoned by both their parents and their country.

Focus on Critical Thinking

1. Answers will hinge on whether students believe that barriers to legal immigration in the United States are too restrictive. Are immigrants who have not passed the difficult test of legality doing something unethical, damaging, or inappropriate enough to merit prohibition by law?
2. Answers will vary. How does consideration for the interests of American-born children of immigrants compare to that of American-born spouses of immigrants?
3. Answers will vary. Students may cite fear of terrorism or fear of immigrants' taking American jobs.
4. Answers will vary.

Writing Practice

1. Have students search the Internet for information about the Department of Homeland Security that supports or refutes Danticat's argument about its actions. Then have students gather in groups to compare their findings and to decide whether they agree with Danticat or with the Department of Homeland Security.
2. Again, you might reflect that students reflect how consideration for the interests of American-born children of immigrants compares with that of American-born spouses of immigrants.

Appendixes

Appendix A provides time-tested strategies to help students make their college experiences more productive and less stressful. It contains practical advice on everything from orienting oneself to the college environment and classroom to what constitutes good study habits to evaluating Web sites. Appendix B provides a succinct overview of the steps involved in academic research, including a sample of a student research paper formatted in MLA style.

Appendix A: Strategies for College Success

This chapter helps students focus on essentials for academic success: preparing early, getting through the first week efficiently, establishing effective day-to-day practices, taking good notes, keeping on top of homework, doing well on exams, practicing effective time management, and using the Internet wisely. Although all students will profit from reading, thinking about, and discussing these topics, first-time college students will find the strategies presented particularly valuable. It is reassuring to learn that one's worries and fears are not unique and that practical strategies exist to deal with actual and potential problems.

Assign this chapter as reading homework early in the semester. Any of the strategies suggested can then provide a focus for small-group or class discussions, as well as for writing assignments and journal entries.

At the end of the semester, consider asking students to reread the chapter and write about what they have since learned, which problems they solved successfully, and which ones they wish, in retrospect, they had approached differently. Another option for an end-of-term assignment is having students write a letter to the textbook's authors suggesting additional information to include in this chapter for the next edition.

Orientation Strategies. Ask students to add to the list of orientation strategies. What did they do prior to starting class that was useful? Looking back, what else do they wish they had done?

First-Week Strategies. Spend some time discussing the kind of notebook organization that you recommend for your class. Explain why, and show samples. Remind students that it will be much easier to get organized in the beginning than to try and retrofit a notebook halfway through the semester so that it accommodates all the loose papers they've been stuffing into it over the past few months.

Day-to-Day Strategies. Tell students where they can get any additional computer instruction or practice needed, such as general student labs or a learning resource center. If your students are of nontraditional age, you may want to spend some extra time talking about the fact that adults typically have problems asking for help (see the "Asking for Help" box) because they feel they should be giving rather than receiving assistance at this point in life. Reassure them that experts (see Cyril O. Houle's "Seven Keys to Effective Learning," p. 157 of this manual) view the ability to ask for help as a key to learning, a sign of strength rather than of weakness.

Time-Management Strategies. Using time effectively is the key to success in all the strategies introduced in this section; help your students take control. Be sure to highlight tip 4, "Learn to enjoy downtime"; worried students often focus only on how to find time for studying, so it is important to remind them that even the tightest schedule must include some relaxation time, or their working hours will become unproductive.

Note-Taking Strategies. Ask students to share any good tips for note-taking that they have developed through past practice or perhaps from study-skills workshops they have attended. One tip is to divide notebook pages as follows:

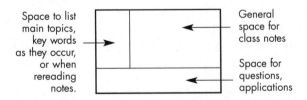

Space to list main topics, key words as they occur, or when rereading notes.

General space for class notes

Space for questions, applications

Homework Strategies. Remind students that one of the biggest wastes of time is spending hours on the wrong assignment, so it is important for them to clarify assignment directions, write them down completely, and review them with the instructor before leaving class,

if necessary. Encourage study group formation, but point out that groups must clarify their roles and purposes or they become bull sessions rather than time-saving learning opportunities. If your students are commuters who have difficulty being in the same place at the same time other than during class hours, you may want to encourage them to start an online study group.

Exam-Taking Strategies. Even if you discuss this section at the beginning of the semester, it is important to review the strategies prior to midterms and again before finals. Consider giving a practice exam to provide a context within which the students can apply and then analyze and discuss the suggested strategies.

Appendix B: Using Research in Your Writing

Even if you do not teach research papers, you may want to use sections of this chapter, especially the discussion on summarizing versus plagiarizing (sections 3 and 4) and advice on making parenthetical references in texts (section 8). Whether or not your syllabus requires essays that contain references, be sure students are aware of the helpful examples for documenting sources because they are likely to be able to use these in future classes. Make it clear, though, that MLA guidelines are just one of several common sets of research instructions and that other instructors may require different formats.

Detailed instructions that break down the research process into separate steps may be helpful for some students:

RESEARCH STRATEGIES

- Choose a Topic
  —Is your topic too broad or too narrow?
  —Is there enough factual information on the topic?
  —Are you interested in this topic?
  —Has your topic been approved by the instructor?

- Locate Sources
  —Break down your research by each type of source you will find, including
     Internet sources
     reference books

      magazines/journals
      newspapers
      books
      experts

- Prepare Bibliography Cards
  —Prepare a separate card for each source you find. Include on each card
    the title of the piece
    where you found it
    the author's name
    page numbers
  —Number each card in the right-hand corner, and circle the number for easy identification.

- Prepare Note Cards
  —Use large note cards, and number these so that they correspond with the right bibliography card.
  —Feel free to use more than one note card for each source, but be sure to number them.

—All notes should be in your handwriting; each quote needs to be *exact* and should be followed by the page number.
—Write legibly, or type your note cards with a typewriter.

- Prepare a Paper Outline
  —Organize this by "Introduction," "Parts of Body," and "Conclusion."
    Title
       I. Roman numerals for topics
         A. Capital letters for subtopics
           1. Arabic numerals for details
             a. small letters for subdetails
  —As you become more acquainted with your topic, revise your outline with more specific information.

- Write the Paper
  —Organize your note cards so that they are in the order of your outline.
  —Follow your note cards as you draft.

PART FOUR
Additional Resources

Writing History Questionnaire

DIRECTIONS: Jot down your answers to the following questions. Don't worry about shaping your ideas into sentences or paragraphs. Just note as much specific detail as possible. You won't have to turn this worksheet in. The information will be used for in-class discussion.

1. **What is your earliest memory of writing?**

2. **What is your best memory connected with writing?**

3. **What is your worst memory connected with writing?**

4. **What different kinds of writing have you done throughout your life?**

5. **What are your biggest concerns as a writer?**

6. **What are your strengths as a writer?**

7. **What do you hope to accomplish in this course?**

Essay Directions for Writing History Assignment

ESSAY 1:   **Due:**

DIRECTIONS: Describe your previous experiences as a writer, from childhood to the present, in a brief writer's autobiography. Include good and bad memories, strengths and weaknesses you've developed, and your main concerns/hopes for this class. Your reading audience will be your classmates and instructor.

PLANNING SUGGESTIONS: Look back over your Writing History Questionnaire and any notes you have from the group discussion of it. Jot down any new ideas that you may have had since that discussion. You might also talk over your general ideas with someone else: for instance, tell a friend what you are going to write about and why. Some writers find it useful to organize ideas in their mind this way before putting them down on paper.

ORGANIZING/DRAFTING SUGGESTIONS: A typical essay has several paragraphs in the main body, along with a brief introduction and conclusion. One way to organize and prioritize ideas for an essay is to do some brainstorming or clustering. On a piece of paper, write the following headings: <u>writing memories from school, work, and home</u>; <u>writing strengths and weaknesses</u>; and <u>concerns and goals</u>. Then, underneath each heading, list all the points you can think of, and circle or highlight the three or four most interesting ones for each topic. You then simply turn those highlighted points into sentences, arrange each group of sentences in a paragraph, and add an introductory paragraph that presents your overall attitudes about writing and a closing paragraph that discusses goals for this class. *Presto*—you'll have an interesting and well-organized essay!

REVISING/EDITING SUGGESTIONS: Review Chapter 12, sections H and I, in *Focus on Writing*. Use these checklists to help you improve your first draft. Try to allow some time to pass between writing your first draft and starting to revise it so that you will be able to see the essay more objectively.

PROOFREADING SUGGESTIONS: After you are satisfied that you have made all the necessary revisions, proofread your essay carefully for spelling, grammar, punctuation, and so on. It often helps to read your essay out loud from the screen. This slows down your eye and allows your ear to catch errors that you might otherwise miss.

Note: Don't worry about saying the wrong thing or not having anything to write about. You're an expert on this topic—no one can give a better description of your writing history than you!

Sample Policy on Plagiarism

Plagiarism is taking another person's words or thoughts and pretending they are your own. Whether intentional or accidental, plagiarism is an academic crime and will result in a failing grade for the paper and perhaps for the course.

Plagiarism may result from lack of research skills, lack of attention, or forgetfulness, as well as from a deliberate attempt to mislead the reader. The reader cannot know what you intended and cannot, therefore, distinguish between deliberate and accidental plagiarism.

Examples of plagiarism include:

- using another person's words without putting quotation marks around those words and without citing their source
- describing another person's ideas in your own words without mentioning that person's name
- following another person's model or structure for your paper without giving that person proper credit
- giving your rough draft to another person to revise and edit

Please note that this does *not* mean that you should avoid discussing your assignments with anyone. Writing is a social act. You are in school to gather information from as many sources as possible, and you should read widely and discuss things with your colleagues, your family, and others. However, once ideas have been gathered, it is *you* who should structure and present them in your own words, giving credit where it is due. If others critique rough drafts of your assignments, please be sure that their help is limited to pointing out places where additional facts would strengthen your argument, passages that need to be clarified, errors in fact or reasoning, or problems with style and mechanics. Other people should just *suggest* changes, not *make* those changes themselves, because doing so would take an important learning opportunity away from you.

Three Sample Essays for Peer Response

These three student essays were written in response to the following directions:

Read Cyril Houle's article titled "Seven Keys to Effective Learning." Then write a brief essay in which you explain which of the seven keys Houle presents is most important to you and why, supporting your choice with examples from personal experience. Write to an audience of college students similar to those in this class (Cyril Houle's article starts on p. 157).

Seven Keys to Learning: Example 1

I selected key Number 5. I feel this particular key describes the learning methods that will be important to me. Some of the experiences, I had encountered upon enrolling in this program was explained in this key.

Seeking help and support from classmates, educators, and groups, I feel, will enhance my chances for the successful completion of college.

My present college experiences, have been hectic, strange and new. Even with these dynamics, I plan for a possitive and rewarding experience. To achieve this goal. I will remain open minded and keep a positive attitude about myself, others and his new environment.

I am making plans to change my place of employment to acommodate this new college experience. With this employment change comes the need to relearn budgeting and thrift skills. This is one of the lifestyle changes I have choosen to complete my learning experience at school.

Note: Students critiquing this essay usually point out its grammar errors, spelling problems, lack of audience awareness—not saying what the "key" was, where it came from, etc.—underdeveloped paragraphs, and lack of specific examples.

Seven Keys to Learning: Example 2

As an adult student, I found the article, "Seven Keys to Effective Learning," enlightening and encouraging.

Key number six, "Learning Beyond the Point Necessary for Immediate Recall," promises to be the most helpful to me while at school as well as in my career. In key six Professor Houle tells us that you can commit things to memory by just repeating to ourselves what it is that we want to remember. Whether or not we continue to remember the information depends on how important it is to you. If we want to remember something permanently, it is suggested we use a technique called over-learning, that is to continue to review or practice what it is that you have learned until there is no chance of it being forgotten.

The most effective way for me to develop my recall is to allow the process to become a habit. I can begin with reviewing new material, whether school or job related, at least 3 times within the 1st week I receive it and twice in the 2nd week and again in the 3rd week if necessary.

The methods suggested in "Key Number Six' may seem time consuming and even boring, however, the benefits gained are worth the effort.

Note: Students critiquing this essay might see as strengths the clear opening sentence, inclusion of specific examples, adequate explanation of the key, and a good general concluding statement. They might point out weaknesses in style, such as the pronoun use in paragraph 2, the lack of explanation of why the technique was important to the writer, and the one-sentence opening and closing.

Seven Keys to Learning: Example 3

In "Seven Keys to Effective Learning," Cyril Houle presents a valuable guide to all adult learners. Within all seven keys, I found something useful for my studies. However, the keys that best represent my station in learning are thinking positively and setting realistic goals. These two keys are interrelated and need to be considered together. First, positive thinking sets the mind for accomplishing one's goals. It eliminates the element of fear that blocks an adult learner's abilities to comprehend. Second, it is important to set realistic tools and standards that emphasize the accomplishment. Ultimately, adult learners need to pace themselves in order to experience the tangible feeling of achievement without feeling overwhelmed. These two keys together generate motivation.

It is reassuring to know that studies have been conducted that suggest that adult learners tend to be better students than young people. According to Houle, adult learners have the capacity to learn as well as young people when effort is invested. Learning is the result of active participation and effort with the subject matter to acquire such knowledge. However, it is important to be in the right frame of mind and to set goals that are obtainable. In the past, I was always frustrated by subjects and assignments that I felt I could not complete without much effort. After reading this article, I realize that the older one gets, the more effort everything requires. Learning should not be an exception. These keys encourage me to try and try again without the high level of frustration that accompanied my learning in the past.

Goal setting and positive thinking are essential to me as a student beginning a journey of learning that is far more comprehensive than others I have encountered in the past. Just absorbing information and recalling it later will not be good enough. In college, more interaction is required from a student than simply memorizing facts. Integrating Houle's advice into my studying and learning process will help me manage both my assignments and my fears, and will help make my college experience successful.

Note: Students critiquing this essay may point out its effective use of personal examples, clear explanations, variety of sentence style, good transitions, and well-developed paragraphs.

Samples of a Variety of Peer Response Group Structures

1. FIRST DRAFT RESPONSE GROUPS

Recommended group size: 5–6

Instructions:

Hand out copies of the first paper. Everyone reads silently. Then each group member will make *all* of the following four kinds of comments, with each member giving his or her four responses before the next member begins. (An alternate method requires everyone to make the pointing responses, then all the summarizing, etc.) The writer should listen without response to all reactions, simply noting comments.

Total time for each person's paper, including reading and response: 10 minutes

Types of response:

1. Pointing: Say which ideas (or words) stood out. (*Not* why.)

2. Summarizing: Explain the writer's main idea in a single sentence.

3. Telling: Tell what happened to you as you read the paper. (Example: "When I got to the third paragraph, I was confused because . . ."; or "I agreed with the point you made at the end and wondered if . . .")

4. Showing: Use two of the following metaphorical exercises. Describe the writing as if you were describing <u>voices</u> (shouting, whining, lecturing), <u>weather</u> (foggy, crisp, rainy), <u>motion or locomotion</u> (marching, dancing), <u>clothing</u> (tuxedo, well-worn sweatsuit), <u>terrain</u> (desert, hills), <u>color</u>, <u>shape</u>, <u>animal or vegetable</u>, <u>musical instrument</u>, <u>part of body</u>, <u>evolution</u> (where it came from and where it's heading), <u>intention</u> (what was the actual intention and what might have been a crazy intention?), <u>substitution</u> (assume author really wanted to write something else; what was it?), <u>environment</u> (assume author did something or something happened before writing—what was it?), <u>author</u> (pretend it was written by someone you've never seen—what is he or she like?), <u>clay</u> (what would you do with it?), <u>doodle</u> (draw picture of the writing), <u>sound</u> (make sound that the writing inspires), <u>jabbering</u> (give it in a language you don't know, or compress it into 30 seconds), <u>dance</u> (make the movements it suggests to you), or <u>meditation</u> (don't think of the writing, but be open to it—what happens?).

Repeat this cycle until all papers have been critiqued.

Note: The fourth activity is generally difficult for developmental writers. If you decide to require it, be sure to give a number of examples and discuss that its purpose is to help writers think and write more creatively.

(Adapted from Peter Elbow, *Writing without Teachers*. New York: Oxford UP, 1973.)

2. CONTENT DISCUSSION: TRIADS

Students take copies of group members' papers home to read and comment on. They then share observations orally in class. (The author of each paper includes at the end of the draft a list of questions that readers should respond to.) Roles rotate within the group so that each student has the opportunity to function as reader, as writer, and as observer.

Time for each cycle: 15 minutes

As writer you will:

1. Ask the questions written on the draft and be sure answers are understood.
2. Ask for clarification of reader's responses if necessary.
3. Use the reader as resource: ask for help with questions as needed.

As reader you will:

1. Summarize the main points.
2. Question any confusing points.
3. Discuss point(s) you find most interesting and say whether or not you agree with them.
4. Give your opinion on the questions the writer asked for responses to.
5. At the end, find out from the writer how useful your feedback has been for generating, expanding, or clarifying ideas.

As observer you will (during the last 5 minutes):

1. Collect data about interaction between writer and reader.
2. Relate these interactions.
3. Infer the degree of usefulness of information gained.
4. Assess the level of specificity of information given by the reader.
5. Summarize what skills, knowledge, or attitudes were the focus of the interaction.
6. At the end, ask the reader and the writer for feedback on their perceptions.

(Adapted from Carol M. Jacko, "Small-Group Triad: An Instructional Mode for the Teaching of Writing." *CCC* 29 [1978]: 290–92.)

3. EDITORIAL GROUPS

This variation on peer response is appropriate for use during a later phase of the writing process. Students work in groups of three, with each student playing the role of author, editor, or proofreader. Roles should be switched so that all students eventually complete each task.

Authors must answer the following:

- Is the topic sufficiently narrow? Can something worthwhile be said about it in a reasonable space and time?

- Did you have enough information about the topic to begin writing about it? Did you have something you really want to communicate?

- What was your purpose in writing? How do you expect to affect the audience? What sort of response are you looking for?

- Have you checked over and revised the draft before sharing it?

Editors must answer the following (concerning structure, organization, logic, and development of ideas):

- What is the main idea? At what point does it become evident?

- What aspects of the main idea does the author develop?

- Does the author use examples, support, or illustration for each aspect of the main idea?

- Are there smooth transitions between ideas? Between paragraphs?

- Do you have a sense of satisfaction at the end of the essay? Do you have any unanswered questions or doubts?

Proofreaders must answer the following:

- Is the language concrete and specific?

- Are all words used conventionally?

- Are conventional capitalization and punctuation used?

- Is the grammar correct: agreement, sentence structure, verb use, etc.?

Note: The proofreading role is difficult for developmental writers and can result in incorrect editing suggestions. One way to make the task a bit more manageable is to require the proofreader to look for only one particular grammar problem (e.g., sentence fragments) or whatever grammar topic the class has been focusing on at that point.

(Adapted from Gene Stanford et al., *How to Handle the Paper Load*. Urbana: NCTE, 1979.)

Advice to Students Giving and Receiving Feedback

ADVICE FOR STUDENTS *RECEIVING* FEEDBACK

- Always read your paper twice if group members haven't read it previously. Allow at least a minute or two after each reading for impressions to clarify.

- Just read the paper through; don't apologize, explain, or give directions. You want to get reactions to the written product as if the other students were reading it in your absence, which is the way it will eventually have to stand.

- Don't reject any views. Listen as if all were true.

- Don't be browbeaten. In the end, you will decide which advice was useful and which was not.

ADVICE FOR STUDENTS *GIVING* FEEDBACK

- Present your reactions as statements rather than questions. This prevents time being wasted by a student answering and telling you what he or she *meant* to write.

- Follow the written instructions provided. All of the directions are there for a purpose.

- Never quarrel with another group member's reaction if it conflicts with yours. This wastes time. Just present your views clearly, and let the writer choose which to follow.

- Give specific reactions to specific parts.

- Tell *what* you felt, not *why* (e.g., "I got confused with all the examples you gave on page 3" rather than "Too many examples tend to get confusing").

- Give full attention to reading and listening. You will want the other group members to do this for you.

- No reaction is no help, so don't leave out ideas that you're unsure of. Something in your discussion may be helpful to the writer, even if you're not completely sure what point you want to make.

Written Response with Rating Scale

PEER REVIEW GUIDE

Name of reviewer _____   Class hour _____

Name of writer _____   Date _____

1. Does the composition include a thesis statement that clearly presents the central idea? Does every paragraph include a topic sentence with a focused controlling idea?

   Rating: (Good) 5   4   3   2   1 (Poor)

   Reason for rating:

2. Does the composition include an effective introduction and conclusion?

   Rating: (Good) 5   4   3   2   1 (Poor)

   Reason for rating:

3. Does the composition include enough specific information to support the thesis statement? Does each paragraph include sufficient information to support the topic sentence?

   Rating: (Good) 5   4   3   2   1 (Poor)

   Reason for rating:

4. Does all the information in the composition directly support the thesis sentence? Does all the information in each paragraph directly support the topic sentence?

   Rating: (Good) 5   4   3   2   1 (Poor)

   Reason for rating:

5. Does the composition have a clear, consistent, and appropriate pattern of organization? Is each paragraph clearly organized? Are transitional words and phrases used where appropriate?

   Rating: (Good) 5   4   3   2   1 (Poor)

   Reason for rating:

6. Is the language in the composition specific and appropriate for the composition's audience, tone, and purpose?

   Rating: (Good) 5   4   3   2   1 (Poor)

   Reason for rating:

7. Does a variety of sentence lengths, structures, and beginnings help make the composition interesting and easy to read?

   Rating: (Good) 5   4   3   2   1 (Poor)

   Reason for rating:

Note: This form works best when filled out prior to oral discussion. As a way to judge group effectiveness, ask the writer to attach all review forms to the revised essay that results from the peer review.

Ranking without Written Comments

To Be Used for Final Draft Review

SA = Strongly Agree; **A** = Agree; **D** = Disagree; **SD** = Strongly Disagree

Writer _____   Class _____

1. The writer has produced a personalized and original draft.
   SA   **A**   **D**   **SD**

2. There is a thesis sentence with a focused controlling idea.
   SA   **A**   **D**   **SD**

3. The entire content of the draft effectively supports the thesis.
   SA   **A**   **D**   **SD**

4. Every body paragraph has a topic sentence with a focused controlling idea.
   SA   **A**   **D**   **SD**

5. All paragraphs are unified.
   SA   **A**   **D**   **SD**

6. The writer wins the respect of readers for his or her point of view.
   SA   **A**   **D**   **SD**

7. Outside sources are effectively used to support the writer's purpose.
   SA   **A**   **D**   **SD**

8. The writer sufficiently develops major supporting points in the essay.
   SA   **A**   **D**   **SD**

9. The writer has provided enough major supporting points to validate the thesis claim.
   SA   **A**   **D**   **SD**

10. The writer has kept the audience for the essay in mind.
    SA   **A**   **D**   **SD**

11. Sentences, paragraphs, and ideas are arranged coherently and logically.
    SA   **A**   **D**   **SD**

12. Errors in grammar and punctuation are kept to a minimum.

    SA   **A**   **D**   **SD**

13. Errors in spelling and typing are kept to a minimum.

    SA   **A**   **D**   **SD**

14. Outside sources are documented fully and correctly.

    SA   **A**   **D**   **SD**

15. The essay meets the requirement for a minimum number of words.

    SA   **A**   **D**   **SD**

16. The manuscript meets all the formatting requirements.

    SA   **A**   **D**   **SD**

Note: This evaluation form can be used in a variety of ways: as a checklist for the author to attach to a submitted essay, as a summary for the instructor's response, or as a peer review sheet to be filled out by group members.

Responding with Written and Oral Feedback
PEER REVIEW DIRECTIONS

DIRECTIONS: Print out two copies of your essay (double-spaced, 14-point font). Give one copy to each of the other two members in your group. You will have <u>30 minutes</u> (15 minutes per essay) to read both essays to yourself silently and write down your answers to the questions below. Fill out one sheet for each essay.

Then the group will reconvene and discuss these responses. You will have <u>30 minutes</u> for this part of the exercise: 10 minutes for two reviewers to present their thoughts on each essay. Please stick to the questions below and give as concrete and specific feedback as possible to your colleagues. I will collect these peer review forms at the end of class, so be sure you make separate notes on any feedback you get.

NAME OF PERSON BEING REVIEWED: _____

NAME OF REVIEWER: _____

1. **Overall Focus**

   Summarize the essay's main message in one sentence.

2. **Beginning and End**

   Is the first paragraph effective? Does it give a clear and interesting introduction to the essay's topic?

   Is the last paragraph effective? Does it bring the essay to a logical and interesting conclusion?

   Do the ideas in the last paragraph match those in the first paragraph without simply repeating them?

3. **Paragraphs**

A. Paragraph focus: In a few words, write down the main theme of each paragraph:

1.

2.

3.

4.

5.

(Continue on back as needed.)

B. Paragraph development

Are there any paragraphs that might be too long? Which one(s)?
Are there any paragraphs that might be too short? Which one(s)?

4. **General Impressions**

A. Which parts (if any) confused you? Why?

B. Where would you have liked more information? Why?

C. What did you like best about this essay?

D. What is the main thing you think the writer should focus on during revision?

Seven Keys to Effective Learning

CYRIL O. HOULE

Cyril O. Houle (1913–1998) was an internationally recognized scholar, professor emeritus of education at the University of Chicago, and Senior Program Consultant for the W. K. Kellogg Foundation. A leading figure in the field of adult education, he was the author of *The Inquiring Mind* (1961), *The Design of Education* (1972), and *Continuing Learning in the Professions* (1980). This excerpt is taken from his *Continuing Your Education* (New York: McGraw-Hill, 1964), a book offering good practical advice to adult learners.

Once in ancient times, a spoiled young king decided to learn geometry, which was then new and very much in vogue. But when his tutor began to reveal the mysteries to him, the king found them hard to understand. He demanded that he be taught not in the usual way but in a fashion appropriate to his station in life. "Sire," the wise man answered, "there is no royal road to geometry."

There is no royal road to anything really worth knowing. Learning can be enjoyable, engrossing, and challenging. Some ways of teaching or of studying are easier than others. And one can occasionally get a surface familiarity with a subject without exerting very much effort. But any learning that is worthwhile requires sustained endeavor, and, in the course of it, there are bound to be times of strain, of darkness, of confusion, or even of a sense of futility. A man who climbs a mountain expects difficulties, but they are all made worthwhile by the exhilaration of the moment when, at last, he stands on top, free and clear, with a great panorama spread before him, which he would never have seen if he had not put forth the effort. In the same way, anyone who wishes the rewards and the exhilaration which come from learning must work for them.

But while there is no royal road to the mountain top, seven key principles will greatly aid your effort to reach whatever summit of learning you may choose as your goal.

1. Act as though You Are Certain to Learn

Nothing so disturbs the beginning adult student as the nagging fear that he will not be able to learn what he would like to know. Nothing is more reassuring than the discovery through experience that he can succeed. Here is the testimony of two men and two women who have learned this lesson:

> Going back after a lapse of time, I was fearful and tense, but that is past.

> My worries lasted only for the one course—after that it became easier. It had been twenty-five years between courses. After receiving a D, I got mad—and now get A's and B's.

> My biggest problem was convincing myself that I could once again maintain a good average in my classes. I felt that I had forgotten how to study effectively. This fear only lasted for the first semester. Once I was convinced that I could keep up, my problem was solved.

> I resumed my study many years after I graduated from a Japanese university. The difference of the language, the customs of the colleges, and the background knowledge added to the difficulty of resuming the study. All these reasons and my shortness of time made me feel an inferiority complex at first and made me nervous. I tried to persuade myself that I had to have confidence from my experience and good grades. But the most important thing was to go through the first semester. The second was easier, and I could regain my own tempo. I wasn't so nervous any more.

Let it be said at once that not everybody can learn everything. People differ from one another in intelligence, bodily strength, dexterity, and special abilities. Only a limited number of people can understand advanced mathematics, play the violin like Heifetz, write novels as well as Tolstoy, or have the philosophical insight of Aristotle or Spinoza. Few adults aspire so high. They know that such talents are extraordinary, and therefore do not worry about not possessing them. What is troubling to many men and women, however, is the fear that they do not have the ability to learn what normal people want to know.

If you have this fear, it may arise from one of two causes. You may think you are no longer as good a learner as you were when young. Or you may believe that some important element has been left out of your makeup—that you do not have enough intelligence to understand difficult ideas or that you have no capacity for a particular subject such as foreign language, mathematics, art, or music. Let us take up these two causes of worry, one after the other.

The relative learning ability of young people and adults has been studied by many investigators. The essential results of this research are: *Adults can learn most things better than children, though it may take them longer to do so.*

. . .

Now to turn to a second possible worry: that you simply do not have the basic capacity to learn what you want to know. You may be right. If so, there is no point in putting yourself under undue strain. If basic inadequacy is your persistent and continuing worry, your best course of action is to try to get a specialized diagnosis of your ability. Consult a counselor, discuss your problems with a teacher, or make arrangements to take the appropriate tests of your aptitude. Then act in terms of what you discover.

Most adults, however, tend to underestimate their ability. They vaguely fear they do not have the capacity to absorb what they want to know. To them one can only say, "How do you know you can't learn unless you try?" Few people become absolute masters of any subject; the great majority fall somewhere short of perfection and yet gain pleasure in what they *have* learned. If you really try to learn in the most effective way, perhaps you will discover that far from having a blind spot in foreign language or mathematics or human relations, you can secure a real sense of satisfaction in studying them, partly because of your new knowledge and partly because you have conquered your fears. Of all the boundaries of the mind, the most limiting are those which it imposes on itself.

The first and basic rule, then, is to act as though you are certain to learn. There will be dark moments and even dark days—but they will pass. Somehow, by acting as though you

were confident, you really will become confident. In an old play, a mother is talking to her shy daughter who is going off to her first ball and is dreading the experience. "My dear," she says, "bite your lips to make them nice and red, throw your shoulders back, hold your head high—and sail right in!" The beginning student may not need red lips, but the rest of the advice is helpful.

2. Set Realistic Goals—and Measure Their Accomplishment

One frequent obstacle to adult learning is that men and women, realizing that they have the full power of their strength and vigor, think that they ought to be able to learn without any effort or strain whatever.

. . .

Now, a forty-six-year-old can probably learn to play the piano almost as rapidly and well as a ten-year-old, given exactly the same instruction and the same number of hours of practice. (As for the old proverb about dogs, it isn't true; an eight-and-a-half-year-old Irish terrier of the author's acquaintance learned two new tricks last summer.) But the child takes it for granted that he will have to practice. Somehow the adult hopes to be exempt from the rule. His goal is so clear-cut! His powers are so great!

If a man and a boy start out to walk a mile, the man will do it much more efficiently than his companion. He is tall enough to see the objective; he has a clear idea of what a mile's distance is and he can pace his progress accordingly; he keeps steadily at his task; and he is strong. The boy cannot see where he is going; he has no real conception of what the word *mile* means; he makes many side excursions; he runs too hard and gets a side ache, or he lags behind; his mind is easily diverted; and his legs are not used to the task assigned. Thus, the man will always be more efficient. But the mile to be walked remains. There is no royal road to learning.

In any learning program, therefore, you must first of all be realistic about what you can achieve. Do not start impulsively on an ambitious reading program, register by mail for an evening school course about which you are poorly informed, purchase a lot of equipment to teach yourself a hobby you are not really convinced you want to learn, or start on a program to get a degree because of a vague belief that it would be nice to have one.

If you are learning because you want to reach some goal, be sure that you really want it; be sure that what you want to learn will help you to reach it; be sure that you want to take on the task of learning. If you are participating in an educational activity because you enjoy doing so, be sure that the activity you choose will give you the satisfactions you want. (If you like to belong to discussion groups, for example, choose groups which really do discuss, which deal in interesting topics, and which are made up of congenial people.) If you learn because you want to know, be sure that what you choose will contribute to your knowledge in the way that you wish.

Having chosen your broad objective and selected the activity which will help you reach it, keep setting specific goals for yourself. As one man remarked, "I always plan ahead and know each night what I expect to accomplish, and when, the next day. I try to adhere to my daily plan." Even the largest building must be built one brick at a time. Some adults are very inventive in planning ways to set up short-range targets. They make each chapter a goal; they work against the clock to see how much can be accomplished each hour; they keep a ledger recording their plan on the debit side and their accomplishment on the credit side; or they divide up a job to be done into separate parts, each of which can be finished in a set period of time or before an established deadline.

Specific goals are important because they provide a feeling of tangible achievement. As one woman explained, "Each lesson well done brings its own rewards." Anyone who feels a sense of accomplishment and who recognizes that he has already gone a part of the way toward the broad goal at which he is aiming has a powerful incentive to continue.

Some adults like to arrange rewards for themselves other than the satisfaction which learning brings. They promise themselves a cigarette, a movie, or an hour of television—or perhaps something even more interesting!—when they complete a given piece of work. There is nothing wrong with such rewards as long as their use is only a game played to whet interest, but matters can go too far. A degree, diploma, or certificate, for example, is a respected evidence that a man or woman has achieved a certain level or kind of education, but it is the learning that counts, not the piece of paper. Whenever an adult reverses those values and seeks not to learn but to have only the evidence of learning, he begins to destroy his ability to gain the greater satisfaction which comes from the development of his own potentialities.

3. Remember the Strength of Your Own Point of View

Your learning is strongly influenced by the point of view you bring to it. Jerome Bruner and Cecile Goodman have shown this to be true in a striking experiment. They cut out gray disks of paper the size of a penny, a nickel, a dime, a quarter, and a fifty-cent piece and asked children to draw circles of the same size. These circles usually did not vary more than 5 per cent from the correct size. Then the investigators used actual coins and gave the same instructions. At once the children's estimates of the size increased. The circles were at least 15 per cent larger than the coins. The more valuable the coins, generally speaking, the more the children overestimated the size. For example, they saw the quarter as being more than 35 per cent larger than it actually was.

An even more striking next step was then taken. The same experiment was carried out with a group of children from wealthy homes and a group of children from poor homes. The wealthy children overestimated the size of the coins from 10 to 20 per cent. The poor children overestimated from 20 to 50 per cent. In both cases, the overestimation of size tended to increase with the value of the coin.

The results of this study seem to show that if an object has no value to a person, he can make fairly good estimates of it, but if it does have value, he sees it as being larger than it is. And the higher the value, the more he will overestimate its importance.

The experiences of all adults have brought them, consciously or not, to many conclusions about what is good and what is bad. Therefore, as mature men and women approach an educational activity, they may lack a proper sense of proportion and a desirable balance of judgment. A labor leader will emphasize some aspects of economics and an industrialist will emphasize others, not necessarily because either really chooses to do so. They simply cannot help their biased viewpoints.

Therefore, as you study, keep in mind the strength of your own point of view. As you make estimates and judgments, be aware that you may be seeing things not in a proper balance and proportion but distorted by the values you have acquired. When bias stands in your way, it is time to change directions.

Turning the matter around, treat the varying points of view of others as a positive value in your pattern of learning. Part of the endless enjoyment of classes and groups is the discovery and rediscovery of the fascinating differences among people. It is rewarding, too, constantly to ask oneself why each individual holds the views he does and what has made him become the kind of person he is.

Most important of all, do not let your established values harden into such fixed beliefs that you cannot tolerate new ideas. When this happens, the process of education ceases. A discussion group may intensely dislike a book which it is asked to read, but if the members can open their minds to it, seek to understand what the author was trying to do and why, and discuss their views as to his success, their understanding will be enlarged. Often they will end up still disliking the book—but out of knowledge, not out of ignorance.

4. Actively Fit New Ideas and New Facts into Context

Your greatest asset as an adult learner is the fact that your experience enables you to see relationships. When a new idea or fact is presented, you can understand it because you have background and perspective. And you can remember it because you can associate it with what you already know and therefore give it meaning. If you doubt this fact, try reading again some substantial work which you first read as a child, perhaps *Ivanhoe, Julius Caesar,* or *David Copperfield.* How that book has changed!

Here is firsthand evidence from two adult students on this point:

> Picking up study again, I find my age (about forty-nine) offers some advantages to education over the younger ages. This is especially so since my field of interest is in business administration. I find that my years and variety of experiences in business are a great help to me in understanding and grasping the basic principles. I really sympathize with young people who are so short on any experience that could be of help.

> To find a technique of study during college was my entire problem in getting through. When I started back in to study again, after some time in the business world, I found I had unknowingly developed the technique of association. I was able to see examples of my course in everyday business working.

The fund of experience of adults is built up gradually and constantly throughout their lives. Everybody, for example, accumulates a set of keys—to the front door, to the car, to the locker or the office door at work, to the tool shed, to the fishing box, to the sewing machine, to suitcases, and to all the other things and places which we think should be kept locked. As each new key comes along, the man who receives it looks at it, establishes its general shape, tries it (incidentally learning at that point whether its flat side should be up or down), and puts it on his key ring. With no ado, his knowledge has been increased and his future behavior changed.

Now think about a man who has grown up in a primitive-tribe society where everything is shared and nothing is private. Consider what he would confront if he went to a city to work. Among the baffling and confusing things that he would before long have to confront would be his first lock and key. We can imagine how complicated they would seem to him, and he would very likely marvel at their strangeness. Soon he would need a second lock and key. Since they were different in design, he might not relate them to his first set. After a while, however, he would gradually come to understand the general idea of locks and keys. And then, perhaps much later, he would reflect about the differences between his village where all good things are shared and his new life where they seem to be jealously guarded.

The same basic situation would occur if an American went to live in a tribal village. To survive, he would need to build a new set of associations and skills. It might be a long time before he adopted all the general practices of the village and even longer before he could understand how the basic ideas and values of the villagers affected what they did.

The ability to learn most easily the information for which a foundation has been laid is illustrated every day in the lives of everyone. How do you read the newspaper? You may say that you read it from cover to cover, but if you were given an examination over what you had read on any given day, great gaps in your reading might be revealed. You have a good understanding of what is going on at city hall, so you read carefully all the stories that have to do with local government—and remember what you read. Since you know nothing about high society, you hastily turn over the pages which have to do with its affairs. Somebody else, with opposite interests and knowledge, would reverse your pattern of reading.

Information also helps to build an understanding of principles. For example, earlier in this chapter, the names of Heifetz, Tolstoy, Aristotle, and Spinoza were used. Did they mean anything to you? If so, you got the point which was being made, and you probably remember it. If not, the names did nothing to help you.

One way to build your understanding, therefore, is always to look for associations between the new matter to be learned and what you already know. This process occurs naturally enough to make most learning experiences immediately significant. When it doesn't, you should deliberately seek to find parallels or to make applications. As one man put it:

> When a subject is being taught in a general fashion, the individual will more quickly grasp the details if he applies his new-found knowledge to a specific problem in his own life. The student then is not only working in familiar ground, where mistakes will be obvious to him, but by seeing an immediate application he is encouraged in his studies.

If a field is completely new to you, the wisest course of action is to spend some time trying to get at the fundamentals so that you have a solid basis on which to build. Suppose, for example, you feel you ought to know more about international affairs. The newspapers, magazines, television, and radio bring floods of information about it—but this information is presented by people who are knowledgeable in the field and is understood best by those who have a similar knowledge. It is taken for granted that you will know the meaning of "balance of power," "sovereignty," the Atlantic Alliance, UNESCO, and other such terms. Suppose you don't! In that case, the meaning is lost to you.

If you want to become knowledgeable about world affairs, you have two major courses of action. One is to go on painfully and laboriously reading about current events, clearing up various terms as you proceed, but, for the most part, accepting new ideas on faith and getting only a crude sense of what is being said, thereby missing the finer shades of meaning. The alternative action (and the more sensible) is to take a course, read a textbook, or in some other fashion get a basic introduction to the subject. When you have laid the groundwork, then all your later reading and viewing will have a deeper meaning than they did before.

You may find it wise deliberately to broaden the base of your knowledge without regard for any immediate purpose. You have learned many things in the past which later on proved to be useful in ways that you did not anticipate when you learned them. If you set your mind to acquiring totally new areas of knowledge, you will usually find in the future that they have values you do not now contemplate. A powerful businessman followed this practice consistently:

> This is a complicated company that I'm head of, and you see relationships everywhere. Of course, I have to stay on top of the new ideas in the field of business and management. But that isn't enough. That's expected of everybody. If I have been able to move out in front, it's because I've deliberately tried to study all kinds of strange things—like modern art or Renaissance painting or the history of ancient Greece or the geography of Africa. You'd be surprised how often these off-beat subjects turn up some new idea or relationship that is really useful to me. And of course I get a great kick out of being able to make associations all over the place and really understanding what all kinds of people are talking about—not just pretending that I do!

Underlying these suggestions is the fact that you must constantly be active in your learning. Here is how four successful students follow this principle:

> I don't accept blindly those statements contained in a text. I ask instead, consciously or not, "What is he trying to say? Is the reasoning good? How does this relate with what has gone before?" As a consequence, the text seems less dry, more interesting, and less like a monologue.

To make the subject more interesting I try to create a broad background of interest. I am studying Spanish. I have read about the history of Mexico—traditions, music, great artists, and so on.

Knowledge is only retained in response to your own mental process of trying to find an answer. In other words, I can "memorize" the fact that Columbus discovered America in 1492, but if memorized only once, this information will gradually be lost. However, if I have really and earnestly asked and wondered in what year Columbus discovered America and have then found out that it was 1492, I will probably never forget it.

Don't just read the assignment. Instead, practice doing what you'll be called on to do later. Write things out, explain the laws, work the problems, apply the formulas. Don't try to learn to swim in an armchair.

This last remark is a fine piece of advice that deserves repeating. Don't try to learn to swim in an armchair!

5. Seek Help and Support When You Need It

Sometimes an adult will choose to learn by himself, and sometimes he will choose to learn with others. A balanced learning program combines many elements, though not all at the same time. But while adults often teach themselves what they want to know, they may run into real dangers if they rely on this method too consistently. John Stuart Mill, the great English economist, put the matter very well when he said, "a clever self-educated man . . . often sees what men trained in routine do not see, but falls into errors for want of knowing things which have long been known . . . he has acquired much of the pre-existing knowledge, or he could not have got on at all; but what he knows of it he has picked up in fragments and at random. . . ."

One time when it is well to seek out a teacher is when you are beginning the study of a new subject. You would not start on an automobile trip without a road map, and you should not begin a journey into an unexplored area of knowledge without the best guidance you can get.

A second time when you need help is when you bog down in your studies. At this point, many people simply stop. They would be wise instead to find someone who understands their particular difficulties. Sometimes this person may be a teacher, sometimes a friend. Sometimes it may be a counselor who can use special techniques to make an appraisal of your abilities and capacities. Other people can help you over difficult places in your study and, even more fundamentally, can assist you to make a realistic judgment about your ability, your knowledge, and your interest.

A third time when it is wise to seek help is when you feel the need of the social stimulation of a class or a group. Sometimes it is wise to turn to reading and independent study as a way of finding quietness and tranquility in the midst of a busy life. At such a time, solitude is the prize. But everybody also needs the sparkle and interest of a shared experience, and the support which comes from realizing that many people share the same interests and problems. As Henry Van Dyke once wrote, "Knowledge may be gained from books; but the love of knowledge is transmitted only by personal contact."

The help and reinforcement of other students may come outside of class as well as in it. One woman said:

> I immediately continue discussions with one of my classmates on the way home, if possible, and always with my husband when I get home. This gives me other people's ideas and impresses the whole thing on my mind so there is less need for later review.

It is very important to have family support and encouragement for any sustained learning program. This point is made very well by a husband and by a mother:

> My wife felt left out and thus enrolled in the basic humanities course. She had been out of school for a long time, and it was not easy for her to adapt to study habits so I taught her to read straight through the *Republic* and then go back and reread again for the essence of the work. It worked too damn well. Now I find I have to define Socrates. So much for higher education.

> My children seem to be quite interested in the fact that Mommy goes to school, too. I think perhaps this has increased their respect for the learning process. They often ask how I did on a quiz and, of course, are very aware of annual examination time.

Still another student recommends "exchanging telephone numbers so that students may exchange ideas and data." Perhaps it should be noted, however, that he is a twenty-seven-year-old bachelor.

6. Learn beyond the Point Necessary for Immediate Recall

We all learn many things we do not really wish to remember—and which we promptly forget. For example, if you are going to call on somebody at an unfamiliar location, you will probably repeat the address several times and remember it until it has served its purpose. Then you will very likely let it slip from your thoughts and your memory. If you go back to the same address again, you will be guided chiefly by your recollection of the appearance of the street and the building.

If you want to remember something permanently, however, you must do what the psychologist calls *over-learning*. Even after you can recall the fact or perform the skill perfectly, you should keep on reviewing it. A day later, review it again. Keep repeating this habit until there is no danger that it can slip from your memory. It may seem wasteful to follow this practice when you could be using your time to better advantage going on to something new. Such is not the case. By over-learning you reinforce the gains you have already made. As one man put it:

> It is the extra 10 per cent that makes a good student. A baseball player hits 260 and we say "lousy hitter." Another hits 300, "good hitter." The difference is four more hits in every 100 times at bat. As a student, go after four more hits.

7. Use Psychological as Well as Logical Practices

You have already had an illustration of this rule. In Chapter 1 you were urged first to skim this book, then to read it, and then to examine it closely. Now it seems illogical to many people not to go through a book thoroughly, digesting a paragraph at a time. Yet research has shown that the way here recommended is better.

The psychological and the logical are not really opposed to one another. When we use a "psychological" approach, we are simply realizing a deeper and more inward kind of logic which applies to what we do. Wisdom comes in knowing that you should sometimes use this deeper logic. Many a scientific investigator has tried again and again to work his way out of a difficulty, using all his resources of knowledge and technique, only to fail each time. But sometime later, when he had ceased thinking about the problem, the clue to its answer suddenly flashed into his mind.

Many psychological methods of approach are suggested throughout this book, and every student will develop his own. Here are a few reported by three successful adult students:

> I do the easy jobs first, the ones I understand. This gives me confidence with the more difficult problems.

> Sometimes I put ideas on paper, or in my mental refrigerator, and let them jell before accepting them. It is good to sleep on ideas. Their absurdity or basic soundness often becomes more pertinent in the next day's cold, clear dawn of reason.

> I'm a great believer in the second wind, so when I hit a snag, I pour another cup of coffee. On a bad snag, I start a game of solitaire. I'm not sure of the psychology of this, but I presume my subconscious mind continues to operate while my conscious mind is taking a breather. I never out-and-out quit working if I get bogged down, or I'd never get this second wind.

Psychological approaches alone are never sufficient. The scientific investigator cannot merely sit around waiting for the answer to come without first stocking his mind with all of the basic factors of which it is composed. And the man or woman who wants to learn must remember that nothing worth knowing can be gained without effort.

In-Class Essay Evaluation Form

CONTENT: response was accurate and thoughtful, ideas adequately developed

Maximum: 30 points   Your score: _____

ORGANIZATION AND STYLE: clear thesis, logical order of ideas, good transitions, clear paragraph focus, appropriate level of formality, good word choice

Maximum: 30 points   Your score: _____

GRAMMAR AND MECHANICS: no pattern of subject-verb disagreements, run-ons, comma splices, fragments, verb construction or verb-ending errors, punctuation errors (missing or improperly placed commas, apostrophes, etc.); adequate proof-reading for spelling, capitalization, etc.

Maximum: 30 points   Your score: _____

FORMATTING: follows assignment directions

Maximum: 10 points   Your score: _____

                                          TOTAL SCORE: _____

SUMMARY COMMENT:

Analytic Essay Evaluation Scale

	LOW		MIDDLE		HIGH
General Merit					
Ideas	2	4	6	8	10
Organization	2	4	6	8	10
Wording	2	4	6	8	10
Flavor	2	4	6	8	10
Mechanics					
Usage	1	2	3	4	5
Punctuation	1	2	3	4	5
Spelling	1	2	3	4	5
Handwriting	1	2	3	4	5

This is the most well known of the holistic rating scales. Developed by Paul Bernard Diederich, it weights factors of content and organization more heavily than mechanics and grammar (see P. Diederich, *Measuring Growth in English.* Urbana: NCTE, 1974). You can adapt this scale by varying the weighting or the categories as necessary to reflect the emphasis of your class.

Pre/Post Essay Evaluation Scale

The following variation of the Diederich scale is an instrument we have used to evaluate the in-class essays students write on the first and last day of class. Because we use this only as a pre/post comparison, we chose to weight all items equally.

Name: _____ Date: _____

EVALUATION SCALE FOR PRE/POST ESSAYS

	LOW		MIDDLE		HIGH
CONTENT (paper has something to say)	2	4	6	8	10
ORGANIZATION (clear thesis)	2	4	6	8	10
ADEQUATE IDEA DEVELOPMENT (main ideas plus supporting details, examples, etc.)	2	4	6	8	10
UNITY AND COHERENCE (logical transitions)	2	4	6	8	10
APPROPRIATE DICTION AND FORMALITY (avoidance of clichés, overused words, jargon)	2	4	6	8	10
STANDARD USAGE (written, not spoken, English)	2	4	6	8	10

	LOW		MIDDLE		HIGH
SENTENCE VARIETY	2	4	6	8	10
(mixture of simple and complex)					
SENTENCE CORRECTNESS	2	4	6	8	10
(avoidance of fragments, run-ons, comma splices)					
VERB CORRECTNESS	2	4	6	8	10
(endings, formation, agreement)					
BASIC MASTERY OF MECHANICS	2	4	6	8	10
(punctuation, capitalization, spelling)					

TOTAL _____

GENERAL COMMENTS:

Sentence-Level Editing Checklist

For each sentence, ask the following questions:

_____ **1.** Does the sentence state the topic?

_____ **2.** Does the sentence add further information to the topic sentence?

_____ **3.** Does the sentence follow a logical order?

_____ **4.** Does the sentence say what I really want it to say?

_____ **5.** Does the sentence sound right?

_____ **6.** Does the sentence show what I really think?

_____ **7.** Does the information sound credible?

_____ **8.** Does the sentence summarize what has been said so far?

_____ **9.** Does the sentence sound like a conclusive comment?

_____ **10.** Will readers see the importance of the sentence?

_____ **11.** Will readers be interested in the sentence?

_____ **12.** Will readers understand what I mean by the sentence?

_____ **13.** Is the sentence clear and to the point?

_____ **14.** Is the sentence connected to the previous one?

Peer Assessment Checklists for Evaluating Paragraphs

Peer Checklist for EXEMPLIFICATION

TOPIC SENTENCE

❐ Does the topic sentence focus on an idea that can be developed in a single paragraph?

❐ Is the topic sentence specifically worded?

❐ Does the topic sentence clearly express what the rest of the paragraph is about?

EVIDENCE

❐ Does the writer include enough examples?

❐ Do all the examples support the topic sentence?

SUMMARY STATEMENT

❐ Does the paragraph end with a summary statement?

❐ Does the summary statement restate the paragraph's main idea in different words?

TRANSITIONS

❐ Are the examples arranged in a logical order?

❐ Has the writer used enough transitional words or phrases?

Peer Checklist for NARRATION

TOPIC SENTENCE

❐ Does the topic sentence focus on an idea that can be developed in a single paragraph?

❐ Is the topic sentence specifically worded?

❐ Does the topic sentence clearly express what the rest of the paragraph is about?

EVIDENCE

❐ Does the writer include enough events?

❐ Do all the events support the topic sentence?

SUMMARY STATEMENT

❐ Does the paragraph end with a summary statement?

❐ Does the summary statement restate the paragraph's main idea in different words?

TRANSITIONS

❐ Are the events arranged in a logical order?

❐ Has the writer used enough transitional words or phrases?

Peer Checklist for DESCRIPTION

TOPIC SENTENCE

❏ Does the topic sentence focus on an idea that can be developed in a single paragraph?

❏ Is the topic sentence specifically worded?

❏ Does the topic sentence clearly express what the rest of the paragraph is about?

EVIDENCE

❏ Does the writer include enough details?

❏ Do all the details support the topic sentence?

SUMMARY STATEMENT

❏ Does the paragraph end with a summary statement?

❏ Does the summary statement restate the paragraph's main idea in different words?

TRANSITIONS

❏ Are the details arranged in a logical order?

❏ Has the writer used enough transitional words or phrases?

Peer Checklist for PROCESS

TOPIC SENTENCE

❏ Does the topic sentence focus on an idea that can be developed in a single paragraph?

❏ Is the topic sentence specifically worded?

❏ Does the topic sentence clearly express what the rest of the paragraph is about?

EVIDENCE

❏ Does the writer include enough steps?

❏ Do all the steps support the topic sentence?

SUMMARY STATEMENT

❏ Does the paragraph end with a summary statement?

❏ Does the summary statement restate the paragraph's main idea in different words?

TRANSITIONS

❏ Are the steps arranged in a logical order?

❏ Has the writer used enough transitional words or phrases?

Peer Checklist for CAUSE AND EFFECT

TOPIC SENTENCE

❐ Does the topic sentence focus on an idea that can be developed in a single paragraph?

❐ Is the topic sentence specifically worded?

❐ Does the topic sentence clearly express what the rest of the paragraph is about?

EVIDENCE

❐ Does the writer include enough causes and/or effects?

❐ Do all the causes and/or effects support the topic sentence?

SUMMARY STATEMENT

❐ Does the paragraph end with a summary statement?

❐ Does the summary statement restate the paragraph's main idea in different words?

TRANSITIONS

❐ Are the causes and/or effects arranged in a logical order?

❐ Has the writer used enough transitional words or phrases?

Peer Checklist for COMPARISON AND CONTRAST

TOPIC SENTENCE

❐ Does the topic sentence focus on an idea that can be developed in a single paragraph?

❐ Is the topic sentence specifically worded?

❐ Does the topic sentence clearly express what the rest of the paragraph is about?

EVIDENCE

❐ Does the writer include enough points of comparison or contrast?

❐ Do all the points of comparison or contrast support the topic sentence?

SUMMARY STATEMENT

❐ Does the paragraph end with a summary statement?

❐ Does the summary statement restate the paragraph's main idea in different words?

TRANSITIONS

❐ Are the points of comparison or contrast arranged in a logical order?

❐ Has the writer used enough transitional words or phrases?

Peer Checklist for CLASSIFICATION

TOPIC SENTENCE

❏ Does the topic sentence focus on an idea that can be developed in a single paragraph?

❏ Is the topic sentence specifically worded?

❏ Does the topic sentence clearly express what the rest of the paragraph is about?

EVIDENCE

❏ Does the writer include enough categories?

❏ Do all the categories support the topic sentence?

SUMMARY STATEMENT

❏ Does the paragraph end with a summary statement?

❏ Does the summary statement restate the paragraph's main idea in different words?

TRANSITIONS

❏ Are the categories arranged in a logical order?

❏ Has the writer used enough transitional words or phrases?

Peer Checklist for DEFINITION

TOPIC SENTENCE

❏ Does the topic sentence focus on an idea that can be developed in a single paragraph?

❏ Is the topic sentence specifically worded?

❏ Does the topic sentence clearly express what the rest of the paragraph is about?

EVIDENCE

❏ Does the writer include enough information?

❏ Does all the information support the topic sentence?

SUMMARY STATEMENT

❏ Does the paragraph end with a summary statement?

❏ Does the summary statement restate the paragraph's main idea in different words?

TRANSITIONS

❏ Is the information arranged in a logical order?

❏ Has the writer used enough transitional words or phrases?

Peer Checklist for ARGUMENT

TOPIC SENTENCE

❐ Does the topic sentence focus on an idea that can be developed in a single paragraph?

❐ Is the topic sentence specifically worded?

❐ Does the topic sentence clearly express what the rest of the paragraph is about?

EVIDENCE

❐ Does the writer include enough evidence?

❐ Does all the evidence support the topic sentence?

SUMMARY STATEMENT

❐ Does the paragraph end with a summary statement?

❐ Does the summary statement restate the paragraph's main idea in different words?

TRANSITIONS

❐ Is the evidence arranged in a logical order?

❐ Has the writer used enough transitional words or phrases?

PART FIVE

Answers to Exercise Items

Chapter 15

◆ **PRACTICE 15-1, page 264**

Answers: **(1)** Derek Walcott **(2)** ancestors **(3)** Walcott **(4)** Writing **(5)** poems **(6)** He **(7)** Walcott **(8)** He **(9)** he **(10)** poem **(11)** poet **(12)** Walcott

◆ **PRACTICE 15-2, page 264**

Answers: **(1)** seeds; plural **(2)** Afghanistan; singular **(3)** industry; singular **(4)** Pomegranates; plural **(5)** fruit; singular **(6)** Officials; plural **(7)** The United States and Europe; plural **(8)** California; singular **(9)** pomegranate; singular **(10)** exports; plural

◆ **PRACTICE 15-3, page 265**

Possible answers: **(1)** I **(2)** passport **(3)** we **(4)** student **(5)** snakes **(6)** car **(7)** water **(8)** birds **(9)** athletes **(10)** police

◆ **PRACTICE 15-4, page 267**

Answers: **(1)** ~~In presidential elections~~, third-party <u>candidates</u> have attracted many voters. **(2)** ~~With more than 27 percent of the vote~~, <u>Theodore Roosevelt</u> was the strongest third-party presidential candidate ~~in history~~. **(3)** ~~In the 1912 race with Democrat Woodrow Wilson and Republican William H. Taft~~, <u>Roosevelt</u> ran second ~~to Wilson~~. **(4)** ~~Before Roosevelt~~, no third-party <u>candidate</u> had won a significant number ~~of votes~~. **(5)** ~~In recent years~~, however, some <u>candidates</u> ~~of other parties~~ made strong showings. **(6)** ~~In 1980~~, <u>John B. Anderson</u>, an Independent, got almost 7 percent ~~of the vote~~. **(7)** ~~With nearly 19 percent of the popular vote~~, Independent <u>Ross Perot</u> ran a strong race ~~against Democrat Bill Clinton and Republican George Bush in 1992~~. **(8)** ~~In 2000~~, ~~with the support of many environmentalists~~, <u>Ralph Nader</u> challenged Al Gore and George W. Bush ~~for the presidency~~. **(9)** ~~In 2004~~, <u>Nader</u> was also ~~on the ballot in many states~~. **(10)** The two-party <u>system</u> ~~of the United States~~ has survived ~~despite many challenges by third party candidates~~.

◆ **PRACTICE 15-5, page 268**

Answers: **(1)** see **(2)** involves **(3)** offers **(4)** distrusts **(5)** enters; wins **(6)** see **(7)** realizes **(8)** returns; saves **(9)** enjoy **(10)** dislike

◆ **PRACTICE 15-6, page 269**

Answers: **(1)** are **(2)** is **(3)** are **(4)** are **(5)** is **(6)** is **(7)** becomes **(8)** seems **(9)** are **(10)** is

◆ **PRACTICE 15-7, page 270**

Answers: **(1)** is **(2)** tells **(3)** is; seems **(4)** loves; is **(5)** lives **(6)** dreams **(7)** dies **(8)** supports; does **(9)** works **(10)** graduates

◆ **PRACTICE 15-8, page 271**

Answers: **(1)** Complete verb: had become; helping verb: had **(2)** Complete verb: had puzzled; helping verb: had **(3)** Complete verb: had become; helping verb: had **(4)** Complete verb: should have been playing; helping verbs: should have been **(5)** Complete verb: would get; helping verb: would **(6)** Complete verb: was called; helping verb: was **(7)** Complete verb: did cause; helping verb: did **(8)** Complete verb: could breathe; helping verb: could **(9)** Complete verb: would remain; helping verb: would **(10)** Complete verb: had reduced; helping verb: had

Chapter 16

◆ **PRACTICE 16-1, page 278**

Possible answers: **(1)** and **(2)** but/yet **(3)** and **(4)** or **(5)** and **(6)** but/yet **(7)** so/and **(8)** nor **(9)** for

◆ **PRACTICE 16-2, page 279**

Possible answers: **(1)** Training a dog to heel is difficult, for dogs naturally resist strict control. **(2)** A bodhran is an Irish drum, and it is played with a wooden stick. **(3)** Students should spend two hours studying for each hour of class time, or they may not do well in the course. **(4)** Years ago, students wrote on slates, so the teacher was able to correct each student's work individually. **(5)** Each state in the United States has two senators, but the number of representatives depends on a state's population. **(6)** In 1973, only 2.5 percent of those in the U.S. military were women, but today, that number is almost 20 percent. **(7)** A "small craft advisory" is an important warning for boaters, for bad weather conditions can be dangerous to small boats. **(8)** A DVD looks like a compact disc, but it can hold fifteen times as much information. **(9)** Hip-hop fashions include sneakers and baggy pants, and these styles are very popular among today's young men. **(10)** Multiple births have become more and more common, and even septuplets have a reasonable chance of survival today.

◆ PRACTICE 16-3, page 280

Possible edits: Diet, exercise, and family history may account for centenarians' long lives, but this is not the whole story. One study showed surprising common traits among centenarians. They did not necessarily avoid tobacco and alcohol, nor did they have low-fat diets. In fact, they consumed relatively large amounts of fat, cholesterol, and sugar, so diet could not explain their long lives. They did, however, share several key survival characteristics. First, all of the centenarians were optimistic about life, and all of them were positive thinkers. They were also involved in religious life and had deep religious faith. In addition, all the centenarians had continued to lead physically active lives, and they remained mobile even as elderly people. Finally, all were able to adapt to loss. They had all experienced the deaths of friends, spouses, or children, but they were able to get on with their lives.

◆ PRACTICE 16-4, page 280

Answers will vary.

◆ PRACTICE 16-5, page 282

Answers will vary.

◆ PRACTICE 16-6, page 285

Answers: **(1)** Andrew F. Smith, a food historian, wrote a book about the tomato; later, he wrote a book about ketchup. **(2)** This book, *Pure Ketchup*, was a big project; in fact, Smith worked on it for five years. **(3)** The word *ketchup* may have come from a Chinese word; however, Smith is not certain of the word's origins. **(4)** Ketchup has existed since ancient times; in other words, it is a very old product. **(5)** Ketchup has changed a lot over the years; for example, special dyes were developed in the nineteenth century to make it red. **(6)** Smith's book discusses many other changes; for instance, preservative-free ketchup was invented in 1907. **(7)** Ketchup is now used by people in many cultures; still, salsa is more popular than ketchup in the United States. **(8)** Today, designer ketchups are being developed; meanwhile, Heinz has introduced green and purple ketchup in squeeze bottles. **(9)** Some of today's ketchups are chunky; in addition, some ketchups are spicy. **(10)** Ketchup continues to evolve; meanwhile, Smith has written a book about hamburgers.

◆ PRACTICE 16-7, page 286

Possible answers: **(1)** Every year since 1927, *Time* has designated a Man of the Year; however, the Man of the Year has not always been a man. **(2)** In the 1920s and 1930s, world leaders were often chosen; for example, Franklin Delano Roosevelt was chosen twice. **(3)** During World War II, Hitler, Stalin, Churchill, and Roosevelt were all chosen; in fact, Stalin was featured twice. **(4)** Occasionally, the Man of the Year was not an individual; for instance, in 1950, it was The American Fighting Man. **(5)** In 1956, The Hungarian Freedom Fighter was Man of the Year; then, in 1966, *Time* editors chose The Young Generation. **(6)** Only a few women have been selected; for example, Queen Elizabeth II of England was featured in 1952. **(7)** In 1975, American Women were honored as a group; nevertheless, the Man of the Year has nearly always been male. **(8)** Very few people of color have been designated Man of the Year; still, Martin Luther King Jr. was honored in 1963. **(9)** The Man of the Year has almost always been one or more human beings; however, The Computer was selected in 1982 and Endangered Earth in 1988. **(10)** More recently, prominent politicians have once again been chosen; for example, in 2001, New York City mayor Rudy Giuliani was *Time*'s Man of the Year (now called Person of the Year). **(11)** In 2003, *Time* did not choose a politician; instead, it honored The American Soldier. **(12)** In 2004, *Time* selected President George W. Bush; now, the magazine was making a more traditional choice. **(13)** In 2005, *Time* wanted to honor the contributions of philanthropists; thus, the magazine named Bill Gates, Melinda Gates, and Bono its Persons of the Year. **(14)** For 2006, *Time* did not choose a specific person; instead, its person of the year was "you." **(15)** For 2008, however, *Time* chose a person again; then, its pick was Barack Obama.

◆ PRACTICE 16-8, page 287

Possible answers: **(1)** Campus residents may have a better college experience; still, being a commuter has its advantages. **(2)** Living at home gives students access to home-cooked meals; in contrast, dorm residents have to eat dining hall food or takeout. **(3)** Commuters have a wide choice of jobs in the community; on the other hand, students living on campus may have to take on-campus jobs. **(4)** Commuters get to live with their families; however, dorm students may live far from home. **(5)** There are also some disadvantages to being a commuter; for example, commuters may have trouble joining study groups. **(6)** Unlike dorm students, many commuters have family responsibilities; in fact, they may have children of their own. **(7)** Commuters might have to help take care of their parents or grandparents; in addition, they might have to babysit for younger siblings. **(8)** Commuters might need a car to get to school; consequently, they might have higher expenses than dorm students. **(9)** Younger commuters may be under the watchful eyes of their parents; of course, parents are likely to be stricter than resident advisors. **(10)** Commuting to college has pros and cons; therefore, commuters are not necessarily at a disadvantage.

PRACTICE 16-9, page 288
Answers will vary.

Chapter 17

◆ **PRACTICE 17-1, page 295**
Answers: **(1)** DC **(2)** IC **(3)** DC **(4)** IC **(5)** IC **(6)** DC **(7)** IC **(8)** DC **(9)** IC **(10)** DC

◆ **PRACTICE 17-2, page 296**
Answers: **(1)** IC **(2)** DC **(3)** IC **(4)** DC **(5)** DC **(6)** IC **(7)** DC **(8)** IC **(9)** IC **(10)** DC

◆ **PRACTICE 17-3, page 299**
Possible answers: **(1)** even though **(2)** After **(3)** where **(4)** because **(5)** because **(6)** when **(7)** in order to **(8)** Although **(9)** as if **(10)** although **(11)** when **(12)** Because

◆ **PRACTICE 17-4, page 299**
Possible answers: **(1)** Although professional midwives are used widely in Europe, in the United States, they are less common. **(2)** When John Deere made the first steel plow in 1837, a new era began in farming. **(3)** Stephen Crane describes battles in *The Red Badge of Courage* even though he never experienced a war. **(4)** When Elvis Presley died suddenly in 1977, thousands of his fans gathered in front of his mansion. **(5)** After Edward Jenner developed the smallpox vaccine in the 1800s, the number of smallpox cases declined. **(6)** As the salaries of baseball players rose in the 1980s, some sportswriters predicted a drop in attendance at games. **(7)** Before the Du Ponts arrived from France in 1800, American gunpowder was not as good as French gunpowder. **(8)** When Margaret Sanger opened her first birth-control clinic in America in 1916, she was arrested. **(9)** Because Thaddeus Stevens thought plantation land should be given to freed slaves, he disagreed with Lincoln's peace plan for the South. **(10)** Even though Steven Spielberg has directed some very popular movies, he did not win an Academy Award until *Schindler's List*.

◆ **PRACTICE 17-5, page 302**
Possible answers: **(1)** Dependent clause: which was performed by a group called the Buggles; relative pronoun: which; noun: video **(2)** Dependent clause: that recorded live studio performances; relative pronoun: that; noun: productions **(3)** Dependent clause: who had been doubtful of MTV at first; relative pronoun: who; noun: executives **(4)** Dependent clause: that featured special effects and large casts of dancers; relative pronoun: that; noun: productions **(5)** Dependent clause: which first aired in September 1984; relative pronoun: which; noun: presentation **(6)** Dependent clause: that featured a group of young people living together in New York City; relative pronoun: that; noun: series **(7)** Dependent clause: who starred in *Newlyweds: Nick and Jessica* in 2003; relative pronoun: who; noun: Jessica Simpson **(8)** Dependent clause: which devotes less and less time to music videos; relative pronoun: which; noun: MTV **(9)** Dependent clause: which feature cast members doing good deeds; relative pronoun: which; noun: shows **(10)** Dependent clause: who challenged MTV to play more videos; relative pronoun: who; noun: Justin Timberlake

◆ **PRACTICE 17-6, page 302**
Possible answers: **(1)** The Harry Potter books, which follow the young wizard from age 11 to 17, have become international best-sellers. **(2)** Readers see Harry in some unusual situations that reveal his magical powers. **(3)** Harry faces many challenges that test his courage and willpower. **(4)** Harry's greatest enemy is the evil Lord Voldemort, who killed his parents with dark magic. **(5)** Harry goes to school at Hogwarts, which is a boarding school for young wizards and witches. **(6)** At Hogwarts, Harry gets to know Ron Weasley and Hermione Granger, who become his closest friends. **(7)** Albus Dumbledore, who is the headmaster of Hogwarts, is Harry's mentor. **(8)** The Harry Potter books, which are filled with magic and witchcraft, are offensive to some people. **(9)** The film adaptations of the books, which star Daniel Radcliffe as Harry, have been very successful. **(10)** The last of the seven books, which was published in 2007, is the longest book in the Harry Potter series.

Chapter 18

◆ **PRACTICE 18-1, page 310**
Answers will vary.

◆ **PRACTICE 18-2, page 311**
Revised sentences will vary. Adverbs: **(1)** however **(2)** first **(3)** often **(4)** generally **(5)** now

◆ **PRACTICE 18-3, page 312**
Answers will vary.

◆ **PRACTICE 18-4, page 312**
Revised sentences will vary. Prepositional phrases: **(1)** during World War II **(2)** in the war's early years **(3)** between 1942 and 1945 **(4)** with this greater responsibility and independence **(5)** after the war

◆ **PRACTICE 18-5, page 313**
Answers will vary.

◆ **PRACTICE 18-6, page 314**
Possible answers: **(1)** In the Cuban-American community, people often mention José Julián Martí as one of

their heroes.   **(2)** José Martí was born in Havana in 1853, at a time when Cuba was a colony of Spain. **(3)** By the time he was sixteen years old, he had started a newspaper demanding Cuban freedom.   **(4)** In 1870, the Spanish authorities forced him to leave Cuba and go to Spain.   **(5)** Openly continuing his fight, he published his first pamphlet calling for Cuban independence while in Spain.   **(6)** He then lived for fourteen years in New York City.   **(7)** During his time in New York, he started the journal of the Cuban Revolutionary party. **(8)** Martí's essays and poems argued for Cuba's freedom and for the individual freedom of Cubans.   **(9)** Passionately following up his words with action, he died in battle against Spanish soldiers in Cuba.

◆ PRACTICE 18-7, page 315

Possible answers: **(1)** Changing from green to red, special lamps in the dorms of one Ohio college warn of rising energy use. **(2)** Capturing methane from dairy cows, a Vermont college now needs less energy from other sources. **(3)** Tending a campus vegetable plot, student gardeners at a North Carolina college supply the cafeteria with organic produce. **(4)** Proving that recycled materials can be beautiful, a building on a California campus is built from redwood wine casks. **(5)** Offering courses in sustainability, some colleges are preparing students to take the green revolution beyond campus.

◆ PRACTICE 18-8, page 316

Possible answers: **(1)** Captured as a young girl by a rival tribe, Sacajawea was later sold into slavery. **(2)** Saved by a French Canadian fur trader named Charbonneau, Sacajawea became his wife. **(3)** Hired by the explorers Lewis and Clark in 1806, Charbonneau brought his pregnant wife along on their westward expedition. **(4)** Skilled in several Native American languages, Sacajawea helped Lewis and Clark on their journey. **(5)** Created in 2000, a U.S. dollar coin shows her picture.

◆ PRACTICE 18-9, page 318

Answers will vary.

◆ PRACTICE 18-10, page 320

Possible answers: **(1)** A playwright who wrote the prize-winning *A Raisin in the Sun*, Lorraine Hansberry was born in Chicago in 1930. **(2)** Hansberry's father, a successful businessman, moved the family from the south side of Chicago to a predominantly white neighborhood when Hansberry was eight. **(3)** Hostile neighbors there threw a brick through a window of their house, an act Hansberry never forgot. **(4)** Such experiences inspired *A Raisin in the Sun*, the story of a family's struggle to escape a cramped apartment in a poor Chicago neighborhood.

◆ PRACTICE 18-11, page 322

Possible edits: Kente cloth is made in western Africa and produced primarily by the Ashanti people. It has been worn for hundreds of years by African royalty, who consider it a sign of power and status. Many African Americans wear kente cloth because they see it as a link to their heritage. Each pattern on the cloth has a name, and each color has a special significance. For example, red and yellow suggest a long and healthy life while green and white suggest a good harvest. Although African women may wear kente cloth as a dress or head wrap, African-American women, like men, usually wear strips of cloth around their shoulders. Men and women of African descent wear kente cloth as a sign of racial pride; in fact, it often decorates college students' gowns at graduation.

Chapter 19

◆ PRACTICE 19-1, page 328

Answers: **(1)** The food in the cafeteria is varied, tasty, and healthy. **(2)** P **(3)** Last summer I worked at the library, babysat my neighbor's daughter, and volunteered at a soup kitchen. **(4)** Pandas eat bamboo leaves and koalas eat eucalyptus leaves. **(5)** P **(6)** A number of interesting people work at the co-op with me, including an elderly German man, a middle-aged Chinese woman, and a teenaged Mexican boy. **(7)** P **(8)** To conserve energy while I was away, I unplugged the television, closed the curtains, and set the thermostat at 65 degrees. **(9)** P **(10)** For several weeks after the storm, the supermarkets had no eggs, milk, or bread.

◆ PRACTICE 19-2, page 330

Answers will vary.

Chapter 20

◆ PRACTICE 20-1, page 336

Answers: **(1)** a game of mahjong; a patch of muddy ground **(2)** rough wooden stools; a faded green folding table; the smooth ivory **(3)** the grassy field; chestnut-colored horses; heavy red and black market bags **(4)** A veil of shimmering white fog; a black umbrella **(5)** wrinkled hands; a frown **(6)** the sharp click; the soft musical talk

◆ PRACTICE 20-2, page 336

Answers will vary.

◆ PRACTICE 20-3, page 337

Answers will vary.

◆ PRACTICE 20-4, page 339

Possible edits: **(1)** Although Robert Frost's home is a national landmark, local teenagers broke into the house in 2007 to have a party. **(2)** By the time the party was over, the teens had caused about $10,000 worth of damage. **(3)** Because a hiker soon discovered the break-in, the police were quickly able to find the suspects. **(4)** After their arrest, the teenagers were found guilty, and the judge in the case had an unusual idea for their sentence. **(5)** After discussing his idea with a local college professor, the judge required the teenagers to take a course in Robert Frost's poetry as part of their sentence. **(6)** At first the professor was not sure that poetry should be used as a form of punishment, but finally he decided that it might do some good. **(7)** The instructor, who had been teaching poetry for many years, knew that usually students could relate to two of Frost's poems: "Out, Out—" and "The Road Not Taken." **(8)** "Out, Out—" catches students' attention because it is somewhat shocking in its portrayal of a mill worker's death. **(9)** "The Road Not Taken" is suitable for these teens because they would always face choices in life, and in this case, they had taken the wrong road. **(10)** This story shows that sometimes the punishment really can fit the crime.

◆ **PRACTICE 20-5, page 340**
Answers will vary.

◆ **PRACTICE 20-6, page 342**
Possible answers: **(1)** Many people think that a million-dollar lottery jackpot allows the winner to stop working long hours and start living a comfortable life. **(2)** In fact, the reality for lottery winners is quite different. **(3)** For one thing, lottery winners who win big prizes do not always receive their winnings all at once; instead, payments—for example, $50,000—can be spread out over twenty years. **(4)** Of that $50,000 a year, close to $20,000 goes to taxes and anything else the winner owes the government, such as student loans. **(5)** Next come relatives and friends who ask for money, leaving winners with difficult choices to make. **(6)** They can either give gifts and loans or lose the friendship of many of their loved ones. **(7)** Even worse, many lottery winners have lost their jobs because employers thought that once they were "millionaires," they no longer needed the salary. **(8)** Many lottery winners wind up in serious debt within a few years. **(9)** Faced with financial difficulties, many might like to sell their future payments to companies that offer lump-sum payments of forty to forty-five cents on the dollar. **(10)** This is usually impossible, however, because most state lotteries do not allow winners to sell their winnings.

◆ **PRACTICE 20-7, page 343**
Answers will vary.

◆ **PRACTICE 20-8, page 344**
Answers will vary.

◆ **PRACTICE 20-9, page 345**
Possible edits: **(1)** Many people today would like to see more police officers patrolling the streets. **(2)** The attorneys representing the plaintiff are Geraldo Diaz and Barbara Wilkerson. **(3)** All the soldiers picked up their weapons. **(4)** Jane Fox is the mayor of Port Lon-

don, Maine. **(5)** Travel to other planets will be a significant step for humanity.

Chapter 21

◆ **PRACTICE 21-1, page 356**
Answers: **(1)** FS **(2)** CS **(3)** CS **(4)** C **(5)** CS **(6)** FS **(7)** C **(8)** CS **(9)** FS **(10)** CS

◆ **PRACTICE 21-2, page 356**
Answers: **(1)** CS **(2)** FS **(3)** CS **(4)** FS **(5)** CS **(6)** CS **(7)** C **(8)** CS **(9)** C **(10)** CS

◆ **PRACTICE 21-3, page 358**
Answers: **(1)** Hurricane Katrina destroyed many homes in New Orleans. It destroyed many businesses, too. **(2)** The city was flooded. High winds damaged the Mississippi and Alabama coasts. **(3)** Americans watched the terrible scenes. Hundreds died waiting for rescuers. **(4)** Many police officers, soldiers, and firefighters acted heroically. Ordinary citizens also took action. **(5)** Residents of flooded communities vowed to return. They knew it would not be easy.

◆ **PRACTICE 21-4, page 359**
Answers: **(1)** Right after World War II, some television programs showed actual scenes of war, and *Victory at Sea* and *The Big Picture* were two of those programs. **(2)** *Hogan's Heroes* was a 1960s comedy set in a German prisoner-of-war camp, so this show was bound to be very unrealistic. **(3)** In the 1970s, *M*A*S*H** depicted a Korean War medical unit, yet the show was really about the Vietnam War. **(4)** The 1980s drama *China Beach* was set in Vietnam, and the main character was an army nurse. **(5)** The contemporary drama *Army Wives* focuses on the home front, but it occasionally shows scenes of the Iraq War.

◆ **PRACTICE 21-5, page 360**
Answers: **(1)** New Mexico governor Bill Richardson has been a U.N. ambassador and a congressman; he also served as U.S. energy secretary. **(2)** César Chávez was a leader of the United Farm Workers Union; Dolores Huerta also became known as a union leader. **(3)** Roberto Clemente was a professional baseball player; Oscar de la Hoya achieved fame as a professional boxer. **(4)** Oscar Hijuelos wrote *The Mambo Kings Play Songs of Love*; Julia Alvarez wrote *How the Garcia Girls Lost Their Accents*. **(5)** Luis Valdez is a noted playwright and film director; his plays include *Los Vendidos* and *The Zoot Suit*.

◆ **PRACTICE 21-6, page 361**
Answers: **(1)** High schools have always taught subjects like English and math; now, many also teach personal finance and consumer education. **(2)** Personal-finance courses prepare students for life; for example,

students learn about money management, online banking, and identity theft. **(3)** Consumer-education courses can be very practical; for instance, students can learn how to buy, finance, and insure a car. **(4)** Some high schools teach students how to avoid credit card debt; in addition, they teach students how to invest their money. **(5)** Academic subjects will always dominate the high school curriculum; however, courses focusing on practical life skills are becoming increasingly important.

◆ **PRACTICE 21-7, page 363**

Possible answers: **(1)** Even though contemporary historians have written about the Harlem Renaissance, its influence is still not widely known. **(2)** Although Harlem was populated mostly by European immigrants at the turn of the last century, it saw an influx of African Americans beginning in 1910. **(3)** As this migration from the South continued, Harlem became one of the largest African-American communities in the United States. **(4)** After many black artists and writers settled in Harlem during the 1920s, African-American art flowered. **(5)** This "Harlem Renaissance" was an important era in American literary history although it is not even mentioned in some textbooks. **(6)** When scholars recognize the great works of the Harlem Renaissance, they point to the writers Langston Hughes and Countee Cullen and the artists Henry Tanner and Sargent Johnson. **(7)** After Zora Neale Hurston moved to Harlem from her native Florida in 1925, she began a book of African-American folklore. **(8)** Because Harlem was an exciting place in the 1920s, people from all over the city went there to listen to jazz and to dance. **(9)** When the white playwright Eugene O'Neill went to Harlem to audition actors for his play *The Emperor Jones*, he made an international star of the great Paul Robeson. **(10)** When the Great Depression occurred in the 1930s, it led to the end of the Harlem Renaissance.

◆ **PRACTICE 21-8, page 364**

Possible answers: **(1)** Nursing offers job security and high pay; therefore, many people are choosing nursing as a career. **(2)** Anne Boleyn was the second wife of Henry VIII, and her daughter was Elizabeth I. **(3)** The Democratic Republic of the Congo was previously known as Zaire; it was previously called the Belgian Congo. **(4)** Housewife Jean Nidetch started Weight Watchers in 1961. She sold the company for $100 million in 1978. **(5)** Millions of Jews were murdered during the Holocaust; in addition, Catholics, Gypsies, homosexuals, and other "undesirables" were killed. **(6)** Sojourner Truth was born a slave, but she eventually became a leading abolitionist and feminist. **(7)** Japanese athletes now play various positions on American baseball teams; at first, all the Japanese players were pitchers. **(8)** Oliver Wendell Holmes Jr. was a

Supreme Court justice; his father was a physician and writer. **(9)** Père Noël is the French name for Santa Claus; he is also known as Father Christmas and St. Nicholas. **(10)** Latin is one classical language; Greek is another.

◆ **PRACTICE 21-9, page 365**

Possible answers: **(1)** Scientists suspected the existence of Pluto as early as 1846. They believed it was causing the changes they observed in Neptune's orbit. **(2)** However, Pluto was not discovered until much later. **(3)** Percival Lowell founded the Lowell Observatory in 1894, and he began searching for a ninth planet in 1906. **(4)** Telescopes caught images of Pluto in 1915, but it was not named a planet until 1930. **(5)** The newly discovered ninth planet made international headlines; in fact, thousands of people sent in ideas for names. **(6)** "Pluto" was suggested by a British girl; the name refers to the Greek god of the underworld. **(7)** Scientists at the Lowell Observatory liked the name because the planet is cold and far away like the underworld. **(8)** They also chose it in honor of Percival Lowell, whose initials are the first two letters of the name. **(9)** Later, Walt Disney borrowed the name for a new cartoon character; in addition, a new element was named plutonium. **(10)** Recently, scientists learned that Pluto does not have enough mass to maintain a stable orbit; as a result, it was reclassified as a dwarf planet in 2006.

Chapter 22

◆ **PRACTICE 22-1, page 372**

Answers: **(1)** F **(2)** S **(3)** F **(4)** F **(5)** F **(6)** S **(7)** F **(8)** S **(9)** F **(10)** S

◆ **PRACTICE 22-2, page 372**

Answers: Items 2, 4, 6, and 7 are fragments. *Rewrite:* Sara Paretsky writes detective novels, such as *Hardball* and *Guardian Angel*. These novels are about V. I. Warshawski, a private detective. V. I. lives and works in Chicago, the Windy City. Every day as a detective, V. I. takes risks. V. I. is tough. She is also a woman.

◆ **PRACTICE 22-3, page 374**

Answers will vary.

◆ **PRACTICE 22-4, page 376**

Answers: **(1)** The U.S. flag was designed by Francis Hopkinson, a New Jersey delegate to the Continental Congress. **(2)** The first flag may have been sewn by Betsy Ross, a Philadelphia seamstress. **(3)** Congress officially recognized the Pledge of Allegiance in 1942, the year after the United States entered World War II. **(4)** In 1814, Francis Scott Key composed "The Star-

Spangled Banner," the U.S. national anthem. **(5)** Some people wanted a different national anthem, such as "America" or "America the Beautiful."

◆ PRACTICE 22-5, page 377

Answers: **(1)** First-born children are reliable, serious, and goal-oriented in most cases. **(2)** More than half of U.S. presidents have been first-born or only children in their families. **(3)** In large families, middle children often form close relationships outside of the family. **(4)** The youngest child is always trying to get attention from the older members of the family. **(5)** Youngest children often take a while to settle down into careers and marriages.

◆ PRACTICE 22-6, page 378

Answers will vary.

◆ PRACTICE 22-7, page 380

Answers: **(1)** Always try to find a store brand costing less than the well-known and widely advertised brands. **(2)** Look for a product's cost per pound, comparing it to the cost per pound of similar products. **(3)** Examine sale-priced fruits and vegetables, checking carefully for damage or spoilage. **(4)** Use coupons whenever possible, keeping them all in one place until they are needed. **(5)** Buy different brands of the same product, trying each one to see which brand you like best.

◆ PRACTICE 22-8, page 381

Answers will vary.

◆ PRACTICE 22-9, page 382

Answers: **(1)** Psychologists need advanced degrees to practice as licensed therapists. **(2)** Schools sometimes close during a flu outbreak to prevent the disease from spreading. **(3)** In 1941, Japan attacked the United States naval base at Pearl Harbor to weaken America's position in the Pacific. **(4)** You should always back up your computer files to avoid losing valuable work. **(5)** Scientists sent remote-controlled robots, called "rovers," to Mars to take photographs of the planet's surface.

◆ PRACTICE 22-10, page 383

Answers will vary.

◆ PRACTICE 22-11, page 386

Answers will vary.

◆ PRACTICE 22-12, page 387

Answers will vary.

◆ PRACTICE 22-13, page 388

Answers will vary.

Chapter 23

◆ PRACTICE 23-1, page 396

Answers: **(1)** know **(2)** need **(3)** include **(4)** appeals **(5)** sell; top **(6)** outsell **(7)** tend; seem **(8)** hosts; draws **(9)** deserve

◆ PRACTICE 23-2, page 396

Answers: **(1)** overlook **(2)** use **(3)** ignore **(4)** maintain **(5)** make **(6)** post **(7)** visit **(8)** miss **(9)** range **(10)** includes **(11)** offer

◆ PRACTICE 23-3, page 398

Answers: **(1)** fill **(2)** come **(3)** grade **(4)** teach **(5)** triggers **(6)** provide **(7)** lead **(8)** walks **(9)** greet **(10)** cheers

◆ PRACTICE 23-4, page 400

Answers: **(1)** have **(2)** is **(3)** has **(4)** are **(5)** do **(6)** are **(7)** is **(8)** do **(9)** has **(10)** has

◆ PRACTICE 23-5, page 401

Answers: **(1)** The <u>roses</u> ~~along the side of the house~~ <u>bloom</u> all summer long. **(2)** <u>Workers</u> ~~in the city~~ <u>pay</u> a high wage tax. **(3)** The <u>tools</u> ~~in my garage~~ <u>belong</u> to a friend. **(4)** <u>Refrigerators,</u> ~~especially those with the freezer on one side,~~ <u>use</u> most of the energy in a typical home. **(5)** A tropical <u>storm</u> ~~with heavy rain and strong winds~~ <u>moves</u> quickly. **(6)** Approximately <u>one</u> ~~out of every four high school students~~ <u>drops</u> out before graduation. **(7)** <u>Workers</u> ~~with a college degree~~ <u>earn</u> more money than those without a degree. **(8)** The <u>president</u> ~~of the company~~ <u>gets</u> a large bonus. **(9)** <u>Vegetarians,</u> ~~especially those who do not eat eggs or cheese,~~ <u>need</u> to be careful to get enough vitamins in their diets. **(10)** A <u>doctor,</u> ~~along with two nurses,~~ <u>staffs</u> the neighborhood clinic.

◆ PRACTICE 23-6, page 403

Answers: **(1)** meets **(2)** provides **(3)** is **(4)** has **(5)** wants

◆ PRACTICE 23-7, page 404

Answers: **(1)** has **(2)** relies **(3)** work **(4)** says **(5)** are **(6)** place **(7)** tend **(8)** understands **(9)** says **(10)** is

◆ PRACTICE 23-8, page 406

Answers: **(1)** Subject: Bering Strait; verb: is **(2)** Subject: compound; verb: does **(3)** Subject: twins; verb: Are **(4)** Subject: Congress; verb: does **(5)** Subject: this; verb: has **(6)** Subject: computer; verb: is **(7)** Subject: people; verb: are **(8)** Subject: books; verb: are **(9)** Subject: reasons; verb: are **(10)** Subject: way; verb: is

Chapter 24

◆ PRACTICE 24-1, page 412

Answers: **(1)** At the start of World War II, 120,000 Japanese Americans were sent to relocation camps because the government feared that they might be disloyal to the United States. **(2)** However, in 1943, the United States needed more soldiers, so it sent recruiters to the camps to ask for volunteers. **(3)** The Japanese-American volunteers were organized into the 442nd Combat Infantry Regiment. **(4)** The soldiers of the 442nd Infantry fought in some of the bloodiest battles of the war, including the invasion of Italy at Anzio and a battle in Bruyeres, France, where they captured over two hundred enemy soldiers. **(5)** When other U.S. troops were cut off by the enemy, the 442nd Infantry soldiers were sent to rescue them. **(6)** The Japanese-American soldiers suffered the highest casualty rate of any U.S. unit and received over eighteen thousand individual decorations. **(7)** Former senator Daniel Inouye of Hawaii, a Japanese American who was awarded the Distinguished Service Cross for his bravery in Italy, had to have his arm amputated. **(8)** The 442nd Infantry received more decorations than any other combat unit of its size and earned eight Presidential Unit citations. **(9)** Today the dedication and sacrifice of the 442nd Infantry is evidence that Japanese Americans were patriotic and committed to freedom and democracy. **(10)** Correct

◆ PRACTICE 24-2, page 414

Answers: **(1)** Young people who want careers in the fashion industry do not always realize how hard they will have to work. **(2)** They think that working in the world of fashion will be glamorous and that they will quickly make a fortune. **(3)** In reality, no matter how talented he or she is, a recent college graduate entering the industry is paid less than $30,000 a year. **(4)** The manufacturers who employ new graduates expect them to work for three years or more at this salary before they are promoted. **(5)** A young designer may receive a big raise if he or she is very talented, but this is unusual. **(6)** New employees have to pay their dues, and they soon realize that most of their duties are boring. **(7)** An employee may be excited to land a job as an assistant designer but then find that he or she has to color in designs that have already been drawn. **(8)** Other beginners discover that they spend most of their time sewing or typing up orders. **(9)** If a person is serious about working in the fashion industry, he or she has to be realistic. **(10)** For most newcomers to the industry, the ability to do what they are told to do is more important than their artistic talent.

◆ PRACTICE 24-3, page 416

Answers: **(1)** A local university funded the study, and Dr. Alicia Flynn led the research team. **(2)** The researchers developed a series of questions about decision making, and then they interviewed one hundred subjects. **(3)** Two-thirds of the subjects relied on intuition, and only one-third used logic. **(4)** After the researchers completed the study, they wrote a report about their findings. **(5)** Many experts read the report, and most of them found the results surprising.

Chapter 25

◆ PRACTICE 25-1, page 422

Answers will vary.

◆ PRACTICE 25-2, page 423

Answers will vary.

◆ PRACTICE 25-3, page 424

Possible answers: **(1)** Driving to work on Interstate 5, my brother was surprised to see a bear. **(2)** Frozen with fear, I saw the dark shape approach. **(3)** The volunteers easily identified the hawks tagged with metal bracelets. **(4)** My sister with a degree in electrical engineering found a job. **(5)** Wearing her warmest coat, Molly went outside to look for her dog. **(6)** Oscar rides to school on a bike powered by a 250-watt battery. **(7)** The brick house at the corner of Huron and Willow is still on the market. **(8)** Hoping to be chosen, Sammy auditioned for the role of King Lear. **(9)** Yelling from the stands, fans cheered on the Detroit Tigers. **(10)** The contestant with the loudest voice won the competition.

Chapter 26

◆ PRACTICE 26-1, page 435

Answers: **(1)** My mother always returned from India with intricate designs on her hands and feet. **(2)** In India, women called henna artists created these complex patterns. **(3)** Henna originated in a plant found in the Middle East, India, Indonesia, and northern Africa. **(4)** Many women in these areas used henna to color their hands, nails, and parts of their feet. **(5)** Men dyed their beards, as well as the manes and hooves of their horses, with henna. **(6)** They also colored animal skins with henna. **(7)** In India, my mother always celebrated the end of the Ramadan religious fast by going to a "henna party." **(8)** A professional henna artist attended the party to apply new henna decorations to the palms and feet of the women. **(9)** After a few weeks, the henna designs washed off. **(10)** In the United States, my mother's henna designs attracted the attention of many people.

◆ PRACTICE 26-2, page 438

Answers: **(1)** came; was **(2)** knew; kept **(3)** went **(4)** got **(5)** became **(6)** saw **(7)** thought **(8)** had **(9)** began **(10)** gave

◆ PRACTICE 26-3, page 439

Answers: **(1)** Correct **(2)** were **(3)** was **(4)** Correct **(5)** were **(6)** Correct **(7)** was **(8)** Correct **(9)** Correct **(10)** was

◆ PRACTICE 26-4, page 441

Answers: **(1)** can **(2)** will **(3)** will **(4)** will **(5)** could **(6)** can **(7)** can **(8)** can **(9)** will **(10)** can

Chapter 27

◆ PRACTICE 27-1, page 447

Answers: **(1)** visited **(2)** offered **(3)** raised **(4)** donated **(5)** joined **(6)** cleaned **(7)** removed **(8)** traveled **(9)** served **(10)** helped

◆ PRACTICE 27-2, page 451

Answers: **(1)** been; been **(2)** heard **(3)** built **(4)** come **(5)** become **(6)** made **(7)** written **(8)** read **(9)** said **(10)** seen

◆ PRACTICE 27-3, page 452

Answers: **(1)** become **(2)** sent **(3)** led **(4)** found **(5)** Correct **(6)** been **(7)** spoken; Correct **(8)** lost; understood **(9)** Correct **(10)** forgiven

◆ PRACTICE 27-4, page 454

Answers: **(1)** visited **(2)** has kept **(3)** belonged **(4)** lost; became **(5)** spoke **(6)** knew; found **(7)** made **(8)** offered **(9)** were **(10)** felt

◆ PRACTICE 27-5, page 454

Answers: **(1)** has changed **(2)** have undergone **(3)** filled **(4)** weighed **(5)** have developed **(6)** have gotten **(7)** invented **(8)** has increased **(9)** have grown **(10)** watched

◆ PRACTICE 27-6, page 456

Answers: **(1)** had raised **(2)** has shown **(3)** had found **(4)** have proven **(5)** has saved **(6)** had bought **(7)** have camped **(8)** had waited **(9)** have learned **(10)** had completed

◆ PRACTICE 27-7, page 457

Answers: **(1)** surprised; preapproved **(2)** Correct; located **(3)** designed **(4)** Correct **(5)** stuffed **(6)** Correct **(7)** concerned **(8)** tied **(9)** acquired **(10)** uninformed

Chapter 28

◆ PRACTICE 28-1, page 465

Answers: **(1)** headaches (regular) **(2)** lives (irregular) **(3)** feet (irregular) **(4)** chains (regular) **(5)** deer (irreg-ular) **(6)** honeys (regular) **(7)** brides-to-be (irregular) **(8)** women (irregular) **(9)** loaves (irregular) **(10)** kisses (regular) **(11)** beaches (regular) **(12)** duties (irregular) **(13)** sons-in-law (irregular) **(14)** species (irregular) **(15)** wives (irregular) **(16)** cities (irregular) **(17)** elves (irregular) **(18)** teeth (irregular) **(19)** catalogs (regular) **(20)** patties (irregular)

◆ PRACTICE 28-2, page 466

Answers: **(1)** travelers-to-be **(2)** lives; Correct; women **(3)** Correct; delays; duties **(4)** Correct **(5)** Correct; boxes **(6)** Correct; tweezers; tools; knives **(7)** Correct; lotions; drinks; quantities **(8)** liquids; Correct; travelers; Correct **(9)** contents; Correct; cups **(10)** Correct; Correct

◆ PRACTICE 28-3, page 468

Answers: **(1)** I **(2)** We; it; we **(3)** we **(4)** it **(5)** It; I; she **(6)** us **(7)** their **(8)** we; it **(9)** they; we **(10)** I; she

◆ PRACTICE 28-4, page 469

Answers: **(1)** Antecedent: campuses; pronoun: they **(2)** Antecedent: crime; pronoun: it **(3)** Antecedent: students; pronoun: their **(4)** Antecedent: students; pronoun: their **(5)** Antecedent: students; pronoun: they **(6)** Antecedent: students; pronoun: they **(7)** Antecedent: students; pronoun: them **(8)** Antecedent: schools; pronoun: they

◆ PRACTICE 28-5, page 470

Answers: **(1)** Compound antecedent: Mary-Kate and Ashley; connecting word: and; pronoun: their **(2)** Compound antecedent: a doctor or a nurse; connecting word: or; pronoun: her **(3)** Compound antecedent: Chinese and Arabic; connecting word: and; pronoun: their **(4)** Compound antecedent: Bert and Ernie; connecting word: and; pronoun: their **(5)** Compound antecedent: Homer or Bart; connecting word: or; pronoun: his **(6)** Compound antecedent: chocolate or oranges; connecting word: or; pronoun: their **(7)** Compound antecedent: Adam and Nathan; connecting word: and; pronoun: their **(8)** Compound antecedent: the chips or the salsa; connecting word: or; pronoun: its **(9)** Compound antecedent: Robins and finches; connecting word: and; pronoun: their **(10)** Compound antecedent: the White Sox or the Cubs; connecting word: or; pronoun: their

◆ PRACTICE 28-6, page 473

Answers: **(1)** Indefinite pronoun: Either; pronoun: its **(2)** Indefinite pronoun: Each; pronoun: its **(3)** Indefinite pronoun: Everything; pronoun: its **(4)** Indefinite pronoun: Everyone; pronoun: his or her **(5)** Indefinite pronoun: Neither; pronoun: her **(6)** Indefinite pronoun: Many; pronoun: their **(7)** Indefinite pronoun: Several; pronoun: their **(8)** Indefinite pronoun: someone; pronoun: him or her **(9)** Indefinite pronoun:

Anyone; pronoun: his or her **(10)** Indefinite pronoun: Both; pronoun: their

◆ PRACTICE 28-7, page 473

Possible answers: **(1)** Everyone has the right to his or her own opinion. **(2)** All students can eat their lunches in the cafeteria. **(3)** Somebody forgot his or her backpack. **(4)** All of the patients had their own rooms, with their own televisions and their own private baths. **(5)** Someone has left his or her car headlights on. **(6)** Simone keeps everything in her kitchen in its own little container. **(7)** Each of the applicants must have his or her driver's license. **(8)** Anybody who has ever juggled a job and children knows how valuable his or her free time can be. **(9)** Either of the coffeemakers comes with its own filter. **(10)** Most people wait until the last minute to file their income tax returns.

◆ PRACTICE 28-8, page 474

Answers: **(1)** Collective noun antecedent: company; pronoun: its **(2)** Collective noun antecedent: groups; pronoun: their **(3)** Collective noun antecedent: government; pronoun: its **(4)** Collective noun antecedent: family; pronoun: its **(5)** Collective noun antecedent: union; pronoun: its

◆ PRACTICE 28-9, page 475

Answers: **(1)** Antecedent: women; pronoun: Correct **(2)** Antecedent: a woman; pronoun: her **(3)** Antecedent: women; pronoun: their **(4)** Antecedent: everyone; pronoun: his or her **(5)** Antecedent: Elizabeth Cady Stanton and Lucretia Mott; pronoun: their **(6)** Antecedent: Fifteenth Amendment; pronoun: Correct **(7)** Antecedent: women; pronoun: their **(8)** Antecedent: women; pronoun: they; Correct **(9)** Antecedent: the U.S. government; pronoun: its **(10)** Antecedent: the House of Representatives and the states; pronoun: their

◆ PRACTICE 28-10, page 477

Answers: **(1)** Subjective **(2)** Possessive **(3)** Subjective **(4)** Objective **(5)** Possessive **(6)** Subjective; Objective **(7)** Possessive; Objective; Objective **(8)** Subjective

◆ PRACTICE 28-11, page 479

Answers: **(1)** I **(2)** Correct **(3)** I **(4)** her; me **(5)** Correct **(6)** They; I **(7)** she; I **(8)** her; him **(9)** her **(10)** they

◆ PRACTICE 28-12, page 480

Answers: **(1)** [they like] him **(2)** she [does] **(3)** [it affected] me **(4)** I [drive] **(5)** [it fits] me

◆ PRACTICE 28-13, page 482

Answers: **(1)** whom **(2)** who **(3)** Whom **(4)** who **(5)** whom

◆ PRACTICE 28-14, page 483

Answers: **(1)** themselves **(2)** ourselves **(3)** himself **(4)** herself **(5)** yourself

Chapter 29

◆ PRACTICE 29-1, page 490

Answers: **(1)** great **(2)** really **(3)** simply **(4)** usually **(5)** passionately **(6)** carefully **(7)** exact **(8)** inventive; differently **(9)** unique **(10)** ultimate; sure; seriously

◆ PRACTICE 29-2, page 491

Answers: **(1)** well **(2)** good **(3)** good **(4)** well **(5)** well **(6)** good **(7)** well **(8)** well **(9)** well **(10)** good

◆ PRACTICE 29-3, page 494

Answers: **(1)** more slowly **(2)** colder **(3)** healthier **(4)** more intelligent **(5)** more distinctly **(6)** taller **(7)** more respectful **(8)** more famous **(9)** wilder **(10)** more gracefully

◆ PRACTICE 29-4, page 495

Answers: **(1)** surest; most shocking **(2)** most daring **(3)** most recent **(4)** most common **(5)** most competitive **(6)** most conventional **(7)** safest; most easily **(8)** latest **(9)** most likely; most visible **(10)** most popular

◆ PRACTICE 29-5, page 496

Answers: **(1)** better **(2)** best **(3)** better; worse **(4)** worst **(5)** better **(6)** worst **(7)** best **(8)** better **(9)** better **(10)** best

Chapter 30

◆ PRACTICE 30-1, page 502

Answers: **(1)** When the first season of the reality show *Survivor* aired, <u>it</u> was an immediate hit. **(2)** Millions of Americans planned their evening so that <u>they</u> could be sure not to miss the next episode. **(3)** <u>It</u> was not surprising to see the many other reality shows that suddenly appeared on the air. **(4)** A recent poll asked viewers: "Do <u>you</u> enjoy reality TV, or has it gone too far?" **(5)** Most viewers thought that reality TV had gone too far even though <u>they</u> enjoyed shows like *Jon and Kate Plus 8* and *So You Think You Can Dance.*

◆ PRACTICE 30-2, page 503

Possible answers: **(1)** The first parts of the Great Wall were built around 200 A.D. **(2)** The Great Wall was built to keep out invading armies. **(3)** The sides of the Great Wall are made of stone, brick, and earth. **(4)** The top of the Great Wall is paved with bricks, forming a roadway. **(5)** The Great Wall is so huge that it can be seen by astronauts in space.

◆ PRACTICE 30-3, page 504
Answers: **(1)** people; dogs **(2)** animals; humans; tasks **(3)** benefits; hours **(4)** dogs **(5)** monkeys; parrots; pigs; horses; people; disabilities **(6)** switches; containers **(7)** chores **(8)** No plural nouns **(9)** attacks **(10)** fish; insects; creatures; humans

◆ PRACTICE 30-4, page 506
Answers: **(1)** Count **(2)** Count **(3)** Noncount **(4)** Count **(5)** Noncount **(6)** Count **(7)** Count **(8)** Noncount **(9)** Count **(10)** Noncount

◆ PRACTICE 30-5, page 509
Answers: **(1)** every **(2)** some major **(3)** A few violent **(4)** Many **(5)** many **(6)** little **(7)** Many **(8)** enough **(9)** some **(10)** a few

◆ PRACTICE 30-6, page 512
Answers: **(1)** A; No article needed **(2)** the; No article needed **(3)** the; a; the **(4)** a; a **(5)** the; No article needed; the **(6)** the; a; the **(7)** No article needed; No article needed; No article needed **(8)** The; a; the **(9)** the; the **(10)** a; a; the **(11)** An; the; an **(12)** the; a; the; the **(13)** No article needed; the; the; No article needed

◆ PRACTICE 30-7, page 515
Answers will vary.

◆ PRACTICE 30-8, page 519
Answers: **(1)** were signing: Correct **(2)** were becoming: Correct; could identify: Correct **(3)** was: Correct; was believing: believed; was: Correct **(4)** know: Correct; is having: has **(5)** study: Correct; want: Correct; have left: Correct **(6)** is: Correct; are liking: like **(7)** are often seeing: often see; are touching: touch; pick up: Correct **(8)** are needing: need; has been damaged: Correct **(9)** weigh: Correct; are deciding: decide **(10)** is collecting: Correct; can compare: Correct; find: Correct

◆ PRACTICE 30-9, page 521
Answers: **(1)** might **(2)** ought to **(3)** should **(4)** would **(5)** should **(6)** must **(7)** Would **(8)** could **(9)** can **(10)** might

◆ PRACTICE 30-10, page 522
Answers: **(1)** Eating **(2)** skating **(3)** cleaning **(4)** swimming **(5)** Quitting **(6)** remembering **(7)** organizing **(8)** singing **(9)** cooking **(10)** practicing

◆ PRACTICE 30-11, page 524
Answers: **(1)** a brand-new high-rise apartment building **(2)** this gifted twenty-five-year-old Venezuelan author **(3)** numerous successful short-story collections **(4)** all her intriguing suspense novels **(5)** the publisher's three best-selling works **(6)** this story's two main characters **(7)** a strong-willed young woman **(8)** the shy middle-aged British poet **(9)** an exquisite white wedding gown **(10)** an elaborate wedding reception

◆ PRACTICE 30-12, page 529
Answers: **(1)** in; in **(2)** In; from **(3)** in; at; to **(4)** On; of; with; of; at **(5)** in; in; in **(6)** to; to; of **(7)** to; in; with; from; to; with; with **(8)** at; about; in **(9)** with; at; of **(10)** to; for **(11)** on; on **(12)** At; to; to **(13)** to

◆ PRACTICE 30-13, page 532
Answers: **(1)** Most fans of the characters in Stephenie Meyer's popular *Twilight* series know that Meyer first thought them up in a dream. **(2)** One night in 2003, Meyer dreamed of a shy teenage girl and the vampire who loved her and stood by her even though he wanted to suck her blood. **(3)** Because Meyer immediately knew their story and just needed to put it on paper, she was able to complete her first book, *Twilight*, in just three months. **(4)** Once her imagination got going, it seemed Meyer could not turn it off. **(5)** Correct **(6)** So, she began writing *Midnight Sun,* a book that went over the same events but told them from the vampire's point of view. **(7)** Unfortunately, the first twelve chapters of *Midnight Sun* showed up online after an unexplained leak. **(8)** Correct **(9)** She promised to return to the draft and assured fans that she was not throwing it away. **(10)** Correct

Chapter 31

◆ PRACTICE 31-1, page 544
Answers: **(1)** The musician plays guitar, bass, and drums. **(2)** The organization's goals are feeding the hungry, housing the homeless, and helping the unemployed find work. **(3)** Correct **(4)** In native Hawaiian culture, yellow was worn by royalty, red was worn by priests, and a mixture of the two colors was worn by others of high rank. **(5)** The diary Anne Frank kept while her family hid from the Nazis is insightful, touching, and sometimes humorous. **(6)** A standard bookcase is 60 inches tall, 36 inches wide, and 9 inches deep. **(7)** Correct **(8)** Young, handsome, and sensitive, Leonardo DiCaprio was the 1990s answer to the 1950s actor James Dean. **(9)** California's capital is Sacramento, its largest city is Los Angeles, and its oldest settlement is San Diego. **(10)** Correct

◆ PRACTICE 31-2, page 545
Answers: **(1)** In the past few years, many Olympic athletes have been disqualified because they tested positive for banned drugs. **(2)** Correct **(3)** In the past, banned steroids were the most common cause

of positive drug tests. **(4)** In recent years, other banned substances have also been used. **(5)** Correct **(6)** Among track and field athletes, doping has been especially common. **(7)** In some cases, athletes' drug use was not uncovered until the games were long over. **(8)** Correct **(9)** Having witnessed many scandals and disappointments, today's fans are suspicious of extraordinary athletic feats. **(10)** Correct

◆ PRACTICE 31-3, page 547

Answers: **(1)** Some holidays are fairly new; the African-American celebration of Kwanzaa, for example, was only introduced in the 1960s. **(2)** This holiday celebrating important African traditions has, however, attracted many people over its short life. **(3)** By the way, the word *Kwanzaa* means "first fruits" in Swahili. **(4)** Correct **(5)** This, of course, can be demonstrated in some of the seven principles of Kwanzaa. **(6)** Kwanzaa is, in fact, celebrated over seven days to focus on each of these seven principles. **(7)** The focus, first of all, is on unity (*umoja*). **(8)** Also, Kwanzaa focuses on personal self-determination (*kujichagulia*). **(9)** In addition, Kwanzaa celebrations emphasize three kinds of community responsibility (*ujima*, *ujamaa*, and *nia*). **(10)** The other principles of Kwanzaa are creativity (*kuumba*) and, finally, faith (*imani*).

◆ PRACTICE 31-4, page 548

Answers: **(1)** Traditional Chinese medicine is based on meridians, channels of energy believed to run in regular patterns through the body. **(2)** Acupuncture, the insertion of thin needles at precise points in the body, stimulates these meridians. **(3)** Herbal medicine, the basis of many Chinese healing techniques, requires twelve years of study. **(4)** Gary Larson, creator of the popular *Far Side* cartoons, ended the series in 1995. **(5)** Correct **(6)** *Far Side* calendars and other product tie-ins earned Larson over $500 million, a lot of money for guitar lessons. **(7)** Nigeria, the most populous country in Africa, is also one of the fastest-growing nations in the world. **(8)** On the southwest coast of Nigeria lies Lagos, a major port. **(9)** The Yoruba people, the Nigerian settlers of Lagos, are unusual in Africa because they tend to form large urban communities. **(10)** A predominantly Christian people, the Yoruba have incorporated many native religious rituals into their practice of Christianity.

◆ PRACTICE 31-5, page 551

Answers: **(1)** Correct **(2)** They built the Alaska highway, which stretches twelve hundred miles across Alaska. **(3)** Correct **(4)** The highway, which cut through some of the roughest terrain in the world, was begun in 1942. **(5)** The Japanese had just landed in the Aleutian Islands, which lie west of the tip of the Alaska Peninsula. **(6)** Military officials who oversaw the project doubted the ability of the African-American troops. **(7)** As a result, they made them work under conditions that made construction difficult. **(8)** Correct **(9)** In one case, white engineers who surveyed a river said it would take two weeks to bridge. **(10)** Correct **(11)** Correct **(12)** Correct

◆ PRACTICE 31-6, page 553

Answers: **(1)** The American Declaration of Independence was approved on July 4, 1776. **(2)** The Pelican Man's Bird Sanctuary is located at 1705 Ken Thompson Parkway, Sarasota, Florida. **(3)** At 175 Carlton Avenue, Brooklyn, New York, is the house where Richard Wright began writing *Native Son*. **(4)** The article originally appeared in the February 12, 2009, issue of the *New York Times*. **(5)** Correct **(6)** The Palacio de Gobierno at Plaza de Armas, Guadalajara, Mexico, houses a mural of the famous revolutionary. **(7)** The Pueblo Grande Museum is located at 1469 East Washington Street, Phoenix, Arizona. **(8)** Brigham Young led the first settlers into the valley that is now Salt Lake City, Utah, in July 1847. **(9)** St. Louis, Missouri, was the birthplace of writer Maya Angelou, but she spent most of her childhood in Stamps, Arkansas. **(10)** Some records list the writer's birthday as May 19, 1928, while others indicate she was born on April 4, 1928.

◆ PRACTICE 31-7, page 555

Answers: **(1)** The capital of the Dominican Republic is Santo Domingo. **(2)** The country's tropical climate, generous rainfall, and fertile soil make the Dominican Republic suitable for many kinds of crops. **(3)** Some of the most important crops are sugarcane, coffee, cocoa, and rice. **(4)** Mining is also important to the country's economy because the land is rich in many ores. **(5)** Correct **(6)** In recent years, resort areas have opened and brought many tourists to the country. **(7)** Tourists who visit the Dominican Republic remark on its tropical beauty. **(8)** Military attacks and political unrest have marked much of the Dominican Republic's history. **(9)** Correct **(10)** However, most Dominican immigrants maintain close ties to their home country and return often to visit.

Chapter 32

◆ PRACTICE 32-1, page 562

Answers: **(1)** Bacteria and viruses, which we can't see without a microscope, kill many people every year, but they are not the only deadly creatures. **(2)** When we speak about the deadliest creatures, usually we're talking about creatures that cause illness or death from their poison, which is called venom. **(3)** After you're bitten, stung, or stuck, how long does it take to die? **(4)** Correct **(5)** The sea wasp is actually a fifteen-foot-long jellyfish, and although it's not aggressive, it can be deadly. **(6)** Correct **(7)** While jellyfish found off the Atlantic coast of the United States can sting, they aren't as dangerous as the sea wasp, whose venom is deadly enough to kill sixty adults. **(8)** A person who's been stung by a sea wasp has anywhere from thirty seconds to four minutes to get help or die. **(9)** Correct **(10)** Also, there's an antidote to the poison that can save the lives of victims.

◆ **PRACTICE 32-2, page 563**

Answers: **(1)** the singer's video **(2)** the students' test scores **(3)** everybody's favorite band **(4)** the boss's office **(5)** the players' union **(6)** the restaurant's specialty **(7)** the children's bedroom **(8)** the tickets' high cost **(9)** everyone's dreams **(10)** the dogs' owner

◆ **PRACTICE 32-3, page 565**

Answers: **(1)** Parents; theirs **(2)** Correct; Correct **(3)** its; weeks **(4)** hers; couples; Correct **(5)** Ryans; years **(6)** Correct; whose **(7)** classes; Correct; your **(8)** Correct; ours **(9)** tests **(10)** Correct; musicians; Correct; subjects

Chapter 33

◆ **PRACTICE 33-1, page 572**

Answers: **(1)** Marsupials have pouches; mothers carry their young in these pouches. **(2)** Marsupials are covered with hair and nursed by their mothers. **(3)** Correct **(4)** Marsupials include the koala, the kangaroo, and the wombat. **(5)** Many thousands of years ago, marsupials were common in South America; now, they are extinct.

◆ **PRACTICE 33-2, page 573**

Answers: **(1)** Four parks with religious themes are the Holy Land Experience, Dinosaur Adventure Land, Ganga-Dham, and City of Revelation. **(2)** The Holy Land Experience is near another popular attraction, which is Disney World. **(3)** An advertisement for Dinosaur Adventure Land describes it in these words: "where dinosaurs and the Bible meet!" **(4)** India's Ganga-Dham is billed as "the world's first spiritual theme park." **(5)** Correct

◆ **PRACTICE 33-3, page 575**

Possible answers: **(1)** In the 1950s, Bob Cousy was a star player for the Boston Celtics. Cousy (an "old man" at age thirty-four) led his team to their fifth NBA championship in 1963. **(2)** During the 1960s, the legendary Wilt ("the Stilt") Chamberlain played for the Philadelphia Warriors. **(3)** Many people still consider game 5 of the 1976 NBA finals—which the Celtics won in triple overtime—the greatest basketball game ever played. **(4)** During the 1980s, five truly outstanding players—Magic Johnson, Kareem Abdul-Jabbar, Larry Bird, Julius ("Dr. J") Erving, and Michael Jordan—dominated the NBA. **(5)** Today, young players (some joining the NBA right out of high school) dream of making names for themselves as their heroes did.

Chapter 34

◆ **PRACTICE 34-1, page 581**

Answers: **(1)** Midwest; Lake; Chicago; O'Hare International Airport; nation's **(2)** Street; Park; museums **(3)** north; Soldier Field; Chicago Bears; Wrigley Field; Chicago Cubs; National League baseball team **(4)** Father Jacques Marquette; Catholic; Ottawa; Huron **(5)** John Kinzie **(6)** Germans; Irish; Italians; Poles; Greeks; Chinese; African Americans; South **(7)** United States; Mrs.; cow **(8)** skyscrapers; John Hancock Company; Sears; Amoco **(9)** mother; Aunt Jean; Uncle Amos **(10)** Introductory Research Writing; High School

◆ **PRACTICE 34-2, page 584**

Answers: **(1)** "The bigger they are," <u>said boxer John L. Sullivan</u>, "the harder they fall." **(2)** "Do you take Michael to be your lawfully wedded husband?" <u>asked the minister</u>. **(3)** <u>Lisa Marie replied</u>, "I do." **(4)** "If you believe the *National Enquirer*," <u>my friend always says</u>, "then you'll believe anything." **(5)** "Yabba dabba doo!" <u>Fred exclaimed</u>. "This brontoburger looks great."

◆ **PRACTICE 34-3, page 585**

Possible answers: **(1)** "Revenge only engenders violence, not clarity and true peace," wrote Mexican-American author Sandra Cisneros. "I think liberation must come from within." **(2)** Talk-show host Oprah Winfrey said, "Luck is a matter of preparation meeting opportunity." **(3)** "Imagination is more important than knowledge," said physicist Albert Einstein. **(4)** At least one character in every *Star Wars* movie says, "May the force be with you." **(5)** "I hate admitting that my enemies have a point," wrote British novelist Salman Rushdie.

◆ **PRACTICE 34-4, page 586**

Answers: **(1)** Sui Sin Far's short story "The Wisdom of the New," from her book <u>Mrs. Spring Fragrance</u>, is about the clash between Chinese and American cultures in the early twentieth century. **(2)** Major league baseball games traditionally open with fans taking their hats off and singing "The Star-Spangled Banner." **(3)** Interesting information about fighting skin cancer can be found in the article "Putting Sunscreens to the Test," which appeared in the magazine <u>Consumer Reports</u>. **(4)** One of the best-known poems of the twentieth century is Robert Frost's "The Road Not Taken." **(5)** Ang Lee has directed several well-received films, including <u>Crouching Tiger, Hidden Dragon</u> and <u>Brokeback Mountain</u>.

(6) It is surprising how many people enjoy reruns of two 1960s television series: <u>Bewitched</u> and <u>I Dream of Jeannie</u>. **(7)** The title of Lorraine Hansberry's play <u>A Raisin in the Sun</u> comes from Langston Hughes's poem "Harlem." **(8)** In his autobiography, <u>Breaking the Surface</u>, Olympic diving champion Greg Louganis wrote about his struggle with AIDS.

◆ PRACTICE 34-5, page 588

Answers: **(1)** When fans of the television show *Lost* voted for their favorite episodes, "Through the Looking Glass," "The Shape of Things to Come," and "The Incident" were in the top ten. **(2)** In 1948, Eleanor Roosevelt delivered her famous speech "The Struggle for Human Rights" and published an article titled "Toward Human Rights throughout the World." **(3)** Before being elected president, Barack Obama wrote and published two books: *Dreams from My Father* and *The Audacity of Hope*. **(4)** English actor Daniel Craig plays secret agent James Bond in the films *Casino Royale* and *Quantum of Solace*. **(5)** *Janis Joplin's Greatest Hits* includes songs written by other people, such as "Piece of My Heart," as well as songs she wrote herself, such as "Mercedes Benz."

◆ PRACTICE 34-6, page 589

Answers: **(1)** The ice-skating rink finally froze over. **(2)** We should be kind to our four-legged friends. **(3)** The first-year students raised money for charity. **(4)** The under-prepared soldiers were at a real disadvantage. **(5)** The hand-carved sculpture looked like a pair of doves.

◆ PRACTICE 34-7, page 590

Answers: **(1)** The doctor diagnosed a case of hypertension. **(2)** November 11 is a federal holiday. **(3)** Derek registered for English literature and a psychology elective. **(4)** The museum was located at the corner of Laurel Avenue and Neptune Street. **(5)** The clinic is only open Tuesday through Thursday and every other Saturday.

◆ PRACTICE 34-8, page 591

Answers: **(1)** Only two students in the eight o'clock lecture were late. **(2)** More than 75% of the class passed the exit exam. **(3)** Chapter 6 begins on page 873. **(4)** The wedding took place on October 12th at 7:30. **(5)** Meet me at 65 Cadman Place.